IMPLEMENTING TOTAL QUALITY IN EDUCATION

IMPLEMENTING TOTAL QUALITY IN EDUCATION TO PRODUCE GREAT SCHOOLS

Transforming the American School System

By

James Lewis, Jr., Ph.D.

National Center to Save Our Schools
P.O. Box 948
Westbury, New York 11590

Library of Congress Cataloging-in-Publication Data

Lewis, James, 1930-
    Implementing total quality in education to produce great schools: transforming the American school system/James Lewis, Jr.
    p. cm.
    Includes bibliographical references (p313) and index.
    ISBN 1-883257-00-X
    1. School management and organization—United States.   2. Total quality management—United States.
3. Educational change—United States.   I. Title
    LB2805.L4146 1993   93-4272
    371.2'00973—dc20   CIP

Dedicated to:

My beloved sister, Sissy
and
my dear father, James

Preface

I owe a great deal of gratitude to some students of a sixth grade quality class in the Goose Creek Independent School District in Baytown, Texas, who inspired me to write this book. These seven students gave a presentation to about 100 teachers and school administrators. They spoke of how they had learned more in one year in a quality class than in all the years they had spent in school. A young girl cried while she related how "good" she felt in the class because she was not failing anymore. Another student said that an education "miracle" had occurred because he was learning so much more. Still another young girl said that she was sensitive to quality whenever she went shopping. The entire group told numerous stories, the theme of which was that learning is fun and enjoyable. I, along with others in the audience, gave them a standing ovation. The superintendent, Harry Griffith, Ph.D., grinned and looked at me, proud as a peacock.

For more than twenty years, I have been traveling around the United States, indicating to audiences the need for public schools to design and implement a process in order to create educational miracles. I always knew that we could produce schools that would enable students to become more than they had ever hoped to be. I thought the journey to excellence would do just that. I know now that I was mistaken. What is needed is a transformation, one that will only come when all students, teachers, school administrators, parents, and other stakeholders are "possessed" by implementing total quality (TQ) in schools across the United States, as well as in their personal lives.

I also want to thank W. Edwards Deming, Ph.D. I found his four-day Quality Institute, held in Cincinnati, Ohio, during the summer of 1992, to be extremely informative and insightful. It led to my own personal transformation. I owe so much to Dr.

Deming. I thought I knew a lot about operating schools. I know now that learning never stops.

I owe a great deal to Theresa May Hicks, a third grade teacher in the Denver Place Elementary School in Wilmington, Ohio. She revealed to me how to implement TQ in the classroom, and gave me the urge to become a teacher again. Further, I am indebted to Lisa Nasiff, my administrative assistant, who helped not only in typing this book, but also in providing some editing and comments to strengthen the contents. I also owe a debt of gratitude to Liza Burby, my editor, who directed and guided me to produce this book.

CONTENTS

INTRODUCTION

The mission of this book is to transform American schools. This transformation must first involve the superintendent of schools, because he or she must become the prime mover of the process. Next, the central school administrators must embrace Total Quality (TQ) with the same level of enthusiasm and commitment as the superintendent of schools. There must be no doubt that those who are "navigating" the school district are ready, willing, and able to bring on the transformation. In addition, the entire school family must be educated and trained in the TQ process, for they will be directly responsible for producing quality services and products. Finally, students cannot be left out of the transformation. There is more to education in a TQ environment than for students to learn their 3 Rs.

Our schools, at least our transformed schools, are where students learn to organize teams to solve classroom and personal problems using the scientific method; to nurture a win-win behavioral style; to undergo education and training in areas not usually taught in the school system; to use basic statistics to understand and to deal with problems; to handle conflict in an effective manner; to become systems thinkers; to understand and improve variations in processes; to understand how to relate to others through good use of psychology; and to utilize the TQ experience to build character.

In 1986, I wrote my best seller, *Achieving Excellence in Our Schools ... By Taking Lessons From America's Best-Run Companies*. I wrote another book entitled *Creating Excellence in Our Schools ... By Taking More Lessons From America's Best-Run Companies*, in 1987. If that was not enough, I wrote my third book on excellence, entitled *Excellent Organizations*, two years later. Obviously my emphasis at that time was on "excellence." As I stated previously, I know now that excellence is not enough.

It was Peter Block, the author of *The Empowered Manager,* who brought to my attention the elevated status of "greatness." He said, "The word greatness is in many ways a very threatening word ... We fear that greatness is simply not in our story, but only in the story of others. Greatness demands that we eliminate caution, that we eliminate our reservations, and that we have hope in the face of the history of our limitations."

To pursue the ultimate in education for our students—to allow them to become more than they ever hoped to be—a transformation must take place in ourselves, board members, school administrators, teachers, and other school people. I know now that one can have school improvement without quality, but that one cannot have quality enhancement without school improvement. Thus, our ultimate goals must be quality enhancement, not school improvement. I have also realized, through my own transformation, that quality has almost nothing to do with excellence. In fact, the term quality is too revolutionary and too transformational to have a good synonym. This is why far too many school administrators are not bent on producing quality schools. They are simply not aware that quality is something completely different than excellence.

You probably don't believe me. Let me see if I can convince you. To achieve excellence, school districts have implemented site-based management, outcome-based education, magnet schools, effective schools, cooperative learning, and a host of other programs and processes. However, these attempts were only a piecemeal approach to improving our schools. For example, site-based management changed the management of the school district and schools, but did little in terms of changing how things are done in the classroom; outcome-based education focused on the achievement of student competencies in the classroom, but, the school district and schools changed very little; effective schools had an overall effect on the school district, schools, and classrooms, but it did not appreciably change how things are done in the classroom; and cooperative learning changed to some degree the teaching arrangement in the classroom, but the management of the school district and schools remained the same.

When TQ is properly installed throughout the three levels of school organizations, we have an integrated system in which the principles and practices of TQ became the foundation not only of the management process of the school district and schools, but also of the teaching process of the classroom. This is one of the reasons why TQ requires a transformation: everything changes. No other program or process does this. Let's take, for example, one of Deming's Fourteen Points: "Eliminate fear ..." This requires school administrators to search for those management practices as well as teaching practices that produce fear and to eliminate them, affecting all three levels of the organization. Let's consider Deming's Theory of Systems, included in the System of Profound Knowledge. Both school people and students are taught to become systems thinkers and to understand that everything and everybody are parts of a system; that is, we are all interrelated and whatever affects one person or component, affects the others. Again, all three levels are affected. Let's explore one of Deming's Seven Deadly Sins (sometimes known as diseases): "Evaluation of performance ..." Here again all three levels of the school organization are affected. Our present system of evaluating teaching performance is outdated and ineffective. Central school administrators develop the system, and principals are expected to execute it, write up a report, and interview the teacher who is being blamed for poor performance. The problem with most current teacher evaluation systems is that we blame teachers for the fault of an ineffective evaluation system. Dr. Deming maintains that more than 90 percent of teacher performance problems can be blamed on the system and the remaining portion on teachers. However, we in education do things backward, we blame all of the faults of the system on the teachers. TQ is the one process that tackles this problem.

This deadly disease does not stop with evaluation of the performance of teachers. It also covers our system of grading and evaluating students. Deming states that the remedy for this disease is substituting cooperation for competition; eliminating grades; ceasing imposing a time limit on learning; and eliminating failure. TQ applies not only to changing the management of the school district, schools, and classrooms, but also its principles and practices can be integrated in the classrooms to make learning fun and enjoyable for both teachers and students.

This is what my colleague Theresa May Hicks, a third grade teacher, has to say about what's going on in her classroom: "I have found the most effective method of introducing the statistical methods and the necessary practice with the Plan-Do-Check-Act (PDCA) cycle and the System of Profound Knowledge is to expand on lessons taken right out of my adopted texts. You may wish to call this activity reinforcement or enrichment, but either way, it gives situations within which I can be creative and still address my course of study. I look at each new lesson as an open door within which I can have student teams either actually produce something, or be involved in a cooperative team-building activity."

I would go on and on explaining why I believe that TQ is like no other processes. However, I believe I have made my point.

Reaching greatness is the practical and realistic manifestation of TQ. It is a systematic, programmatic, strategic, and operational process for school organizational greatness. It is a human endeavor designed to identify and to accommodate the needs of all of the customers: students, parents, teachers, communities, industries and others. TQ is not a passing fad, because it is the natural evolution of all the effective management principles and practices currently being applied in the best-run industries, service organizations, and in school districts in the United States. It is not a destination. It is a journey, because it requires total commitment on the part of the superintendent and his or her central school administrators to use proven and practical techniques to accommodate the present school organizational culture. Finally, all of the answers that we have been searching for to produce great school districts for our most treasured resources—our students—are right before us if we take ownership of TQ.

Someone once wrote: "All that remains beyond our physical being is the spiritual, for the heart is the source of our will. It is the spirit, the will to act, that defines greatness. It is the spirit that differentiates schools. It is the symbols we project, the reputation we earn, the stature of our deeds that conveys to others an aura of greatness."

I wrote this book because I am convinced that TQ can and will transform American schools so they can become educational/social science organizations capable of reaching every student, regardless of his or her God-given abilities, interests, and talents. To perform this feat, we must do as Dr. Deming says. To do this, we must treat TQ as a new religion, one that will save our young souls, if we treat this process like no other and embrace its philosophy with a deep and penetrating religious belief.

I only wish that I had the opportunity to have attended a TQ school—how much better I would have been treated as a human being. So, I give guidance through this book for others to plan, launch, and sustain the quest for TQ. In each chapter, there are figures and bulleted lists to enhance your understanding of TQ, as well as checklists for making the transition to TQ. Discussed is a systematic approach for developing a master plan for implementing TQ not only on the district and school levels, but also on the classroom level. I discuss how to demonstrate a strong commitment to and support for TQ through words, actions, and deeds to empower both school and community people to initiate quality efforts. A guidance system for TQ is explained and illustrated. A checklist is included to assist school districts to develop their own TQ process model to meet the specific needs of the school and community. Considerable attention is given to the core of the TQ process, the quality service measurement system, so that school administrators can easily devise one for their own school districts. Most school administrators have received their training in detecting and closing one performance gap (instructional). I go further and devote a chapter to detecting and closing not one, but five performance gaps that may appear in a school setting. With the encouragement of a number of teachers who have received my training, I have included a chapter on implementing quality in the classroom. Specific suggestions are highlighted to integrate TQ principles and practices with course content. I conclude with a chapter on educating and training school and community people in TQ, and another chapter on recognizing and rewarding individuals and teams for their quality victories.

Chapter One

Introducing Total Quality In Education

America has still not reached the take-off stage in making quality a national obsession. I do not know why, in the face of overwhelming evidence of the benefits, more organizations do not institute full-blown quality processes. Models ... validated by a five-year record of continually increasing success, prove that quality is not a mysterious, unattainable goal. Quality can be achieved. Practical steps can be taken - NOW.

—Tom Peters

In a total quality (TQ) context, the standard for determining quality is meeting and exceeding customer needs, requirements, and expectations on a continual basis. There are many potential requirements and expectations that customers have, depending upon the particular product or service and needs of the customer. Rather than the school district attempting traditionally to specify what it views as quality, a TQ approach to quality systematically inquires of its customers what it is they want, and strives to meet, and even to exceed those requirements. Such an approach helps to identify the elements of quality that are of paramount importance to customers. It also recognizes that customers' expectations may change over time.

IN THIS CHAPTER, I WILL INTRODUCE TQ IN EDUCATION BY:

- Explaining the origin of the quality movement
- Defining TQ
- Providing an understanding of quality
- Defining quality
- Identifying the types of quality
- Extending the quality process
- Defining customer-provider interface
- Describing operating practices of quality
- Identifying the characteristics of a quality educational organization

EXPLAINING THE ORIGIN OF THE QUALITY MOVEMENT

It would be wonderful if I could claim giving momentum to the quality movement in education; however, I cannot. I do not know what school district is responsible for being the first to implement TQ. However, some practitioners maintain that the Mt. Edgecumbe High School in Sitka, Alaska, is the first school to do so. I do know that no school district has of yet fully implemented it on all levels of the school organization. However, throughout his lectures, an American named W. Edwards Deming, Ph.D., has frequently espoused that quality can become operational in all organizations, even schools. Dr. Deming is responsible for helping Japan build its economy after World War II by awakening the Japanese consciousness to quality. Later on, Joseph M. Juran, Ph.D., gave more impetus to the quality movement. Another person who is respected as a guru in the quality movement is Philip B. Crosby, Ph.D. All three of these contributors are discussed below.

Why are the theories of the three gurus appropriate for education? It's rather simple. In the past, education reforms often developed from ideas that began in industry. In fact, the area of educational administration originated from the scientific management movement in the early 1900s. As a result, educational administration is closely aligned with the principles and practices of business and industry. The reason for focusing on the three gurus is that their systems for improving quality services and products have worked. Repeatedly, their principles and practices have produced great organizations, and will do so in education.

W. Edwards Deming, Ph.D., is the 93-year-old statistician best known for setting Japanese business upon the course that has made them number one in quality throughout the world. In the 1950s, he went to Japan to help the United States secretary of war conduct a population census, and was invited to lecture to top business leaders on statistical quality advice. The rest is history, and today the highest quality award in Japan is named after Dr. Deming. He has been called the "founder of the third wave of the Industrial Revolution," and often sounds like a crusader for quality with statements such as, "it is time to adopt a new religion in America."

According to Dr. Deming, good quality does not necessarily mean high quality. He says it is, rather, "a predictable degree of uniformity and dependability, at low cost, and suited to the market." He recognizes that the quality of any product or service has many scales, and may get a high mark on one scale and a low mark on another. In other words, quality is whatever the customer needs and wants. Further, since the customer's requirements and tastes are always changing, the solution to defining quality in terms of the customer is to constantly conduct customer research.

Dr. Deming's basic philosophy on quality is that productivity improves as variability decreases. Since all things vary, he says, that is why the statistical method of quality control is needed.

"Statistical control does not imply absence of defective times. It is a state of random variation, in which the limits of variation are predictable," he explains.

He is extremely critical of U.S. management, and is an advocate of worker participation in decision making. He claims that management is responsible for 94 percent of all quality problems, and points out that it is management's task to help people work smarter, not harder.

"The first step is for management to remove the barriers that rob the hourly worker of his or her right to do a good job," he says.

Since the substance of this book deals with Dr. Deming's philosophy and principles, the next chapter is exclusively devoted to his work. However, the works of two other men, Drs. Joseph M. Juran and Philip B. Crosby, deserve mention.

Joseph M. Juran, Ph.D., was born eighty-nine years ago in Rumania, and came to the United States in 1912. After studying electrical engineering and law, he rose to chief of the inspection control division of Western Electric Company and professor at New York University. Dr. Juran, like Dr. Deming, is credited with part of the quality success story of Japan, where he went in 1954 to lecture on how to manage quality. He is the author of numerous books on quality and management, as well as editor of the *Quality Control Handbook*. In 1979, he founded the Juran Institute, which conducts quality training seminars.

According to Dr. Juran, there are two kinds of quality: fitness for use and conformance to specifications. To illustrate the difference, he says a dangerous product could meet all specifications, but not be fit for use.

Dr. Juran was the first to deal with the broad management aspects of quality, which distinguished him from those who espouse specific techniques, statistical or otherwise. In the 1940s, he pointed out that the technical aspects of quality control had been well covered, but that firms did not know how to manage for quality. He identified some of the problems as organization, communication, and coordination of functions — in other words, the human element.

According to Dr. Juran, "An understanding of the human situations associated with the job will go far to solve the technical problems; in fact, such understanding may be a prerequisite of a solution."

For example, he says, "an inspector may incorrectly interpret the specifications, and thus subvert quality control efforts, or worse, he may knowingly protect favored operators or suppliers."

Dr. Juran talks about three basic steps to progress: structured annual improvements combined with devotion and a sense of urgency, massive training programs, and upper management leadership. In his view, less than 20 percent of quality problems are due to workers, with the remainder being caused by management. Just as all managers need some training in finance, all should have training in quality in order to oversee and participate in quality improvement projects.

"Top management should be included, because all major quality problems are interdepartmental. Moreover, pursuing departmental goals can sometimes undermine a company's overall quality mission," Dr. Juran says.

The Juran Institute teaches project-by-project, problem-solving methods of quality improvement, in which upper management must be involved.

"The project approach is important," says Dr. Juran. "When it comes to quality, there is no such thing as improvement in general. Any improvement in quality is going to come about project by project, and no other way."

Dr. Juran's ten steps to quality improvement are:

1. Build awareness of the need and opportunity for improvement.
2. Set goals for improvement.
3. Organize to reach the goals (establish a quality council, identify problems, select projects, appoint teams, designate facilitators).
4. Provide training.
5. Carry out projects to solve problems.
6. Report progress.

7. Give recognition.
8. Communicate results.
9. Keep score.
10. Maintain momentum by making annual improvement part of the regular systems and processes of the company.

Philip B. Crosby, Ph.D., is the 67-year-old quality expert best known for coming up with the concept of zero defects in the 1960s when he was in charge of quality for the Pershing Missile Project at Martin Corporation. In 1965, he went to International Telephone and Telegraph (ITT) as director of quality, and left in 1979 to form Philip Crosby Associates. He got into consulting and writing because he "was tired of hearing how the United States was going down the chute." His book, *Quality Is Free*, has sold more than one million copies.

According to Dr. Crosby's definition, quality is conformance to requirements, and it can only be measured by the cost of nonconformance. "Don't talk about poor quality or high quality. Talk about conformance and nonconformance," he says. The approach means that the only standard of performance is zero defects, which means to examine and to adjust the attitude of defect prevention; that is, to do the job right the first time.

If he had to sum up in a single word what quality management is all about, Dr. Crosby says the word would be prevention. Whereas the conventional view says quality is achieved through inspection, testing, and checking, he says that prevention is the only system that can be utilized. And when Dr. Crosby says prevention he means perfection. There is no place in his philosophy for statistically acceptable levels of quality.

"People go to great elaborate things to develop statistical levels of compliance," he says. "We've learned to believe that error is inevitable, and to plan for it. But," he adds, "there is absolutely no reason for having errors or defects in any product."

Dr. Crosby talks about a quality vaccine that firms can use to prevent nonconformances. The three ingredients of this vaccine are determination, education, and implementation. He points out that quality improvement is a process, not a program, saying, "Nothing permanent or lasting ever comes from a program."

One misconception concerning Dr. Crosby is that he is primarily advocating inducing workers to perform better. He explains the root of this misconception, saying, "Unfortunately, zero defects was picked up by industry as a motivation program." In 1964, the Japanese adopted zero defects, and Dr. Crosby says they were the only ones who correctly applied it—as a management performance standard rather than as a motivation program for employees.

Dr. Crosby's fourteen steps to quality improvement are:

1. Make it clear that management is committed to quality.
2. Form quality improvement teams with representatives from each department.
3. Determine where current and potential quality problems lie.
4. Evaluate the cost of quality and explain its use as a management tool.
5. Raise the quality awareness and personal concern of all employees.
6. Take actions to correct problems identified through previous steps.
7. Establish a committee for the zero defects program.
8. Train supervisors to actively carry out their part of the quality improvement program.
9. Hold a zero defects day to let all employees realize that there has been a change.
10. Encourage individuals to establish improvement goals for themselves and their groups.
11. Encourage employees to communicate to management the obstacles they face in attaining their improvement goals.
12. Recognize and appreciate those who participate.

13. Establish quality councils to communicate on a regular basis.
14. Do it all over again to emphasize that the quality improvement program never ends.

To implement TQ in education requires a transformation by all school administrators. Most school administrators have been trained in the above traditional management principles and practices to achieve a level of excellence. In fact, some of them have received rewards for doing so. The job of achieving greatness in education is a herculean task that cannot be achieved unless school administrators and other school people have undergone a transformation, whereby they are guided by a System of Profound Knowledge. (See Chapter Two for more on this.)

IS TQ THE ANSWER?

Only time will tell if TQ is the answer to our educational system. It has gone beyond being just a phenomenon. It is a movement that has spread in every industry, business, and service organization. Today, it is beginning to spread into public education. In fact, it is spreading throughout the world. Why? Because TQ involves everyone within the school district, from board members to volunteers, in a daily search for incremental improvements that provide every school person with the education, training, and authority needed to identify, analyze, and solve problems; to establish quality goals and objectives, and to measure results; and to focus the strategic vision on the needs, requirements, and expectations of its customers. With TQ implementation, everything a school organization does, every service, every product, every program, and every process is designed to reach greatness.

There are a multitude of definitions for the term quality. C. Philip Alexander states that quality "... is the invisible and intangible expression of human excellence." Dr. Crosby defines quality as "the total of expenditures devoted to preventing and correcting errors." Leonard L. Berry maintains that quality is "both reality and perception—a chemistry of what actually transpires in the service encounter and how the customer perceives what transpires based on service expectations." Howard S. Gitlow says, "Quality is a judgment by customers or users of a product or service; it is the extent to which the customers or users feel that product or service surpasses the needs of customers." Dr. Deming maintains that quality means "anticipating the needs of the customer, translating those needs into a useful and dependable product, and creating a system that can produce the product at the lowest possible price."

Quality deficiencies anywhere in the school organization can have an impact on any component of the system. For example, students who are unable to read after the third grade will be unable to master their subject elsewhere along the continuum of learning. That is why any quality improvement efforts must be total, involving everyone within and out of the school district. These efforts must also entail changes in the way things are done in the school organization, which is the responsibility of school administrators. Hitherto, school administrators tried to make improvements in isolation. In many instances, these improvement efforts have many components, and any of these components can and have undercut isolated improvement efforts. In addition, traditional improvement efforts usually do not have a support network to deal with problems and to ensure continuity if something goes wrong. School organizations that truly embrace the TQ concept are not fraught with these problems.

Quality in education refers to a cooperative system in which both customers (students, teachers, and parents) and providers (school administrators, teachers, and others) mutually agree to, and meet the needs, requirements, and expectations of customers on a continuous basis.

TQ encompasses four basic principles:

1. a focus on internal and external customers;

2. a commitment to education and training;

3. the empowerment of all school people; and,

4. the goal of continuous improvement.

To achieve these principles requires the transformation of school and community people to dream, speak, breath, and perform TQ and greatness.

IDENTIFYING TYPES OF QUALITY

Gitlow identifies three types of quality: design/redesign, conformance, and performance. Each is described below.

Quality of Design/Redesign

Gitlow says: "Quality of design begins with research on, and analysis of the needs, requirements, and expectations of customers to provide either a service or product. Next, requirements are established for the service or product through interfacing among various schools, departments, and units within the school district."

Research on the customer may be conducted internally within the school district. For example, a service support team conducts a survey among teachers to determine the specific education and training needs that lead to improvement of the ability of teachers to perform in the classroom.

An analysis of the needs, requirements, and expectations of the customer is the systematic investigation into any problems the customer currently has with the service or product. A critical review of the needs, requirements, and expectations indicates what has to be changed in the service or product to satisfy and surpass the needs of the customer. For example, a focus group of students is organized to obtain information on why students are unhappy about meals in the high school cafeteria. This information is transmitted to a team for review and action.

Quality of Conformance

Quality of conformance is the degree to which a school district and its providers exceed service or product requirements to meet the needs, requirements, and expectations of customers. Once service or product requirements are determined through quality-of-design analysis and studies, the school district, school, department, or unit continuously strives to exceed these requirements. The primary goal of continuous improvement in education is to create services or products that produce great school districts. For example, during the initial year of the process, teachers agree on a 95 percent score on all tests as an acceptable level of quality; the second year, a 96 percent score; and, the third year, a 97 percent score.

A quality of conformance study can detect two sources of loss in quality. First, it can detect when services or products result in quality requirements below the needs of the customer. For example, the design, development, and implementation of a reading program that does not appreciably improve student achievement. This loss may be eliminated by replacing the current reading program with one that meets the needs of students.

Second, a loss in quality may result when a process generates services or product quality characteristics that are not uniform. That is, when the service or product creates high variation among customers. For example, a performance quality study in a reading class of twenty-five equally adept students revealed that six students made significant gain, four made "some" gain, ten made "little" gain, and the remaining students made no gain.

This loss in quality is due to a lack of uniformity that can be reduced by understanding and dealing with the causes of variation using statistical techniques. The two causes of process variation are briefly described below.

A process similar to people, programs, and procedures varies over time. In fact, everything varies. The extent to which the process varies is due to either common causes or special causes. Take the example of John's appetite. Some days John is hungrier than other days. Some days, John may eat less than usual. His appetite varies from day to day. This variation is due to common causes. However, if John were to go on a diet or become seriously ill, which would dramatically alter his eating pattern for a period of time, and he lost a considerable amount of weight, this would be due to special causes. If he had not deviated from his usual pattern, he would have continued on a previous path of common variation. Common causes can be caused by such things like poor training, poor planning, poor design, or poor lighting. Special causes can be caused by absenteeism, new school persons, defective equipment, and more.

Quality of Performance

Through customer research and analysis, quality of performance determines how the school district's service and products are performing. Quality of performance may include a teacher's ability to teach, a secretary's telephone manners, a student's success after graduation, or effectiveness of support services for teachers. The continual flow of information generated by quality of performance studies helps to clarify the gap between customer research and analysis, and the constraint of service and product requirements.

Extending the Quality Process

Implementing TQ in a school district is highly dependent on a school administrator's ability and propensity to create an environment that demonstrates a commitment to understanding, and to accepting responsibility for school improvement and quality enhancement. The quality environment encourages teamwork, open communication, research, problem solving, trust, empowerment, security, pride of professionalism and workmanship, and continuous improvement. An esprit de corps prevails in this type of culture.

In the quality environment, school people are no longer afraid to identify and discuss problems of the school district, school, department, or unit. School administrators are actively involved with all school people in the quest for TQ and greatness. All school people learn to participate and cooperate as team members, and to speak the language of TQ. School people are responsible for communicating their concerns to school administrators so they can take appropriate action. Continuous quality improvement eventually leads to enhanced student achievement and greater satisfaction for all school people at reduced cost. The quality environment includes more than the school district, school, department, or unit. It also means providers, external customers, the community, and the board of education.

DEFINING CUSTOMER-PROVIDER INTERFACE

Since TQ relates to the customer-provider relationship, which is relatively new in education, attention should be given to how the customer relates to the provider and what services are provided by the provider. Figure 1.1 illustrates the interface between the customer and provider. Customer and provider are further defined as "I" for internal and "E" for external. The terms customers and providers are discussed below.

A provider is any person or group on which the quality improvement (QI) team depends for input that is used to deliver a service to satisfy its customer or to produce a product. Input includes things like resources, materials, information, equipment, services, and products. An internal provider is any person or group that works in the school district to satisfy a customer. For example, the staff development department of the school district inputs data from various persons and groups within (and sometimes outside) the school district about staff development needs, and it receives advice about its budget from the business department. These two sources are internal providers.

FIGURE 1.1
Customer-Provider Interface

Customer	Type	Provider	Type	Services
Students	I	Teachers	I	Instructions, counseling, guidance, leadership, materials, supplies, space, technology, equipment, safe and secure environment
Teachers	I	School administrators and all support staff	I	Multiple support
School Administrators	I	Board of Education	I	Multiple support
Parents	E	School district	E	Knowledge, experience, wisdom, skills, character
Community	E	School district	E	Knowledge, experience, wisdom, skills, character
Colleges and universities	E	School district	E	Minimum academic skills, characters
School district	E	Vendors	E	Materials, supplies, equipment, technology

I = Internal
E = External

At the same time, the staff development department might decide to bring in consultants and prepare training materials from a publisher. These sources are considered external providers.

A customer is any person or group to which the QI team delivers either a service or product in order to meet and exceed a need, requirement, or expectation. There are two types of customers: internal and external. An internal customer is a person or group located within the school district who receives a service or product. Most school people are aware that students are internal customers. However, a few do not relate to teachers as customers. When a member of the staff development department provides some service in terms of training to a group of teachers, the teachers become internal customers, and the staff development people become internal providers. Parents are also external and internal customers. For example, when parents send their children to school they become external customers. When they participate on the QI team, they become internal providers.

DESCRIBING THE PRINCIPLES AND PRACTICES OF TOTAL QUALITY

There are a few TQ operating principles and practices that comprise the substance of this book. These are consistent with criteria from the Malcolm Baldrige National Quality Award. The Baldrige criteria identify a complete and "nondenominational" framework of what it takes to become a quality organization. The three principles of TQ to maximize customer satisfaction are to:

1. Focus on achieving customer satisfaction.
2. Seek continuous and long-term improvement in all the school organization processes and outputs.
3. Take steps to assure the full involvement of all school people improving quality.

Put another way, the essence of TQ is involving and empowering all school people to improve the quality of services and products continuously in order to satisfy and even delight the customer. To achieve this goal requires identifying customers and their needs, having a clear idea of how the school organization plans to go about meeting expectations, and making sure that everyone in the school organization understands the customers' needs and is empowered to act on their behalf. There are few quick fixes for improving quality. Experience shows that it takes years to create a new environment, or culture that places a premium on greatness; to build structures that will sustain and manage change; and, to provide education to drive the effort.

How does a school district achieve a commitment to TQ that meets the above description? This approach to TQ emphasizes several elements or practices that, when integrated as a strategy for quality improvement, result in the fundamental changes required. These include central school administration leadership and support, strategic planning, customer focus, measurement and analysis, commitment to training, school people empowerment and teamwork, and quality assurance.

Central School Administration Leadership and Support

The first and most critical element of TQ is leadership and support from central administration. School administrators at the central office must be directly and actively involved in establishing an environment that encourages change, empowerment, innovation, risk-taking, pride in work, and continuous improvement on behalf of all customers. These school administrators set the tone, determine the theme, and provide impetus. They also communicate quality policies and goals throughout the school district. This means providing an active, visible presence to all school people, and the resources, time, and training essential for the school organization to improve quality. Central school administrators must ensure that communications are open and effective throughout the school organization, among all school people, and among customers and providers.

Effective school administrators involve school people, including union/association leadership where applicable, in the early stages of the quality planning process. They empower school people to make decisions. They shift their efforts from directing and controlling how the operations will be carried out to identifying and removing barriers that prevent school people from meeting customer needs, requirements, and expectations the first time and every time. They lead the fundamental change in the school organization culture from crisis management to continuous improvement.

Not only do standards of quality vary among the above dimensions, they also frequently change over time. Once customers become accustomed to a new, higher level of quality than had previously been available, their expectations often increase so that what is considered acceptable quality also increases as well.

Strategic Planning

Strategic planning drives the school organization's improvement efforts. Planning for quality improvement is integrated into the strategic planning process, so that planning and achieving quality improvement become a part of the day-to-day management of the operation. Furthermore, establishing a dynamic, participatory planning process is as important as developing the plan itself.

A critical objective of TQ is to develop a climate or culture in the school organization that encourages pursuit of greatness on behalf of customers, and which nurtures risk-taking and direct participation by school people.

A primary goal of the strategic plan is to map out the long-term strategy necessary to bring about the cultural change. The plan establishes the goals for attaining superior levels of customer satisfaction and school organizational performance. Thus, it looks outward to the customer, and focuses inward on the school organization's processes. The plan, which is updated periodically, defines how the school district intends to fulfill customer expectations over the next one, two, five, or even ten years.

Everyone in the school district contributes ideas to the plan and is aware of its implications for their own areas of responsibility. In organizations in which school people are represented by union officials, both school administrators and school people benefit from the active involvement of unions/associations in planning and carrying out the quality improvement process.

Focus on the Customer

Effective school organizations seek not only to meet customer expectations, but also to go the extra mile and delight the customers. Since the strategic plan sets out the goals for meeting customer expectations, actively involving customers and finding out exactly what they want is central to a quality management effort. A strategy based solely on a school organization's perception of its customers' needs is not likely to measure accurately what customers really want or what they think of current services and products. Only the customers know, and their expectations are likely to change over time. When needs, requirements, and expectations relate to curriculum and instruction, school and community people should form a partnership to mutually agree to student outcomes.

Every school organization should have a wide range of methods for obtaining and assessing customer feedback, such as customer surveys, in-depth interviews of customer groups, follow-up of customer complaints, collection of customer feedback at time of service delivery, and third-party analysis of customer feedback. Customers should have easy access to the school district for obtaining information and resolution of their problems at the school, department, or unit level. The school organization should balance fairly the conflicting needs of different customer groups, and should set priorities for how those conflicting needs will be met. When the school district is barred by policy, law, or regulation from meeting customers' stated requirements, it should seek a waiver.

The concept of customer focus applies to both internal and external customers. Within a school district, the process of schooling is normally organized so that the student of one teacher is passed on to another before a final service is delivered. Under a TQ approach, any teacher who delivers a service or product to someone else sees that person as a customer and attempts to determine his or her needs, requirements, and expectations in order to improve the quality of the final service or product.

Measurement and Analysis

A system should be put in place to allow the school organization to determine systematically the degree to which school services please customers, and then focus on internal process improvement. Data should be collected on features of customer satisfaction such as student competencies described in the Secretary's Commission on Achieving Necessary Skills (SCANS) report, which is a report of the secretary of labor that delineates necessary skills for teachers to incorporate in their curriculum and instruction. The measurement systems should also focus on internal processes, especially on those that generate variation in quality and time. When customer data indicates a problem, or when the school organization wants to raise the level of customer satisfaction, the school district should focus on improving the processes that deliver the product or service.

In order to assure that processes are always improved, data should be collected and analyzed on a continuous basis, with particular attention paid to variation in processes. The causes of variation are examined to determine if they result from special circumstances, such as failure of textbooks to arrive in time during an effort to improve reading achievement, or from recurring or common causes, such as teachers not being trained properly to begin a new reading program. Different strategies should be adopted to correct each occurrence.

The immediate objectives of the analysis and measurement efforts are to reduce rework and waste, and to improve cost-effectiveness and accuracy. The ultimate objectives, of course, are to insure that school people understand the extent to which customer satisfaction is being realized, where there are deficiencies, and why, and to isolate causes that can be attacked systematically. A critical feature of the quality improvement process is collecting and reporting customer feedback. This information identifies deficiencies in services and end products, and is used to isolate causes and potential solutions.

Commitment to Training

Often the key element that is missing in efforts to improve processes is the education and training that will enable school people to do the job right. This includes adequate training to ensure that school people have the requisite skills to perform their jobs. It also includes education and training in quality management concepts and skills, such as teamwork, problem solving, and methods for collecting and analyzing data using basic statistical tools.

School people (and parents, too) who make contributions to quality improvement should be recognized and rewarded in ways that are meaningful and timely. Reinforcing positive performance is a key ingredient for developing service greatness. A school organization that claims to be focused on quality, but measures and rewards other things such as conformance to schedule without regard to quality, is sending conflicting messages to its school people.

Non-monetary awards and recognition can have a powerful and lasting impact on school people's motivation and commitment. The experience of many school districts facing stringent budget constraints and rigid compensation systems is that creative recognition systems can go a long way toward achieving school people participation in service improvement.

School People Empowerment and Teamwork

Once the superintendent has made the commitment to TQ, the most important and critical ingredients to achieving a quality commitment throughout the school organization are school people involvement, empowerment, and teamwork. Improving processes will be fully successful only when all school people in the school district, across vertical and horizontal levels, are involved in making it happen. When the intelligence, imagination, and energies of all school people are engaged in pursuit of the school organization's goals, amazing results can be realized. People closest to the problems usually have the best solutions. School people are an almost unlimited source of knowledge and creativity that can be used, not only to solve problems, but also to continuously improve the quality of services and products.

School people involvement and empowerment is not unique to TQ. Indeed, many school administrators claim to support the idea. Too often, actual implementation falls far short of the goals; more so in this area than in many others. Efforts often fall short also, not because of the absence of good intentions on the part of school administrators or school people, but because school administrators have not adopted specific systems and procedures to make school people involvement routine.

The first step in achieving empowerment is to involve school people systematically in identifying and solving problems. Possible approaches include teams of school people working on specific process or operating issues, cross-functional problem-solving teams, self-managing teams, and active suggestion systems. The key to all school people involvement mechanisms is that everyone be empowered to make real and lasting changes on the spot, which is usually done after the school organization has some experience with school people involvement.

One of the most powerful school people involvement techniques is to engage teams of school people and parents (often called QI teams or quality action (QA) teams) in addressing immediate operational issues that the team itself helps to identify and resolve. When school people participate in identifying and solving problems that are affecting the quality of the work they perform, they experience the satisfaction of making tangible contributions to the quality of their performance, and are frequently motivated to make continuing and lasting improvements to the job they do. Obviously these results will not occur without the active support and responsiveness of the central school administrators.

The school people involvement efforts of QI teams should be supported and reinforced by building into the school district's management system explicit recognition and support for teams. Frequently, a quality steering (QS) committee and other bodies are established that are responsible for approving teams at the outset, assigning resources to let the teams perform their mission, and perhaps most importantly, authorizing changes in overall systems and policies necessary to implement solutions.

The school people involvement strategy should include the unions/associations at all stages in the process so that team leaders understand what is planned and can support the effort. School administrators must be prepared to listen, and where possible, to adopt recommendations of school people, delegating greater responsibility to other levels in the school organization. If they do, everyone will feel "ownership" of QI, and will exhibit personal pride in the quality of their performance.

Quality Assurance

In order to meet customer quality requirements, the processes used to produce their products and services must be designed to prevent problems and errors from occurring in the first place. Quality assurance in a TQ environment focuses on the front end of processes, beginning with inputs, rather than the traditional controlling mode of inspecting and checking services or products at the end of operations, after errors are made. Processes are designed both to prevent errors and to detect and correct them as they occur throughout the process. As part of the emphasis on prevention and early detection, school people should be trained to hire competent teachers, and to analyze incoming equipment and supplies. The school organization establishes a partnership with providers and customers to assure continuous improvement in the quality of the end services and products.

CITING CHARACTERISTICS OF A QUALITY SCHOOL ORGANIZATION

When the conditions cited in this chapter have been adopted by school organizations, the results should not only be startling, but great. School people at all levels focus on their customers' needs and become committed to and involved in the quest for quality. Principals and other school people (and parents and students) form a team in seeking continuous improvement. The cumulative result of these changes frequently is a profound change in the overall culture and atmosphere of the school organization. As school organizations become more streamlined, a larger percentage of school people are involved in school or unit operations, and there is a greater spirit of cooperation and working toward common goals. Perhaps most significantly, a spirit of energy and excitement, even fun, permeates the school organization. As a sixth grade student in a quality classroom said, "an education miracle has occurred."

Some specific contrasting characteristics that frequently result are summarized below:

Traditional Management Approach	TQ Approach
The school organization is hierarchical and has rigid lines of authority and responsibility.	The school organization becomes flatter, more flexible, and less hierarchal (five levels or less).
Focus is on maintaining the status quo ("don't fix it if it ain't broke").	Focus shifts to continuous improvement in systems and processes (continue to improve it even if it "ain't broke").
Teachers perceive the principal as controller.	Teachers perceive the principal as coach and facilitator; principal is seen as an educational leader.

Principal/teacher relationships are characterized by interdependency, fear, and control.	Principal/teacher relationships shift to interdependency, trust, and mutual commitment.
The focus of teacher efforts is on individual effort; teachers view themselves as competitors.	The focus of teacher efforts shifts to team effort; teachers see themselves as teammates.
School administrators perceive school people training as costs.	School administrators perceive school people as an asset and training as an investment.
School administrators determine what quality is and whether it is being provided.	School people and customers form a partnership, define quality, and develop measures to determine if customers' requirements are met.
Primary basis for decision making is off-the-top-of-head, by-the-seat-of-the-pants, gut-feeling or instinct.	Primary basis for decision making shifts to facts, reasearch and systems.

Most school administrators are not knowledgeable about Dr. Deming's work, and believe that TQ is similar to other programs, such as site-based management, participatory management, etc. In fact, when I asked a superintendent in Texas if he was committed to TQ, he said, "I am committed to the tools of TQ," as if the philosophy, principles, diseases, obstacles, and System of Profound Knowledge—which I equate with the soul of TQ—were unimportant. Superintendents who are committed to the tools of TQ need to attend one of Dr.

Deming's four-day institutes. Unless they do, I am afraid their school and community people will be denied a great education.

Superintendents beginning a TQ effort should bear in mind that to realize the full potential of TQ requires a fundamental cultural change. When the transformation has occurred, everyone in the school organization is continuously and systematically working to improve the quality of services and processes, and the processes for delivering them, in order to maximize customer satisfaction. TQ becomes a way of managing that is embedded in the culture and environment of the school organization, not simply a set of specific management techniques and tools.

It follows that a successful approach to quality improvement requires a long-term commitment and recognition that the effort is an unending journey. Although some early successes can be achieved, a cultural transformation to full use of the TQ approach will occur only gradually.

A TQ approach to greatness represents a unique blending of the objective, practical, and quantitative aspects of management (e.g., focusing on processes and relying on quantitative data and statistical analysis for decision making) and the "soft" aspects of management (e.g., providing visionary leadership, promoting a spirit of cooperation and teamwork, fostering empowerment, and practicing participative management). Many school organizations, when deciding to undertake a TQ effort, focus on one or several of these general approaches. A fully successful effort requires balanced attention to both.

Although many of the principles and operating practices summarized above are familiar, and many school administrators believe they already practice them, many aspects of TQ are in fact unique. For instance, many school administrators encourage school people involvement and empowerment, but few school organizations adopt the specific practices that bring them about, such as reliance on teams of school and community people to identify and resolve specific operating problems. Where teams are used, few have been delegated sufficient authority, have made changes, or have been trained to use the full array of TQ tools.

Although many school organizations recognize the importance of measurement and analysis to decision making, many measure the wrong things. Also, few school organizations focus on internal processes across functions in order to assure that quality is built into the service system on a continuing basis.

Some school organizations claim to serve the customer first, but few systematically and rigorously identify the needs of customers, both internal and external, and monitor the extent to which those needs are being met.

Many school organizations do not treat teachers as internal customers. As a result, teachers do not get the quality of support due them by school administrators.

DESCRIBING TOTAL QUALITY DIFFERENCES BETWEEN EDUCATION AND INDUSTRY

Although most of the concepts, procedures, principles, and practices for implementing TQ are identical for school organizations to that of other organizations, there are some differences that should be discussed. The major differences fall into the following six categories, including establishing a partnership to determine customers' needs, using basic statistical tools for solving problems, allocating more funds for education and training, implementing TQ in the classroom, making everyone responsible for TQ, and involving the school as a whole.

Establish a Partnership to Determine Customers' Needs

Unlike industrial, manufacturing, and service organizations in which the customers determine their needs, in education, both the customers (parents and students) and providers (school administrators and teachers) reach mutual agreement on needs, requirements, and expectations. There is a sound reason for this. School administrators and teachers are the professionals who have been trained and certified to have some knowledge of what students need today. They must also look into the future to determine what students need to become productive members of society. However, parents, who are the customers of the school district, also know what they want for their children. That is why it is absolutely necessary for a partnership to exist between the school district and parents in order to decide on student needs, requirements, and expectations.

This reminds of the time when New York City Chancellor of Schools Joseph Fernandez was defending himself before the board and some irate parents challenged his posture on including gays in the curriculum and distributing condoms to students. One parent approached him and said, "You forget that we are the customers." Chancellor Fernandez should have listened more to his customers. Perhaps he would have remained in his position for another contract period. It will take time before school administrators understand that we must not impose our will on the customers, but meet with them to reach some common ground.

Use Basic Statistical Tools for Solving Problems

In many organizations, advanced statistical techniques are applied to tackle complex problems. Although basic statistical techniques are useful for solving school-related problems, there is not a strong need to use advanced statistical techniques. If advanced statistical techniques are warranted in a particular situation, a consultant should be hired.

Allocate More Funds for Education and Training

Most school districts are under-funded for education, training, and development. As a result, additional funds must be allocated to this category. A formula to be considered is one to two percent of the payroll. In addition, school administrators, teachers, secretaries, clerks, and other members of the school family should be required to engage in a minimum number of hours of TQ education, training, and technical training.

Implementing TQ in the Classroom

An essential feature of the TQ process that is not done in other organizations is the implementation of TQ in the classroom. Most of the principles and practices in TQ can be applied in the classroom.

Make Everyone Responsible for TQ

Unlike site-based management, in which teachers have the option to become involved in the process or not, with TQ teachers, in fact, no one has the right not to participate. Quality is everyone's responsibility.

Involve the School as a Whole

Keep the school as a whole involved in quality decisions. Since quality is everyone's responsibility, this concept should be embraced by all schools. In reality, this means that before a major decision is implemented, it should be brought to the entire school family for discussion and agreement. As a result, teams will not get the stigma of being an elitist group that can doom the quality improvement efforts.

SUMMARY

To introduce TQ in education, our whole education system must change. We need first and foremost committed superintendents of schools who are supported by a ready and willing central school administration, to do whatever is necessary to support the principals, teachers, and parents in their pursuit of great school districts. We will need to respond to students, parents, and teachers as customers, and school administrators and teachers as service providers. We need to define the meaning of quality and TQ, as well as to understand the different types of quality. We need to establish a quality service measurement system in order to deliver quality teaching and services. We need to employ a number of methods to listen to our customers in order to identify and meet their needs, requirements, and expectations. We need to integrate in the classroom the principles and practices of TQ with course content. We need to establish teams to develop and execute plans to deliver quality services and products. We need to perform all these tasks through the transformation called for by Dr. W. Edwards Deming. His philosophy and principles are elaborated on in the next chapter.

Checklist for Making the Transition to TQ

The following activities are necessary to embrace TQ in order to successfully implement it throughout all levels of the school organization:

1. Become familiar with the various definitions of quality in order to develop a definition appropriate to the school district.
2. Be able to actualize the various types of quality.
3. Create a TQ environment by including subunits of the school organization.
4. Define all internal and external customers and providers, and disseminate the list throughout the school district.
5. Understand the principles and practices of TQ, and insist that they are implemented, beginning with a pilot study.
6. Make a list of desirable characteristics of a quality school organization, and use them as guidelines to plan, develop, implement, and evaluate the school district's TQ model.
7. Know the various principles of the TQ gurus, and adopt those that are appropriate for meeting the needs of your school district.

CHAPTER TWO

Understanding Deming's Philosophy And The System Of Profound Knowledge

Given the same capital, labor, and technology, one firm can produce better quality with higher and continually improving productivity than another if it possesses profound knowledge and the other does not.

—*Rafael Aguayo*

D r. Deming has developed Fourteen Guidelines, Seven Deadly Sins, Thirteen Obstacles, and a System of Profound Knowledge, all of which he says are needed in order to transform a school district from one state into another, the same way that a caterpillar can metamorphose (not my words, though I wish they were) into a butterfly. According to Dr. Deming, "the transformation will lead to the adoption of what I call a system and the need to optimize the performance in an effort to fulfill the aim of the system." He stresses the need for the system and individual components to be cooperative instead of competitive. He also uses statistics and some basic planning tools to improve the system. The transformation that he calls for is more like a religion. In fact, he continually calls for a new religion to transform organizations. Unfortunately, many school administrators who are not thoroughly familiar with the works of Dr. Deming admire the "tools" of quality, but do not become "baptized" by his philosophy and guidelines.

IN THIS CHAPTER, I WILL COVER THE FOLLOWING:

- Deming's Fourteen Points
- Identifying the Seven Deadly Sins and Thirteen Obstacles
- Understanding the System of Profound Knowledge

DESCRIBING DR. DEMING'S FOURTEEN POINTS

Since Dr. Deming's Fourteen Points were originally designed for manufacturing companies, some school officials have found them difficult to translate for educational purposes, because they could not relate statistics, variations, systems, etc., to the instructional process. I was fortunate to attend one of Dr. Deming's four-day institutes, and have translated his principles so they can be applied to your school district.

Create Constancy of Purpose for Improvement of Service

Constancy of purpose means developing a network of aims (guidance system) to govern the behavior of school people to stay in business through innovation, research, and education; developing continuous improvement of products and services; maintaining equipment, furniture and fixtures; and aiding production in the organization. There are thirteen steps to this guideline. They are:

1. Develop a mission statement for your school district, schools, departments, and units.

2. Create a strategic vision as the umbrella for your entire school district, and a superintendent's vision, school visions, and student visions as action plans to realize your strategic vision.

3. Develop core values for your district, and shared values for individual schools. Make them measurable, and evaluate them annually.

4. Prepare a quality policy and principles for your school district.

5. Prepare a service strategy for your school district.

6. Identify all internal and external customers and providers of your school district, and of each school, department, and unit.

7. Define operational definitions.

8. Establish an education and training program to translate constancy of purpose.

9. Translate constancy of purpose to school and community people through five-minute stump speeches.

10. Develop a strategic quality plan for your school district, and operational quality plans for each school, department, and unit.

11. Evaluate all school administrators partially on their ability to translate and actualize the constancy of purpose.

12. Insist that members of the board of education embrace the constancy of purpose in everything they say and do on behalf of your school district.

13. Involve your unions/associations in preparing the constancy of purpose statement.

Adopt the New Philosophy

Adopt a new religion in which the superintendent is the "prophet" preaching the TQ philosophy and the "fourteen commandments" of Dr. Deming, and your central school administrators and principals perform as "disciples" of the superintendent.

As a result of this new religion, six steps need to be taken. They are:

1. Base all your decisions on research, facts, and data. School people can no longer live with commonly accepted levels of mistakes.
2. Train all school administrators to embrace the new philosophy.
3. Replace artificial methods of training with coaching, tutoring, and mentoring.
4. Allocate more funds to education, training, and development.
5. Train all school people to embrace the new philosophy.
6. Insist that the board of education in your community allocate more funds to accommodate this new philosophy with a strong and everlasting commitment to training.

Cease Dependence on Mass Inspection

Quality comes not from inspection, but from improving the process. Inspection is not the answer. There are five steps to achieve this point. They are:

1. Require statistical evidence of quality from providers when you purchase items such as textbooks, reference material, equipment, food, furniture, fixtures, and educational supplies.
2. Eliminate rework programs, such as remedial classes and detention programs.
3. Compute the cost of poor quality and act to improve the process.
4. Eliminate the harmful effect of rating school people and grading students.
5. Eliminate departments established by the state department of education to monitor your schools. Provide services to improve existent processes.

End the Practice of Awarding Business Based on the Price Tag Alone

It is high time that school districts take a stand that price alone has no meaning. You should deal with vendors who can provide statistical evidence of control. The state requires that school districts accept bids on items at low cost. If necessary, get a waiver from the state, and purchase all items based on quality, not necessarily on the lowest bid.

Without adequate resources of quality, school business is usually given to the lowest bidder, which ultimately results in higher cost. Focusing on quality rather than on cost will in all likelihood cause a reduction in the number of bidders. Your school district must also work with vendors so they understand the new focus on quality and must understand the procedures used by vendors in order to reduce the number of defects.

Improve Constantly and Forever Your System of Production and Service

Quality enhancement is not a one-time effort. School people are obligated to continually look for ways to reduce waste and improve quality. The following are six points that address this principle:

1. Require school people and students to establish quality standards and to upgrade them continuously.
2. Survey customers frequently to determine how to improve school services and products.
3. Construct control charts to determine if processes are in or out of control. If they are out of control, you should determine and eliminate the cause. If they are in control, improve the process continuously.
4. Implement Kaizen, that is, require all school people on all levels of your school organization to implement at least one meaningful change daily.

5. Establish a formal suggestion program.
6. Form a partnership with unions and/or associations to improve service.

Revise Your Training Agenda

The traditional training received by school people for achieving excellence is insufficient. In order to make the transformation to TQ, school people need education and training in different areas, such as those indicated below:

1. Develop school administrators and supervisors as coaches, mentors, and tutors.
2. Teach school people methods of statistical control.
3. Insist that central school administrators receive the same training as other school people.
4. Train all school people until they reach a level of statistical control; that is, when all performance is charted within control limits on a control chart.
5. Train all school people to become systems thinkers.

Institute Supervisory Leadership

Supervision is the first function of leadership. The TQ system must be supervised, and this is the function of school administrators. The following are six steps to this point:

1. Train all school administrators to communicate constancy of purpose through delivery of stump speeches to school and community people.
2. Require all school administrators to base all decisions on research and facts, not on hunches, seat-of-the-pants, or off-the-top-of-the-head planning.
3. Concentrate supervision on school people that are out of statistical control, and not on low performers. When members of a team or in a school are in statistical control, there will always be low performers and high performers.

4. Train school administrators how to use the results of customer surveys.
5. Train support staff how to develop customer surveys, and how to use the results of customer surveys.
6. Enable school administrators, directors, and supervisors to gain a better understanding of their role as members of your support staff.

Drive Out Fear

Do away with old practices of blaming school people for problems of the system. School administrators are the ones who can change the system. Hold them responsible for faults of the system. There are fifteen steps to this point. They are:

1. Allow school people to fail. Failing is an indication that they are doing something for students.
2. Applaud school people who learn from mistakes.
3. Discourage gossip.
4. Do not segregate school people based on their classification. Every school person is an important member of the system.
5. Seek suggestions from school people and act on them.
6. Replace fear with trust.
7. Establish an egalitarian setting that enables school people to perform their jobs without close supervision.
8. Share information and feelings that are directly related to either jobs, responsibilities, functions, tasks, activities, or issues with school people.
9. Reduce external controls by giving school people the opportunity to monitor and correct their own performance.
10. Allow school people to perform tasks, chores, or activities without fear of outcome.
11. Give more responsibilities to school people.
12. Provide more freedom for school people to use their own discretion in performing a job.

13. Ask school people to identify trust indicators, then use the results to train school administrators to foster them.

14. Keep working at it; trust will not occur overnight. Attitudes, once acquired, are difficult to change, and this will only occur when school administrators are consistent in their behavior.

15. Ask your unions and/or associations for assistance.

Breakdown Barriers

It is important to break down barriers between schools, departments, and units; between school administrators and teachers; and between teachers and students. Determine the problems among the various levels of the school organization, and between school people and students. Use focus groups, surveys, and other forums, and act on these problems. Here are sixteen ways to do so:

1. Allow school people to switch jobs from time to time.

2. Recognize and reward cooperation.

3. Conduct periodic meetings for kindergarten through grade twelve throughout the school year.

4. Walk around the school and inquire about the concerns of school people.

5. Encourage school people to intermingle by having district-wide meetings, events, and other activities.

6. Allow school people to cause change that will improve your school environment.

7. Communicate thoughts, ideas, and feelings to school people.

8. Travel a lot, listen a lot, and receive uninhibited communication from school people.

9. Show school people trust, concern, and respect.

10. Be responsible for the secure and comfortable life style and welfare of school people and their families.

11. Bring problems directly to the superintendent without going through channels.

12. Establish good will between school people and school administrators, and make it unnecessary to make any special effort to maintain it.

13. Encourage all school administrators to share themselves with school people.

14. Encourage all school administrators to know school people so well that they can usually predict their behavior and feelings, and vice versa.

15. Encourage all school people to tell school administrators openly how they feel about anything without fear of being penalized.

16. Encourage all school people to reveal their weaknesses to school administrators without fear of adverse effects.

Eliminate Slogans and Posters That Encourage School People to Do a Good Job

Slogans and posters that encourage school people to do a good job should be eliminated. As an alternative, display the accomplishments of school administrators in terms of what they are doing, have stopped doing, and have done differently to help school people improve their performance. A good place to start is with these Fourteen Points.

Eliminate Numerical Quotas That Establish Standards

Numerical quotas that establish standards should also be eliminated. This is true for both school administrators and students. For school administrators, this means substituting quality for quantity, which will require the elimination of management by objectives, the traditional performance evaluation method, the requirement of lesson plan submission, the offering of differentiated diplomas, and the increase of test scores.

For teachers, this means eliminating a time span for learning a lesson, avoiding competitions between students in classwork and physical work, ignoring the different intelligence levels of students (such as focusing only on the language arts and math intelligence level without regard to the six other intelligence levels, like spatial, the ability to perceive and manipulate the visual world; bodily-kinesthetic, skills in using one's body; musical, the ability to think in sound; interpersonal or social skills; and intrapersonal skills, the ability for self-understanding), and recognizing only one or two percent of the student body for academic achievement.

Remove Barriers to Pride of Workmanship

School people are willing to do a good job, and are disappointed when they cannot. Usually when they cannot, it is because of inept, untrained, and misguided school administrators who create barriers, such as demeaning and debilitating policies; who require outmoded practices; and who mandate continuation of programs and processes that do not work.

Institute a Vigorous Program of Education and Retraining

School people must feel secure about their jobs. To this end, you need to institute a vigorous program of education and retraining. They must understand that new skills help to some degree to secure their jobs.

School administrators must receive education and training in:

- TQ;
- supervision, coaching, mentoring, tutoring, and facilitating;
- team-building, conflict resolution, group dynamics, meeting management, and consensus;
- problem solving tools such as the Pareto chart, cause-and-effect analysis, force-field analysis, control chart,

run chart, scatter diagram, histogram, and flow chart; and,

- empowerment, delegating, sponsoring, communicating, listening, and supporting.

Teachers must receive training in:

- TQ;
- technical skills;
- team building, conflict resolution, meeting management, and consensus; and,
- problem-solving tools such as the Pareto chart, cause-and-effect analysis, force-field analysis, control chart, run chart, scatter diagrams, histogram, and flow chart; and,
- principles of Total Quality.

Students must receive education and training in:

- TQ;
- team building, conflict resolution, and meeting management, and consensus;
- problem-solving tools such as the Pareto chart, cause-and-effect analysis, force field analysis, control chart, run chart, scatter diagrams, histogram, and flow chart;
- System of Profound Knowledge; and,
- cooperative learning.

Establish a Steering Committee

To put all school people to work to carry out the transformation you need to establish a steering committee. Like quality, transformation is everybody's responsibility. You should follow these six steps:

1. Start the transformation at the top, beginning with your board of education.

2. Plan the transformation using the Shewhart/Deming Plan-Do- Check-Act Cycle. The cycle has four steps. The first is to plan a change of whatever you are trying to change. The second is to carry out the change on a pilot study. The third step is to study the result. The fourth step is to study the results and decide what you have learned from the change.

3. Encourage your superintendent to explain to a critical mass of school and community people why the transformation is necessary, and that it will involve everybody.

4. Transform your school district using continual improvement of methods and procedures.

5. Hire only school administrators who have the traits and characteristics to transform the school district.

6. Include representatives from unions and/or associations on the steering committee.

SEVEN DEADLY SINS

In his TQ plan, Dr. Deming also identifies seven "deadly diseases" and obstacles likely to doom a school district if they are not considered and eliminated. These are briefly described below.

Lack of Constancy of Purpose

A school district without a guidance system—which Dr. Deming refers to as constancy of purpose—to govern school people's behavior on the short- and long-range is doomed for failure.

Emphasis on Short-term Results

A school district that is interested in short-term results at the expense of long-term results will go nowhere. Short-term results can have devastating effects on long-term results.

Evaluation of Performance, Merit Rating, and Annual Review

Dr. Deming is absolutely opposed to management by objective (MBO) programs, performance evaluations, merit rating, and student grades. He maintains that these processes discourage risk-taking, build fear, undermine teamwork, and pit people against people for the same rewards. He maintains that the school administrators' role is to lead by dealing with variations in processes and to shrink the variations.

Mobility of Central School Administrators

The mobility of central school administrators' disease has two implications for education: 1) Schools of education are failing to properly train central school administrators, and they need additional training to make the transformation suggested by Dr. Deming; 2) the average tenure of a superintendent in urban school districts and some suburban school districts is three years. How can meaningful long-term change be implemented if the superintendent is not present long enough to monitor the change?

Operating a School District on Visible Figures

Measuring the success of a school district is important, but it is not everything. What is probably more important, as well as more difficult to measure, is the intangible effects of the TQ process that enables students to become more than they ever hoped to be.

Excessive Medical Costs and Excessive Costs of Warranty Fueled by Lawyers Who Work on Contingency Fees

Dr. Deming maintains that two of the seven deadly diseases are beyond the scope of most school organizations. For some organizations, excessive medical costs are the largest single expenditure. Further, he states that the United States is the most litigious country in the world, which makes warranty costs excessive.

THIRTEEN OBSTACLES

In order for a school district to pursue greatness, a critical mass of school people must not only understand Dr. Deming's Fourteen Points and System of Profound Knowledge, and avoid his Seven Deadly Sins, they must also beware of his fourteen Obstacles, which are cited below.

- Fail to engage in strategic quality planning and the transformation necessary to do so.

- Assume that quick fixes, problem solving, technology, gadgets, and new machinery will transform the school district.

- Only school people who have been educated and trained in TQ can solve deep-rooted problems.

- Emulate other school districts without determining why they succeeded or failed, which can be devastating.

- Believe "our problems are different," which is often heard from large urban school districts. It is an excuse.

- Use professors of educational administration as leaders. (Higher education institutions are often staffed with retiring school administrators who do not stay abreast of changing times and conditions. As a result, colleges of educational administration do not take the lead in restructuring or reforming schools, but are followers.)

- Rely on quality control departments. (Quality is everyone's responsibility.)

- Blame the wrong school people for problems. (Dr. Deming maintains that school administrators are responsible for 94 percent of the problems in schools. Changing the school system is the responsibility of school administrators.)

- Evaluate quality by performance rating and grading. (School districts that depend on performance rating and grading to improve will not get there.)
- Have false starts. (Initiating change without a change in the school organization's philosophy is a false start. Another false start is implementing TQ without the superintendent's commitment of support.)
- Have an unmanned computer. (Although the computer is important, if the data is never used, it is of no value.)
- Meet specifications. (Although meeting specifications (state standards) is an accepted way to operate school districts, it is insufficient if quality and productivity are to improve.)
- Do inadequate testing of prototypes. (Often a program or process works extremely well in one school, but may not work well in another. It must be adopted to meet the specific needs of the school district.)
- Believe "anyone who comes to try to help us must understand all about our school district." (Although this statement is heard in many school districts, it is not necessarily valid. Help toward improvement can come only from some other kind of knowledge.)

SYSTEM OF PROFOUND KNOWLEDGE

Dr. Deming maintains that the prevailing style of management is necessary, but insufficient. School administrators must know what changes to make in order to transform public schools in the United States. He maintains that with any journey, there is an origin and a destination. The origin is the prevailing style of management, and the destination is the transformation.

The System of Profound Knowledge must be used as a guide to begin the journey. Usually, profound knowledge originates from the outside of the organization and by invitation. Because a system cannot understand itself, the journey must have leaders.

The System of Profound Knowledge is comprised of four component parts, and each is related to the other. If one component is absent or poorly conceived, the entire system is impractical. The four components are indicated and discussed below. They are:

- Theory of Knowledge;
- Theory of Systems;
- Theory of Psychology; and,
- Theory of Variation.

The Theory of Knowledge

The Theory of Knowledge basically means that management in any form makes a prediction. For example, a superintendent who is interested in getting the board of education excited about implementing TQ in the classroom makes a prediction that if he gets several students who are in a quality classroom to appear before the board and present their "quality experiences" to them, that the board will most likely favor a district-wide quality initiative. The Theory of Knowledge teaches that a statement conveys knowledge if it predicts future outcome, either right or wrong, and if it fits without future observations of the past.

Dr. Deming says: "Theory is a window into the world. Theory leads to prediction. Without prediction, experience and examples teach nothing."

To use another school's success as a standard without understanding why it was successful may not lead to success. For example, a high school was experiencing difficulty with students who arrived to class on time only when the bell rang. A council of teachers was organized to study and solve the problem. After several meetings, a plan was developed and implemented. The problem was solved. However, another high school principal tried to implement that plan in his high school. The attempt was a disaster.

Any rational plan is a prediction that conceives conditions, behavior, performance of school people, procedure, equipment, materials, and environment. Interpreting data from a survey, audit, or experiment is also a prediction. Prediction will pose the question, What will happen if I do this? The strength of the prediction depends largely on knowledge of the subject matter. The more knowledge of the subject matter, the better the prediction.

William W. Scherkenback states, "Dr. Deming has said many times that management's prediction increases knowledge, and knowledge is a prerequisite for action. When the predictions and the actions coincide, this increases wisdom. In order to predict, you must have data. To collect data, you must first ask a question. To ask a question, you must first have a theory."

For information to convey knowledge, it must have temporal spread and come from theory. Without theory, there is no way to use the information. The Theory of Knowledge identifies basic assumptions that should be understood and embraced by the principal and his or her teams as cited below:

- A rational plan requires prediction.

- A statement devoid of prediction conveys no knowledge.

- Theory should lead to questions. Without questions, experience and examples teach absolutely nothing.

- Numbers of themselves do not establish a theory.

- There is no such thing as a fact regarding empirical observation.

The Theory of Systems

A system is a complexity of interdependent components that strive to achieve the aim of the system. Without an aim, there is no system. The aim must be communicated and understood by everyone in the system. A school system consists of parents, students, teachers, administrators, support staff, and board members.

The components of the system need not be clearly defined; people operating within that system may merely do what must be done. As a result, management of the system needs knowledge of the interrelationships between all the components and the school people within that system. The aim of the system should be for everybody to gain over the short- and long-range trends. With respect to school people, this aim might be to provide an educational environment in which school people are empowered to do their very best, have opportunities for education and training, are recognized and rewarded for their quality efforts, and make contributions to their job in school and personal life.

One requirement of a system is interdependence between components. The greater the interdependence, the greater the need for communication and cooperation. Failure of a school administrator or team to understand the interdependence between components will sub-optimize the system. The efforts of the various schools, departments, or units in a school system are not additive. Their efforts are interdependent. Each one has a specific function that serves to put the entire system into operation.

Competition among components is not allowed. Competition must be replaced by cooperation. Dr. Deming says: "We have been sold down the river in terms of competition. Because we are all a part of the system, if one component of that system fails because of competition, we all fail. On the other hand, if all components of that system are cooperating successfully, we will all be successful."

Optimization of the system—the process of orchestrating the efforts of all components to achieve the aim or purpose of the system—is the responsibility of school administration and teams. When the system is optimized, everybody wins. Failure to optimize, called sub-optimization of the system, causes everybody in the system to lose. Optimization occurs over time and space. Although optimization, similar to greatness, can never be achieved, school leaders must always strive for it.

In order to begin the process of optimizing the system, it must be based on the social memory. Without it, there can be no differentiation between special and common causes of variation. Social memory helps to facilitate the performance efforts that will bring a feeling of anticipated success to the team—rather than to the individual.

Sub-optimization has been used in school districts from the beginning of public education in the United States. Some examples of routine sub-optimization of the school system are as follows:

- School is only in session in most communities for nine out of twelve months a year.

- School is in session for students in some high schools from only 8:00 A.M. to 1:00 P.M.

- Computer equipment is inoperable if a room becomes overheated.

- The school library is underheated by an inefficient burner.

- The entire school has to be closed because of a sewage back-up.

Systems thinking conveys the knowledge that a system contains interrelated components or parts that depend on each other to achieve a collective aim. As a result, there are some basic assumptions inherent in any system, as indicated below:

- The interrelationships among parts of a system are more powerful than the individual parts.

- Improving a part without considering the whole system can have devastating effects.

- Information that comes back into the system changes the way the system behaves.

- A system will resist changes to any of its parts.

- Improving one part of a system without considering the other parts can be devastating.

- How a system handles its problems comes from the design of the system.

The Theory of Psychology

Psychology helps school people to understand other school people, and the interaction between people and circumstance, between customer and provider, between school administrators and teachers, and between teachers and students. As everyone knows, no two persons are exactly alike, not even identical twins.

School people learn in different ways and at different speeds. Some school people are practical learners, which means they learn by doing, while others are cognitive learners who learn by reading. Others learn by a combination of these two methods. School administrators and teams must understand and appreciate these differences, and use them to optimize all school people's abilities to fulfill the purpose of the school organization.

There are numerous psychological theories designed to induce school people to effect change in order to begin the journey to TQ. The following are some of the most important, including the theory of personal goal fulfillment, theory of human zones, theory of human addictions, theory of empowerment, theory of equity, theory of goal setting, theory of expectancy, and self-esteem.

It is human nature for all people to fulfill their personal goals before any other goals, even if the goals are those of their mother, father, spouse, or children. Obviously, this is also true in regard to school goals. As a result, the best way to achieve school goals is to enable school and community people to achieve their personal goals while at the same time achieving school goals. This also applies to initiating change. School and community people must see the change as fulfilling their personal goals. The most effective approach to performing this feat is to involve school and community people in the change so that they produce the change.

All human beings have three zones: the goal of acceptance, the goal of indifference, and the goal of rejection. To get school and community people to accept change, their zone of acceptance has to be increased, causing a corresponding decrease in the zone of rejection. To widen the zone of acceptance, you should understand and apply appropriate theories of psychology.

All human beings are endowed with three basic addictions. These are security, sensation, and power. The security addiction is related to food, shelter, clothing, or whatever you equate with your personal security. The sensation addiction is concerned with finding happiness in school and in life by providing you with more and better measurable sensations and activities. The power addiction is concerned with dominating people and situations, and increasing your prestige, wealth, status, and pride, in addition to other subtle forms of manipulation and control.

When initiating change, all three addictions must be taken into consideration, particularly the security addiction.

Many school administrators equate empowerment with the law of thermodynamics, the law of physics, or zero-sum assumption; that is, if power is shared or distributed, power is lost. However, the principle of empowerment should be rightfully equated with the law of synergy, because empowerment is an interactive process. When two or more school people get together, and share, interact, and agree, the results lead to positive gain. This interactive process gives all parties involved a sense of power to change.

The theory of equity rests on the premise that school people are motivated to change if there is a sense of equity. Equity satisfies, while inequity does not. Equity or fairness exists when input results in equality of outcome. Inequity or unfairness exists when a person perceives that the ratio of input to outcome is not even, as compared to the ration of another person. When evaluating fairness or unfairness, a person mentally makes an inventory and compares the sum total of his or her input and the resultant output with the sum of the input and output of another person. In the fairness equation, skills include training, seniority, age, effort, and risk taking. The unfairness equation includes reward items such as pay, nature of work, quality of supervision, benefits, status, power, and respect.

When a person perceives inequity in a given situation, he or she is dissatisfied. If the inequity is devoid of any reward, the dissatisfaction usually takes the form of anger. A feeling of inequity usually creates a state of tension in proportion to the amount of perceived inequity. As a result, this tension becomes the motivating force directed toward removing the inequity. The equity theory sets up the hypothesis that teams encourage equity and discourage inequity. People are motivated to function fairly or equitably. However, the intensity of the need to achieve equity varies with the individual, based on circumstances. In order for a school administrator to behave equitably, two conditions must prevail: 1) There must be clear understanding of input such as effort, performance level, and qualifications; 2) The school administrator must be able to determine how the individual is performing based on some reference.

Equity theory is supported by empirical research. People are more productive and more apt to change when they perceive they are being treated fairly, and usually when school administrators are motivated to behave equitably toward their people.

Another theory under the Theory of Psychology is that of goal setting. The hypothesis behind this theory is that when a person sets specific goals (for change) or performance standards (to change), he or she will perform more than if goals or standards were not set. Although incentives and participation are important, what is most important is the setting of the goal.

Performance is higher when difficult, but achievable, goals are set. If the person is highly motivated, then he or she can set his or her own goals. If not, then the supervisor should set them. At times, when people are permitted to set their own goals, they will tend to set easy goals with the resulting effect of lower performance.

Goal setting energizes and focuses people's energy and efforts. It was found to be more important than feedback or knowledge of results regarding performance. Job satisfaction is a function of the degree to which people attain their goals. The closer a person attains preset goals, the greater the satisfaction. On the other hand, goals should not be set so high that they are unattainable. The greater the discrepancy between set goals and actual performance, the greater the job dissatisfaction.

In order for the goal-setting theory to work, the job must contain some degree of intrinsic satisfaction. If the job is too routine, repetitive, or boring, setting difficult goals may not work. An important point to realize regarding the goal-setting theory is that it may hinder teamwork. When individual goals are set, there is less need for communication with others. As a result, people focus on goals rather than teamwork. In TQ, teams need to set group goals mixed with individual goals.

A person does what he or she expects will lead to a goal, for example, if he or she perceives that high productivity will be a high producer. If, on the other hand, he or she perceives that low productivity is the path to attaining the desired goal, he or she will be a low producer. Obviously this theory is compatible with the positive thinking of philosophy; that is, select a goal, visualize enjoying the fruits of the goals, and follow a conscious plan and your intuition in achieving this goal, and the probability will be high that you will reach your goal.

Although the expectancy theory makes good sense, it is not widely practiced by many school administrators. However, it is widely advocated by psychologists, primarily because it fits with older theories and common-sense experiences. Their four points are stated below:

1. Stay positive.
2. A person gets what he or she expects from others.

3. A person becomes what he or she thinks he or she is, so expect the best.

4. Expect what you want.

Do not underestimate the powerful effects of self-expectancy, a person's concept of his or her own ability is a better indicator of ability than IQ. As a result, positive thinking is a strong motivator for improving productivity. Not only do we mold our own behavior, we also mold the behavior of how others perceive us. To this end, people aid us in attaining the outcome we anticipate. This, in essence, is the Pygmalion effect, or the self-fulfilling prophecy, which maintains that when a person predicts an event, the expectation of that event changes the behavior of a person in such a manner that the event actually occurs.

What does this mean for team leaders? The most productive team members are those who have high expectations for themselves. These people may already have high expectations due to the attitudes and behavior of the team leader. As a result, to achieve a high level of performance, it is absolutely necessary for the team leader to have high expectations of team members, and to have them set difficult group and individual goals. Productivity is to some degree related to self-esteem. In order for a team to be productive, its members need to possess good attitudes about themselves and their capabilities. This good attitude includes self-acceptance, self-respect, and self-confidence. Productive team members respect themselves and expect others to respect them. Self-esteem is a key psychological trait that is a fundamental part of the personality of productive school people.

Productive school people possess higher self-esteem and tend to achieve more. They are seldom influenced by the opinions of others. In essence, they tend to be their own persons. High achievers have a positive attitude about themselves, their environment, and their future. Because self-esteem and productivity are to some degree related, school people can be more productive by increasing their self-esteem.

The Theory of Variations

Analyzing a process for variations is relatively new to school administrators. The Theory of Variations emphasizes the need not only for school administrators, but for all school people to understand and apply this concept in order to transform schools. Without this knowledge, the transformation will be short-changed.

There are seven concepts about variation that all school people should understand:

1. All variations are caused. There are specific reasons why people's behavior may fluctuate, and why one school person consistently performs better than others. Some of these reasons could include training, tools, praise, punishment, working conditions, etc.

2. There are four types of causes to be considered. First, common causes are those factors that contribute to small changes in day-to-day outcomes. The total number of common causes is frequently called a system variation because these small causes depict the expected variation inherent in the system.

   Special causes represent factors that cause a *significant* change in the system. They can be determined if the reason is identified when analysis is performed to determine its origin.

   Structural variations are expected and systematic changes in output due to trends and seasonal patterns.

   Tampering causes are additional variations caused by adjusting the system to compensate for common cause variation.

3. Different action is required for each type of cause. Therefore, it is imperative that school people are able to distinguish between types of causes. Without understanding the different types of causes, school people will not be able to improve the process.

4. Special causes can be detected if timely data is generated. Investigation should be conducted as soon as it has been

determined that a general cause is in effect. Knowledge about these special causes can assist school people in reducing the number of negative outcomes, and in increasing the number of good outcomes in the future.

5. In-depth knowledge of the process is necessary to analyze common-cause data.

6. The process is within statistical control when all variations within the system are due to common causes.

7. The total system variation can be determined by using the process data to perform a statistical analysis. This method can be used to identify control limits necessary to determine statistical control.

Variations by chance will behave in a random manner over time. As a result, they will not show cycles, runs, or any other definable pattern. No future variations can be predicted from knowledge of past variations. Variation by chance does, however, follow the laws of statistics. Therefore, variations produced by a system can be predicted using a basic control chart theory.

When data is found to conform to a statistical pattern, and is assured to be produced by chance causes, it can be assumed that no special causes are present. As a result, the conditions that produced this variation are considered to be under control. However, if the variations do not conform to the data, then the conditions that yield this variation are considered out of control. In this case, it can be assumed that one or more special causes are present in the data.

Based on the nature of processes, most data that deserves attention and analysis can be assumed to follow a normal distribution. The upper- and lower-control limits are defined to be some multiple of the standard deviation for the standard normal distribution (mean = 0, variance = 1). Areas under the curve for different multiples of standard deviations are used for control limits of a control chart.

By applying limits to a control chart, it can be determined if only change causes are present. The probability of a single point or observation falling above the upper-control limits (using three sigma limits) is approximately one-tenth of a one percent change, and the probability of a point falling below the lower-control limit is 0.001. Although three sigma limits are most often used, the actual limits should be based on the nature of the process and the quality of the analysis desired. In addition, upper- and lower- control limits may not necessarily be the same distance from the mean.

School administrators have been conditioned to recognize and reward school people who perform better than others, and to reprimand those whose performance falls below the average with little or no analysis of the reason for the poor performance. All people are different, and some will perform above average while others will perform below average. As a result, the concept of variation can assist the principal and team to understand how to deal with this situation.

In a school setting, instead of reprimanding "low performers," the principal should track the performance of individual teachers using the same process on a control chart. If any points are outside of the below-control limits, then teachers should receive training to improve their performance. If any points fall outside the upper-control charts, the principal should review these teachers' performance to determine why they are high performers, and then use that information to improve the performance of all teachers. On the other hand, if no points fall outside the control limits, then either he or she should leave the process alone, or improve it.

Dr. Deming maintains that it is the school administrator's responsibility to determine which school people are performing above or below the control limits. However, the teams are also responsible to do likewise.

When a school person consistently performs significantly better than others (as identified by appearing above the upper-control limits of a control chart), that person should be questioned and critically analyzed to determine what it was that enabled him or her to achieve success. There are a number of characteristics about a person that can be examined, which can help either the principal or team, and therefore be useful in improving better school people performance in a school program. The following are some of these characteristics:

- improved training and/or education;
- improved tools;
- better procedure or methods;
- improved human match with the tasks, job or program; and,
- improved communication sources.

Unless these factors are examined and ruled out, school people should not assume that above-control-limits performance is due only to a highly motivated school person. Once the true reason behind superior performance has been ascertained, the principal or team should then attempt to improve performance of the group with similar methods. If, on the other hand, the principal or team discover that motivation was the key to superior performance, then the focus should be on the motivational aspect of TQ. The principal or team should also analyze the superior person's motivational level to ascertain if the motivational strategy of the principal should be revised for other school people.

Similar to superior performance, there may be certain characteristics about school people who perform below the control limits of a control chart that may be useful in improving performance when they are critically analyzed by either the principal or the team. The following are some of these characteristics:

- poor training and education;
- ineffective tools, methods, or procedures;
- poor human match with the task, job, or program; and,
- poor communication.

When the problems and causes are determined, the principal or team should make use of this information to improve the school person's performance level. This information may be useful in improving the performance level of other school people as well. However, if no cause can be found from the critical analysis, the principal or team should consider revising the motivational strategies employed with this particular school person.

A control chart can be used as an analysis tool. It is not only a tool for obtaining a state of statistical control, but also a device that can be used to determine when the studied process is out of control. Therefore, if all points in the control chart fall within the control limits without varying in a non-random manner within the limits, then the process can be judged to be within control at the level indicated by the chart. Non-random is indicated when trends are discovered within the control chart data; the point making up the trend should be analyzed and given a cause.

The fact that no points fall outside either the upper- or lower-control limits does not necessarily mean that special causes are not present. It suggests, however, that the cost of additional analysis to look for special causes is not worth the effort. A point falling outside the control limits means that the process is out of control. As a result, an analysis should be conducted to find the cause. If the cause is determined, then the problem causing the variation can be resolved, thus improving the process and reducing the likelihood that the problem will occur again in the future. If the problem is not related to the data, then the control chart can continue to be used. If there is a relationship between the problem and other data, resolving the process to account for the problem will provide an even greater improvement to the system. It is therefore advised that a new control chart be developed in the future that reflects this improved process.

The following is a partial list of common causes of variation:

- Use of poor design of product or service.
- Failure to remove the barriers that rob school people of the right to do a good job and to take pride in their work.
- Use of poor instruction and poor supervision.

- Failure to measure the effects of common causes and reduce them.
- Failure to provide school people with information in statistical form that shows performance can be improved.
- Incoming materials that are not suited to requirements.
- Procedures that are not suited to requirements.
- Equipment that is out of order.
- Equipment that is not suited to requirements.
- Use of poor lighting.
- Existence of uncomfortable working conditions, such as noise, confusion, awkward handling of materials, unnecessary extremes of heat of cold, poor ventilation, and poor food in the cafeteria.
- Constant shift of school administrator emphasis from quantity to quality, back and forth, without understanding how to achieve quality.

There is a critical shortage of school people today who have an understanding of the Theory of Variation. In summary, the knowledge entails the following assumptions:

- Everything has variation at one time or another.
- There are several causes of variations.
- There are two major mistakes frequently made to improve results: to treat outcomes as if they come from common causes; and, to do so when they actually come from special causes.
- A process is either stable or unstable.

Knowledge about the interaction of forces is necessary:

- Do forces reinforce or nullify efforts?
- Use of data requires an understanding of the numerous studies of information about a frame such as the census and analytic problems, and the interpretation of a test or experiment, such as change in process or procedure.

- If data indicates that the process is stable or under statistical control, then the chance to affect the future is better than if the process were unstable.

- If data indicate that the process is unstable, then the prediction of the future is based on previous knowledge of the subject matter.

- A process varies over time and from customer to customer.

There are several advantages of a stable process (within statistical control) over an unstable process, as highlighted below:

- The process is predictable. It has a measurable and communicable capability.

- Cost can be predicted.

- Regularity is inherent in the process.

- Productivity is maximum with the present system.

- The impact of change in the system can be measured with a greater speed and reliability.

SUMMARY

You are probably asking yourself why I devote most of the contents of this book to the works of Dr. Deming. For one thing, this is where I have received most of my training. For another, Dr. Deming has appeared in schools relating his philosophies and principles to the educational family. In addition, Dr. Deming's Fourteen Points touch many of the concepts that are wrong with our public education system. I am referring to principles such as eliminating fear in the classroom, breaking down barriers between schools, departments, etc., removing barriers of the profession, ceasing dependence on grades, etc. His Seven Deadly Sins and Thirteen Obstacles, if followed by school people, would in themselves appreciably improve the education environment. Finally, his System of Profound

Knowledge consists of guidelines that would truly transform our schools to greatness.

CHECKPOINTS FOR MAKING THE TRANSITION TO TOTAL QUALITY

The following activities are suggested to enable you to implement Dr. Deming's principles and System of Profound Knowledge, and to avoid his Seven Deadly Sins and Thirteen Obstacles. Dr. Deming's works can be adopted and implemented in education by carrying out the following:

1. Apply Dr. Deming's philosophy of Fourteen Points to the school district's planning process for implementing TQ.
2. Check to determine the extent to which Dr. Deming's Seven Deadly Sins exist in your school district.
3. Review the present practice in the school district to determine if any resemble the obstacles cited by Dr. Deming, and then eliminate them.
4. Master the System of Profound Knowledge in order to make the transformation to TQ. Make certain the school district master plan reveals each of the basic theories of profound knowledge.

Chapter Three

Implementing Total Quality In Education

American companies all too often have jumped to implement "hot" new solutions to their problems. They tend to spend too little time, thought, and energy on developing the corporate policy and planning needs to implement their actions. The Japanese, for example, spend two-thirds of their effort on building consensus, developing understanding of the client's needs, and reviewing options for implementation. Then they think through all the steps needed to implement this change or process. In America, companies tend to spend one-third of their efforts on planning, then jump into the implementation phase and continue to "fight fires" to resolve the errors and inconsistencies that with proper planning they could have avoided. The concept of doing things right the first time depends on realistic, thorough planning.

—V. Daniel Hunt

The master plan for implementing TQ is a management system for the integration of quality principles, practices, techniques and tools into the school organization. Just as TQ must be built into the services and products delivered to customers, so must the quality process be built into the school organizational structure and day-to-day activities. Board members, school administrators, and other school people must understand that the quality improvement process is a continuous one, and a never-ending service of activities based on new theories, principles, and practices that will result in great schools. Everybody must work together to consistently provide the best services and products to customers.

IN THIS CHAPTER, I WILL COVER THE FOLLOWING:

- Identifying strategies for implementing TQ
- Understanding the initial steps to TQ
- Developing an organizational structure for TQ
- Selecting an approach to TQ
- Assessing school organization readiness for TQ
- Developing a strategy for implementing TQ
- Commenting on TQ training

THERE IS NO SIMPLE FORMULA FOR GREATNESS

Products and services that satisfy a customer do not happen by accident. Neither does TQ—it is greatness by design. It takes a lot of hard work, careful planning, listening to the customer, teamwork, the involvement of everyone in the process (from the top of an organization to the bottom), special training, systematic examination of ways to improve, performance measurement, and an esprit de corps that comes from people in the organization who feel appreciated. All of these factors need to build on each other and to be guided by a shared vision of what is important and what is needed to achieve it.

Quality deficiencies anywhere in a school district can have an impact on its services and products. That is why an improvement effort needs to be *total;* it has to involve everyone, and it has to involve changes in the way things are done, which is the responsibility of school administration. If an improvement is made in isolation, it is unlikely that the improvement will be long lasting because too many factors can undercut it. There will be no supportive network to ensure continuity if something goes wrong or if you leave. That is why it is so important to integrate all the changes that must take place.

TQ is built on management fundamentals learned from experience. A lot of them are probably familiar to you. For example, the need to properly train people so that they can carry out their job responsibilities is not new. Neither is the idea of strategic planning. Improvement techniques that have shown some results in the past should not be abandoned. TQ builds on techniques that have been successful, and adds other dimensions (e.g., customer focus and continuous improvement) that help to integrate them into a sensible, systematic management approach.

TQ is used to ease communications. Yet, by doing so, school people are sometimes misled into thinking that its essence can be boiled down into a sentence or two; that is, follow step one through ten. TQ is being implemented as a process and not a program. There is no magic formula. It is learned by education and training (e.g., reading, attending seminars, listening to others), and then by practice.

IDENTIFYING INITIAL STEPS FOR IMPLEMENTING TOTAL QUALITY

There are a number of ways to implement TQ. The approach selected should be based on the specific needs of the school district. The following are some of the basic steps for implementing TQ, including gaining central school administration commitment, determining school organization readiness, creating a strategic vision and guiding principles, conducting the superintendent retreat, involving principals, and initiating early discussion with union representatives. Others can and should be included as needed.

Gain Central School Administrators' Commitment

The first step for implementing TQ is to obtain a strong commitment and support from the superintendent and his or her assistant superintendents. TQ is a value-driven culture, and all central school administrators must be involved in planning, developing, launching, maintaining, and evaluating it. Dr. Juran has said, "In our experience, no quality improvement effort has ever been successful without top management involvement." Peter Drucker has stated, "When I want something done, I want a maniac with a mission." Thus, the superintendent and his or her assistant superintendents must be obsessed with TQ. They must demonstrate this obsession through giving stump speeches on TQ, walking the talk, talking the talk, catching school and community people doing the right things in TQ activities, and recognizing and rewarding them.

Determine School Organization's Readiness

This second step, determining a school organization's readiness, is aimed at taking a look at the school organization as it presently exists to determine if it is ready to embark on the TQ journey. The basic questions you should ask are:

- Are central school administrators sufficiently committed?

- Is central school administration likely to change within the next few months?

- Is a reorganization imminent?

- Is there a current crisis that for a time will absolutely override all other efforts?

- Are there long-standing intransigent, interpersonal conflicts at the central school administrative level that would impede cooperation?

School organizations often use central school administrators to consider these questions and others. Benefits result when they do so. First, communication among team members is enhanced as they focus on issues of common concern. Second, the team increases its commitment to change as they weigh the significance of existing problems. Third, the open discussion of problems may lead to earlier solutions. Answering these questions will provide a cursory assessment to help the school organization decide if it is ready to begin TQ or if preliminary steps should be taken. If the school district decides to proceed with TQ implementation, it will need to make a more detailed assessment later as a foundation for developing the TQ strategy.

Create a Strategic Vision and Guiding Principles

A key step in the TQ process is the creation of a common understanding about what you want the school organization to look like in the future, and about what principles will guide the actions you take to achieve the desired future. These agreements will become the basis for formal statements of the school organization's guidance system (mission, vision, values, service strategy, quality policy, etc.).

The strategic vision is a clear, positive, forceful statement of what the school organization wants to be in five, or even ten years. It allows the school organization to stretch and aim for a high target, and must be powerful enough to excite people and to show them the way things can be. A well-crafted vision supported by action can be a powerful tool for focusing the school organization towards a common goal. Consider the following vision:

> "To enable our students to become more than they ever hoped to be through a total quality educational system."

Conduct the Superintendent Retreat

An effective method for galvanizing commitment to TQ is the superintendent retreat. Typically, members of the board of education and central school administrators are gathered for one to three days outside the school district, away from the normal distractions of the daily operations. Because TQ affects every level of the school organization, each key department or unit needs to be represented. Sometimes, the superintendent has been known to invite "movers and shakers" of the community, and to involve them in the commitment process. The retreat can be used for the following purposes:

- To gain an understanding of TQ.
- To determine initial readiness of the school district and community.
- To achieve consensus or aspects of the constancy of purpose.
- To develop a tentative action plan.
- To discusses the process of planning, implementing, and evaluating.
- To gain the support of respected members of the community.

For instance, during a two-day retreat, an organization conducted a detailed analysis of its organizational systems, and developed strategic goals and short-range objectives. The conditions that would influence the organization in the short- and long-terms were analyzed. Consideration was given to the strategic vision and values that were implicit in the management of the organization and the customers it serves. The organization developed a set of guiding principles that would be the foundation for all decisions and actions. These guidelines consisted of the following:

- We want to deliver our products and services on time, within cost, and in conformance with all requirements.
- We exist to satisfy the requirements, needs, and expectations of our customer
- People are our greatest assistance.
- We ensure a safe work place.
- We attain equal employment for all.
- Teamwork is our hallmark.
- First-time quality (conformance to requirements) increases productivity and reduces cost.
- We relentlessly pursue continuous improvement.

- We are customer-oriented.
- We thus earn our customers' trust and our community's respect.

Several long-range goals were set to be achieved within five years. When the plan was reviewed one year later, a fifth goal was added to improve the educational level of the people considered to be vital to the organization's mission and continuous improvement.

Five long-range goals are:

1. Establish a process to improve quality and productivity.
2. Maintain a quality of work-life improvement program.
3. Reduce the cost of poor quality by 25 percent while maintaining schedule and time.
4. Develop a master plan for capital investment for facilities and equipment.
5. Improve the education level of our people.

Although the strategic vision is an important component of the guidance system, there are other components, such as the mission shared values, service strategy and quality policy. All components are elaborated on in Chapter Five.

Involve Principals

The active involvement of principals is essential to the success of the TQ effort. They are accountable for achieving the school performance goals, and they form the enduring links in the communication chain from central school administrators to the other school people. They influence daily the climate within which school people provide services to customers. More than one observer has noted that without a principal's early and active support, a number of promising quality initiatives have failed.

Recent research also confirms that long-term performance is highest in those school organizations that practice a participative approach to management. However, many school districts over the years have selected and rewarded those who more closely fit the traditional authoritarian model. For these school administrators, the change from the familiar and formerly successful behavior to a more participative personal style may be difficult to make.

Central school administrators need to ensure that school administrators at all levels have the imminent opportunity to develop ownership in the quality improvement effort, and a chance to acquire the insight and skills necessary to become leaders instead of controllers of school people. Later, rewards and recognition should be structured clearly to reinforce school administrators who demonstrate the ability to become key participants in the new approach to quality achievement.

Initiate Early Discussion With Union Representatives

Central school administrators should have early discussions with union/association representatives on TQ. Central school administrators should also involve union/association leaders by sharing with them their quality effort progress. School administrators may also involve union/association leaders in setting common goals, and may work together on quality improvement activities.

DEVELOPING AN ORGANIZATIONAL STRUCTURE FOR TOTAL QUALITY

Developing a parallel organizational structure that will institute, sustain, and facilitate expansion of the quality improvement effort is an essential element for success. The structure is the vehicle for focusing the energy and resources of the school organization toward one common goal: continuous improvement of the products and services it provides to the customer. Successful school organizations tailor the structure so that it maximizes strong points and accommodates their unique mission, culture, and approach for improving quality. As a result, several common practices emerge that are described below, including forming a QS committee, using the existing organizational structure, linking organizational elements, establishing QI teams, and creating quality action (QA) teams.

Form a Quality Steering Committee

During the early stages of implementation, most school organizations that have successfully introduced TQ have formed a QS committee composed of a slice of school and community people. By establishing a QS committee, central school administrators provide identity, structure, and legitimacy to the QI effort. It is the first concrete indication that the superintendent has recognized the need to improve, and has begun to change how the school organization operates. The direction this change will take becomes clear when the committee publishes its vision, guiding principles, and mission statement.

The committee is usually chaired by the superintendent of schools, or his or her designee. The committee is responsible for launching, coordinating, and overseeing the QI effort. For instance, in some manufacturing and industrial organizations, a two-tiered approach is used. If the top tier of the organization is designated as a quality committee, the second tier is labeled the quality sub-committee or executive steering committee. Organizations that have labeled the top tier the executive steering committee, use the term quality management board to represent the second tier unit. Depending on the complexity of the organization, there may be several sub-committees representing major functional areas.

The purpose of this second tier is to allow the QS committee to concentrate on quality strategy rather than on tactical issues or problem solving.

Use the Existing Organizational Structure

Some school organizations find it advantageous to overlay the TQ organization onto the existing organizational structure. This allows the school organization to use the existing lines of authority, and communicate to foster the QI efforts while avoiding major disruptions in the school district.

Rather than requiring a major revamping of the school organization, the TQ process can improve the effectiveness of the structure that is already in place. For example, cross-functional teams that identify customer requirements in each step of a process learn how the process or product of each school or unit impacts on the quality of the next or other school unit's performance. Such knowledge leads to process improvements while reducing the frequency of disputes over "turf."

One modification some organizations make to the existing structure is to form a quality staff that reports to the QS committee. Typically, this is a small staff that helps to promote, coordinate, and track the quality improvements that are underway. They can also serve as in-house consultants and trainers. However, care should be taken to avoid the appearance that this unit is solely responsible for quality. It must be clear that all school people, including part-time people and volunteers, are responsible for improving the quality of the process in which they work.

The same caution holds true for any quality assurance departments that may exist. These departments can be a valuable resource for school administrators if used properly. Since the quality specialists working there are often the statistical process control experts, they can become the nucleus for expanding the knowledge and use of these tools and techniques throughout the school organization. With their help, all school people can learn to solve problems using data. It is important to foster the view that everyone needs to be comfortable using the statistical tools, and that analytical problem solving is no longer the responsibility of a quality assurance staff.

Link Organizational Elements

Three-level tier linkage is advocated for large school districts, and is accomplished by having a member of a central school administration-level quality council serve as chairperson of a second-tier quality steering committee. In turn, a member of one or more QI levels, in turn, chairs a third-tier level or leads a QI action-level team. For example, the two-tier level is desirable for smaller school districts. It is similar to the three-tier level. The difference is the absence of a quality council.

Horizontal linkage is accomplished by having members of different functional departments (e.g., personnel, administration, finance) serve together on cross-functional teams. These teams are sometimes called quality management boards.

This type of structural linkage offers a number of benefits to the school organization:

- It helps the school organization stay focused on pursuing the same goals, rather than having functional units working at cross purposes.

- It fosters better teamwork and less internal competition.

- It improves communication throughout the school organization, and a better understanding of how all the pieces fit together.

- It improves the ability to replicate ideas and standardize solutions that have applicability to processes in other areas of the school organization.

Establish Quality Improvement Teams

Participative management places a premium on teamwork as the way to solve problems and initiate process improvements, especially issues with cross-functional implications. The focus is on teamwork and process rather than on individual efforts and tasks. Teams that work on process improvement can be called school improvement teams, QI teams, etc. There are numerous variations of this team approach.

Create Quality Action Teams

Usually there are too many management problems in a school to leave it solely to the QI teams to solve. Most school districts encourage the QI team to organize QA teams to solve problems. Although there are some permanent QA teams, usually these teams are established to solve a specific problem, and are then dissolved. More is covered on QI and QA teams in Chapter Six.

SELECTING AN APPROACH TO
IMPLEMENTING TOTAL QUALITY

Once a readiness has been determined for TQ, the superintendent or steering committee will need to implement TQ on a district-wide level, or implement one or more pilots. It is also possible to tailor a combination of the two approaches to accommodate the specific needs of the school district after realistically assessing a number of key factors involving the following:

- The intensity of the support and commitment of the superintendent of schools.
- The size and complexity of the school district.
- The available resources (time, money, and people) that can be allocated to plan, implement, and sustain TQ efforts.
- The amount of resistance that can be anticipated.
- The level and intensity of support for TQ throughout the school and community.

Implementing TQ on a district-wide level, particularly in a large school district, such as Chicago, New York City, or Los Angeles is a major undertaking. It requires significant allocation of time, money, and people, and in many school organizations, substantial operational and cultural changes. Obviously, the larger the school district, the more massive the change. However, there are some advantages to implementing TQ on a district-wide level, as described below:

- It promotes consistent implementation, since each school organization element uses the same TQ philosophy.
- Barriers are removed, because the decision to implement TQ district-wide demonstrates strong commitment by the superintendent.

- The TQ organizational structure can be implemented throughout the school district, thereby providing linkage between the central school administrators and individual schools.

- It provides economics of scale when retaining consultants that provide within-district training, support, etc.

- It allows the school district to capitalize on its people to support implementation. For example, specialists at the central school administration office can be used to provide technical assistance to schools and other units.

When making the selection of the pilot schools, the district should try to match the characteristics desired in a TQ environment with those school principals who have the desired criteria. However, the most important criteria for selecting the pilot schools is leadership style. A large number of school districts use a host of other criteria to select their pilot schools.

There are several advantages for first initiating TQ as a pilot effort. For one thing, the intention of a pilot project is to demonstrate the effectiveness of TQ without requiring a heavy initial commitment of resources from the school.

The pilot project also allows the superintendent or steering committee to select those schools that have a higher potential for success. It stands to reason that if there is a greater success in the pilot study, there is a greater probability of acceptance and success when expanding the process.

Finally, the possibility of embarrassment and the expense of failure throughout the school district are avoided. If a district-wide attempt at TQ should fail, it may preclude another attempt at a later date. On the other hand, a smaller failure of a pilot study should not prevent undertaking a second attempt with other schools at a later date.

There are numerous methods for selecting a pilot project for implementing TQ as indicated by the following:

- Student achievement
- Teacher attendance
- School climate
- Expulsions/suspensions
- Instructional leadership
- Discipline
- Student attendance
- Parent support
- School culture
- Community reaction
- Instructional focus
- District's demographic make-up
- Recommendations from teachers or other professionals
- High expectations
- Leadership style
- Letter of intent
- Noting the frequency and kinds of problems
- Essay by the principal
- Selection by proposal
- Performance approval reports of the principal for the last three years
- Interviews
- Innovativeness
- Positive vote from teachers
- Capability of teachers
- Selection by the superintendent

Most school districts that use these methods include a combination of the following:

1. An application packet containing many of the items stated above.
2. A review of the school's or unit's performance.
3. One or more interviews with individuals and/or committees.
4. A final interview with the superintendent.

However, when TQ is implemented as a pilot study, it may produce some problems, as cited below:

1. The pilot project may be supported with money, but sometimes lack committed attitudes and climate.
2. The pilot school or unit may be dissimilar to the rest of the characteristics of the school district.
3. The pilot techniques may not be tied to specific program objectives.
4. Often a pilot project is planned, financed, and implemented without adequate training of school and community people to carry it out.
5. A pilot project may threaten roles and not deal with this side effect.
6. A pilot project may ignore the teachers union/association concerns and issues, therefore making them the targets of animosity and opposition.
7. There may be principal turnover. This is deadly to a young program.
8. Non-participating schools may suffer "star envy," and may undermine the pilot project.
9. Ongoing central school administration commitment may be lacking.

ASSESSING SCHOOL ORGANIZATIONAL
READINESS FOR TOTAL QUALITY

Prior to implementing TQ, many school organizations have conducted in-depth assessments intended to identify the existing culture and management style of the school district. An assessment also helps to identify those vital processes that require change and provide a baseline measurement for evaluating progress. Assessments can take a variety of forms, and they frequently involve identifying and surveying the school organization's internal and external customers and providers, school administrators, and other school people. The following are some issues that are usually assessed:

- What is the key consideration for assessing school organizational readiness for TQ?

- What are the mission, vision, and core values of the school district, and to what extent are they evaluated and adjusted?

- What services and products are provided?

- Who are internal and external customers and providers?

- What measurement systems are in place?

- Does the school organization measure its success based on the extent to which it satisfies its customers' needs, requirements, and expectations?

- How well does the school organization communicate with its customers and providers?

- How much emphasis is placed on proactive planning as opposed to reactive planning?

- How does the school district generate ideas for improvement?

- What type of suggestions program is in place? How effective is it? How many suggestions are generated per school person?

- What does the school organization recognize and reward? Is the recognition and reward program tied to core values?
- To what extent is teamwork used, encouraged, and recognized?
- To what extent are school people empowered and able to be empowered?
- What is the relationship of the administration with the unions/associations?
- How well do schools and units cooperate?
- How well do school administrators walk the talk?
- Do the superintendent and his or her central school administrators have credibility in the eyes of principals and other school people?
- What type of management style is employed by the superintendent? By principals? By other unit leaders? Is it autocratic or participative?
- How much discretion do school people have in making decisions?
- What is the superintendent's attitude toward training?
- What is the attitude of the superintendent, principals, and unit leaders toward quality? Is the focus on quality prevention?
- Are the school organization's strategic vision, core values, goals, objectives, policies, and procedures clearly stated and widely known?
- Does the school organization have a multitude of priorities, or have vital few been identified and communicated?

School districts may opt to produce their own assessment instruments using the criteria stated above or using V. Daniel Hunt's book entitled *Quality in America: How to Implement a Competitive Quality Program*, Homewood, Illinois: Business One Irwin, 1992, pps. 145-182, or the Federal government has different types of assessment tools available that can be augmented to help school districts assess their readiness for TQ. (See the reference section at the end of this book.)

Many of these documents can be obtained from the Federal Quality Institute Resource Center, located at P.O. Box 99, Washington, D.C. 20044-0099, (202) 376-3747.

Assessment Tool

There are different types of assessment instruments that can be adapted to accommodate the specific needs of school districts. These can be obtained from any one of the professional associations indicated in the reference section of this book. However, Hunt's book, mentioned above, contains comprehensive instruments for assessing all phases of TQ.

There are several strategies used by school and other organizations to implement TQ, including the guru approach, the organizational mode approach, the TQ element approach, and the prize criteria approach. There are probably others.

The guru approach is the experience of adopting the training and writings of one or more of the leading quality thinkers in the country and using them as a benchmark to determine where the school district has problems and where to make appropriate changes. For example, one school district may adopt Dr. Deming's Fourteen Points. Another may adopt some of Dr. Deming's points, and some of Dr. Crosby's Fourteen Principles.

In the organizational mode approach, school people in the school district visit schools and other organizations that have taken a leadership role in TQ to determine what successes they have had and how they have achieved them. The school district then investigates the success of other organizations, and develops its own model.

The element approach takes key ideas, components, systems, organizations, and tools of TQ, and uses them to implement their own version of TQ. For example, a school district using quality tools and statistical process control would be adopting this approach.

A school district implements the prize criteria approach when it adopts the criteria of either the Deming Prize or Malcolm Baldrige National Quality Award to identify QI areas.

IDENTIFYING APPROACHES FOR DEVELOPING AND IMPLEMENTING TOTAL QUALITY

You have probably heard this statement before: There is no one right way to successfully implement TQ in a school district. Perhaps the best approach is a synthesis of various approaches informed by TQ gurus, and those successfully used by both public and private organizations. The approach and principles and practices advocated in this book are only intended as guides in developing strategies and related plans to affect these strategies. I recommend a flexible approach, one that capitalizes on the strengths of the school organization to allow synergy to be focused on those essential key elements and improvement opportunities.

Because the missions, cultures, and management styles of school districts vary so greatly, it would be inadvisable to attempt to develop one "ideal" plan or school organizational structure to implement TQ. Furthermore, it would be useless to graft the experience of one school organization wholesale onto another, without tailoring it to meet the unique needs of that school district.

The best approaches are those that result in action, action that improves the processes of the school organization and results in better services and products for the customer. A simple plan that generates action and gets results is better than an elaborate plan that collects dust. Some initial TQ actions might consist of specific projects designed to address system-wide problems that have potential for expanding to other processes of the school organization; or, they might be efforts to implement TQ in one or more school organizational components. Examples of such efforts might include:

- Conduct customer identification efforts and customer survey and feedback efforts to be reflected in quality and timeliness indicators.

- Designate quality teams to address specific operating problems.
- Conduct organizational assessment, leadership development, and group dynamic efforts.
- Direct involvement of some teachers, parents, and other school people in implementing a form of QI effort reflected in the overall strategic plan.

It is a good idea for a school organization to have at least initiated in some key areas the process of identifying customers and their requirements, and reviewing quality indicators for products and services. This might occur in school organizational components where TQ will be implemented initially, or on a more wide-scale basis in anticipation of future TQ implementation.

One of the most important decisions the superintendent or steering committee will have to make when developing a TQ implementation strategy is whether to begin the process from the top-down or bottom-up approach. This decision will have to be made whether or not a pilot study is utilized. If the pilot study involves less than eight schools, the decision becomes less important, because TQ will sooner or later involve everyone. However, if the process is going to be implemented district-wide from the onset, or the pilot study involves school departments, schools or units, the top-down approach is preferred. The purpose of this top-down approach is to improve the school district's chances of making a significant positive impact early in terms of meeting and exceeding the needs of customers.

There are at least two ways to begin the implementation of TQ. These include the strategic planning approach, and the QI team approach.

Strategic Planning Approach

Begin by replacing the ordinary planning process with strategic quality planning. An effective way to begin is to first identify all the reasons why a customer may use the services of the school district. Then, in respect to each customer, conduct research with customers to determine their need requirements and expectations from each contact. Once these steps have been completed, change can be determined to meet the varied needs of the customers. It must be stressed that each and every time a customer has contact with the school district, school, or unit, a perception is shaped and formed by the customer's mind as to the quality of service. For example, parents send their children to school for a multitude of reasons. Some of the most common are:

- To give their children an excellent education.

- To enable their children to become productive members of society.

- To fortify children with the knowledge necessary to get into higher education.

- To enable children to eventually obtain a job.

- Parents have numerous questions or concerns in mind as they think about sending their children to schools, questions or concerns that translate to needs.

A careful examination of customer concerns and expectations relating to the needs of the customer will reveal some clear indications of what should be in place in order to meet the needs of the customers. Therefore, a thorough review of the school district as seen through the eyes of the customers will provide numerous opportunities for creating more customer-friendly systems and processes. However, this review should not be conducted solely by the school district. Customers should be involved in some manner. For example, one of the best companies in the United States, Northwestern Mutual Life Insurance Company, invites on an annual basis a group of its policyholders into the organization to conduct an "audit" of its operations. School districts can do likewise by establishing a meeting between customers (parents and students) and providers (teachers and administrators) to review the school district's translation of the customers' questions and concerns, and to determine if it truly represents the needs, requirements, and expectations of customers.

Quality Improvement Team Approach

The QI team approach involves a large number of school people in the TQ process right from the onset. Therefore, these people are exposed more quickly to the principles, concepts, and tools of QI, and are more likely to produce measurable results that build momentum and enthusiasm for TQ. However, quality planning should begin soon after the introduction of QI teams. As a result, QI teams identify and strive to solve quality issues. Quality planning helps to provide quality service, and helps to become involved in quality projection selection on the most pressing problems in the school district, school, or unit.

Colonial Penn Insurance Company initiated QI teams at the top level of the organization and implemented these as a pilot study with 350 people. School districts can take a cue from Colonial Penn and begin their TQ process with two or three cross-functional teams at the central school administrative level, a few QI teams at the school level, and some at the unit level. In this way, the team approach would be used to "test" TQ on all three levels of the school organization.

TQ represents a major change in school organization and management philosophy for most school districts in the United States. Simply deciding to do it, and attempts at understanding it will not produce great schools. Someone once said, "Insight alone does not produce change." Similar to other major undertakings, a school district needs a master plan to implement TQ. The scale, scope, and magnitude of the transformation needed to create schools through TQ requires a master plan, which is developed, directed, and supported by the board of education, superintendent, other central school administrators, union/association officials, and movers and shakers of the school district. The master plan should not focus on quality services and products alone, but should be linked to the process by which these services and products are planned, produced, and delivered.

COMMENTING ON TOTAL QUALITY TRAINING

Training is essential to the success of the TQ effort. Because it is so significant, Chapter Ten will be devoted to this topic. However, it is important to note here that during the early stages of implementation, attention should be given to developing a plan for training.

Ted Cocheu, writing in the January 1989, issue of *Training and Development Journal*, says: Quality experts ... all agree that a comprehensive training curriculum is critical to providing everyone in the organization with the knowledge and skills necessary to fulfill his or her QI responsibilities.

Training must include:

- explaining the need for improvement as well as its individual and collective benefits;
- communicating the organization's quality goals;
- developing a common language to talk about quality-related issues;
- defining the structure and process through which QI will take place;
- clarifying everyone's responsibilities; and
- providing people with tools and techniques to manage the quality of their work.

All school people must understand their jobs and their roles in the school organization and how their performance will change with TQ. Such understanding goes beyond the instruction given in manuals or job descriptions. School people need to know where their job fits into the larger context: how their job is influenced by other school people, who precedes them, and how their work influences school people who follow.

The school district's training plan should be an outgrowth of the TQ implementation strategy, and should be directed to the school organizational units or projects where central school administrators have focused the implementation effort in the first year.

To prevent surprises and delays in implementation, the training plan must include reasonably accurate estimates of the schedule and required resources.

DEVELOPING AN IMPLEMENTATION PLAN

To implement TQ in a school district requires an implementation of a master plan that is developed, directed, and supported by the central school administrators. There are a variety of different strategies/plans being used by numerous organizations to implement TQ. The following plan, illustrated in Figure 3.1, is one that I recommend, with or without changes.

Figure 3.1
Implementing Total Quality In Education

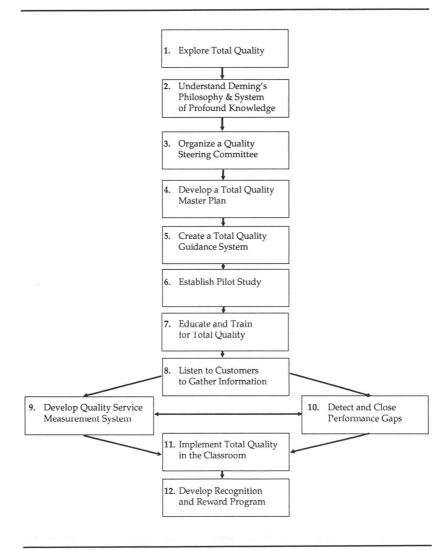

Step 1: Explore Total Quality

In order to implement TQ, central school administrators must become committed to the process, decide the readiness of the school district to implement TQ, and reach a consensus on whether or not to proceed, and how. The exploration phase usually involves the superintendent and his or her central school administrators. However, other school people should be considered for involvement in this step, such as members of the board of education, the union/association, and prominent people in the school and community. Activities that are helpful in exploring TQ are visiting recognized TQ school districts and organizations; attending conferences and workshops on TQ; reading books, magazines, and articles on TQ; and speaking to TQ practitioners, consultants, and trainers. (See Figure 3.2.)

FIGURE 3.2
Step 1: Explore Total Quality

Step 1: Explore Total Quality

Activity	By Whom	Duration
• Read TQ books, magazine, journals	All school administrators, directors, and supervisors	Throughout the school year
• Attend conferences, seminars, and workshops on TQ	Central school administrators, union/association officials, and selected stakeholders	Continuous
• Visit TQ schools and other organizations	Board members and central school administrators	Once or twice a year
• Determine school organizational readiness for TQ	Board members and central school administrators	1 week
• Reach a consensus on how to proceed	Central school administrators	1-2 days
• Appoint or select quality coordinator	Superintendent of schools	1 day

Step 2: Understand Dr. Deming's Philosophy and System of Profound Knowledge

Although Dr. Deming's philosophy was originally adopted for business, he has proclaimed that his principles, deadly sins, obstacles, and System of Profound Knowledge are also appropriate for school districts. Since very little progress is being made using traditional principles and practices, and organizations in this country and around the world have field-tested Dr. Deming's philosophy and have had extraordinary results, it would seem foolish for educators in the United States not to capitalize on his work and make the transformation to TQ school environments. However, it would not be easy. Dr. Deming indicates that it will require school districts to accept this change as a new religion in which school people and parents are guided by a System of Profound Knowledge. To effect these steps, school districts will need to translate Dr. Deming as well as other prominent people's works in TQ for classroom use. (See Figure 3.3.)

FIGURE 3.3
Step 2: Understanding Dr. Deming's Philosophy and the System of Profound Knowledge

Step 2: Understand Dr. Deming's Philosophy and the System of Profound Knowledge

Activity	By Whom	Duration
• Study and Practice Dr. W. Edwards Deming's *Fourteen Points*	All central school administrators and all other school people	Continuous
• Avoid Dr. Deming's *Thirteen Obstacles*	All central school administrators	Continuous
• Avoid Dr. Deming's *Seven Deadly Diseases*	All central school administrators	Continuous
• Study and practice Dr. Deming's *System of Profound Knowledge*	All central school administrators	Continuous

Step 3: Organize a Quality Steering Committee

It is essential to the success of TQ for the superintendent or his designees to organize a QS committee to plan, guide, and direct the activities of TQ to give life to the process. In business and industry, this steering committee is usually comprised of members of top management. In education, the steering committee is usually comprised of a cross-section of the school and community people. The superintendent is usually the chairperson of the QS committee, and the quality coordinator orchestrates the activities of the QS committee.

A structure must be established for forming the QS committee, choosing a quality coordinator, creating various other teams, and, if appropriate, selecting pilot schools and/or units. When organizing for TQ, a parallel organization structure is developed to plan, guide, launch, and evolve total quality efforts. It is highly recommended that another committee known as the quality service support (QSS) team be organized to provide support for all total quality efforts. (See Figure 3.4.)

FIGURE 3.4
Organize a Quality Steering Committee

Step 3: Organize a Quality Steering Committee

Activity	By Whom	Duration
• Determine composition of quality steering committee	Superintendent	1 day
• Form quality steering committee	Quality coordinator	1-5 days
• Train quality steering committee	Quality coordinator and consultant/trainer	40 hours
• Launch TQ process	Quality steering committee	90 minutes
• Conduct quality steering committee meeting	Quality steering committee chairperson	90 minutes
• Establish a quality service support team	Quality steering committee and quality coordinator	2 weeks
• Create quality improvement teams	Quality coordinator	As needed
• Establish quality action teams	Quality improvement teams	As needed
• Establish any other appropriate component	Quality steering committee	As needed

Step 4: Develop a Total Quality Management Plan

Now that the QS committee has been organized and the quality coordinator has been appointed or selected, a TQ master plan must be developed by the quality coordinator and approved by the QS committee. This plan should be based on the extent to which the superintendent desires to implement TQ, available resources, knowledge gains through education, training, and visitation to TQ schools and organizations. (See Figure 3.5.)

FIGURE 3.5
Develop a Total Quality Master Plan

Step 4: Develop a Total Quality Master Plan

Activity	By Whom	Duration
• Gain knowledge of other TQ plans by reading books, attending events, and acquiring other TQ plans	Quality coordinator	2-3 weeks
• Identify critical issues	Superintendent and other stakeholders	1 day
• Outline sequence of activities to prepare the plan	Quality coordinator	1 day
• Develop the plan	Quality coordinator	3-5 days
• Approve the plan	Quality steering committee	1 day

Step 5: Create a Guidance System for Total Quality

The first, and perhaps the most important, step in implementing TQ is the creation of a TQ guidance system, referred to by Dr. Deming as constancy of purpose, to guide and direct all human efforts in the school organization. The TQ guidance system is a network of aims that spells out the primary reason for the school district, school, or unit's existence and future directions, and ensures that everyone is working together. (See Figure 3.6.)

FIGURE 3.6
Create a Guidance System for Total Quality

Step 5: Create a Guidance System for Total Quality

Activity	By Whom	Duration
• Prepare the mission	Departments, schools and units	1-8 weeks
• Create the vision	School district and schools	1-8 weeks
• Formulate shared values	Departments, schools and units	1-4 weeks
• Prepare quality service strategy	School district	1-2 weeks
• Develop quality policy	School district	1-2 weeks

Step 6: Establish a Pilot Study

Most school districts will probably want to initiate TQ as a pilot study. Select ten percent of your schools to perform the pilot study. Although some superintendents are inclined to select their poorest schools to do it, this is not the recommended procedure. Only your top principals and schools should be selected for the pilot study. In essence, "put your best foot forward" is the approach which should be used to "field test" TQ. (See Figure 3.7.)

Figure 3.7
Establish a Pilot Study

Step 6: Establish a Pilot Study

Activity	By Whom	Duration
• Develop criteria to select pilot schools	Quality coordinator and quality service support team	1 week
• Interview candidates	Quality coordinator	2 weeks
• Approve criteria and select schools based on recommendation of quality coordinator	Quality steering committee	1-2 days
• Train pilot schools	Quality coordinator, quality service support team, and consultant/trainer	2 weeks
• Allocate a budget for each pilot school	Quality steering committee	1 weeks
• Execute pilot study	Quality coordinator	Continuous

Step 7: Educate and Train for Total Quality

There is a high correlation between education, training, and commitment to TQ. As a result, a comprehensive education and training is essential to an effective TQ process. In those schools and other organizations that have not been successful in implementing TQ, the superintendent and central school administrators have failed to realize the true value of education and training for gaining a commitment, as well as a passion, for using TQ as a process for reaching greatness. (See Figure 3.8.)

FIGURE 3.8
Educate and Train for Total Quality

Step 7: Educate and Train for Total Quality

Activity	By Whom	Duration
• Conduct orientation sessions in TQ	Superintendent and consultant/trainer	1-3 weeks
• Conduct TQ awareness session	Central school administrators, quality service support team, consultant/trainer	1-4 weeks
• Conduct in-depth training in TQ	Consultant/trainer and quality service support team	Continuous
• Other TQ training	Quality service support team	As needed

Step 8: Listen to the Customers to Gather Information

This step is usually combined with Step 9. However, because it is such an important one, I felt the need to separate it as a critical implementation step. A number of strategies must be devised to listen to customers by collecting appropriate data for the purpose of identifying their needs, requirements, and expectations. TQ organizations engage in interviewing, surveying, using complaint cards, acting as "mystery parents," and numerous other ways to stay in tune with customers. School districts must emulate these strategies if they are to become sensitive to their customers on the way to greatness. (See Figure 3.9.)

FIGURE 3.9
Listen to the Customers to Gather Information

Step 8: Listen to the Customers to Gather Information

Activity	By Whom	Duration
• Survey existing customers	Quality steering committee and teams	1 month
• Survey providers	Quality steering committee and teams	1-2 weeks
• Identify quality opposition	Quality steering committee, principals and supervisors	1-2 weeks
• Divide customer demands into related groups	Quality steering committee and teams	1-2 days
• Validate and determine reliability of information	Quality steering committee, quality service support team, and teams	2 weeks

Step 9: Establish a Quality Service Measurement System

The case of a TQ process is the quality service measurement system. It is this system that will pinpoint the service areas, characteristics, measures, standards, and performances to identify, track, and evaluate whether or not TQ has been performed as decided jointly by the customers and school district, and if it has been measured by the customers. (See Figure 3.10.)

FIGURE 3.10
Establish a Quality Service Measurement System

Step 9: Establish a Quality Service Measurement System

Activity	By Whom	Duration
• Brainstorm quality service areas	Either by quality steering committee or teams	1-2 days
• Use nominal group process to identify and describe service measures	Either by quality steering committee or teams	102 days
• Match quality standards to measures	Either by quality steering committee or teams	1-2 days
• Identify ways to continue to satisfy customers	Quality steering committee schools and units	2-3 days and quarterly

Step 10: Detect and Close Quality Service Performance Gaps

TQ requires that performance be measured multi-dimensionally; that is, it should be measured in terms of customers expectations and school district perceptions of the customers' service expectations; school district's perceptions of customers' expectations and the translation of perceptions into quality service standards; service delivery and the translation of perception of customers' service expectations; service delivery and external communications to customers; and customers' expected service and perceived service. Once all performance gaps have been reviewed and closed, the next step involves increasing quality standards and customer satisfaction. (See Figure 3.11.)

FIGURE 3.11
Detect and Close Quality Service Performance Gaps

Step 10: Detect and Close Quality Service Performance Gaps

Activity	By Whom	Duration
• Review all possible performance gaps	Quality steering committee, departments, schools, and units	Continuous
• Close all performance gaps	Quality steering committee, departments, schools, and units	Continuous
• Increase quality standards	Quality steering committee, departments, schools and units	Continuous
• Increase customer satisfaction	Quality steering committee, departments, schools, and units	Continuous

Step 11: Implementing Total Quality in the Classroom

Classrooms in the schools of the United States need a boost to make learning fun and enjoyable for students. Many of the principles, practices, and activities in a TQ organization can be integrated with course content to produce what I believe are great schools. The philosophies and works of Drs. Deming, Juran, and Crosby are appropriate and can easily be translated to enhance the learning process. Not only will students be more productive in a TQ classroom, but their personal lives will also be enhanced. Implementing TQ in the classroom will require adopting appropriate TQ principles and practices; understanding the System of Profound Knowledge; preparing a quality service measurement system; using scientific method; arriving at students', teachers', and principals' expectations; and designing and engaging a host of activities to incorporate instruction with principles of TQ. (See Figure 3.12.)

FIGURE 3.12
Implement Total Quality in the Classroom

Step 11: Implement Total Quality in the Classroom

Activity	By Whom	Duration
• Identify and practice appropriate TQ principles	Teacher and students	1-2 week
• Master and use a System of Profound Knowledge	Students	Continuous
• Develop quality service measurement strands	Quality service support team, teachers and students	Continuous
• Learn and use Shewhart/Deming cycle	Students	Continuous
• Reach mutual agreement and practice TQ expectations	Principal, teacher and students	Daily
• Relate Dr. Deming's interaction triangle to classwork	Teacher and students	Continuous
• Integrate TQ activities with course content	Teacher	Ongoing

Step 12: Develop a Recognition and Reward Program

Recognizing and rewarding quality efforts, expressing gratitude for quality accomplishments, and celebrating quality successes must be performed in a timely and sincere fashion. This can vary from a handshake to giving those who earned them lavish gifts. It must be reflective of the involvement and gratitude of central school administrators, and it must be engaged. A recognition and reward program for those who produce quality is essential. (See Figure 3.13.)

FIGURE 3.13
Develop a Recognition and Reward Program

Step 12: Develop a Recognition and Reward Program

Activity	By Whom	Duration
• Allocate a budget for recognition and reward program	Quality steering committee	2 days
• Develop recognition and reward program	Quality coordinator	3 weeks
• Obtain feedback from appropriate school people on program	Quality steering coordinator	1 week
• Approve recognition and reward program	Quality committee	1-7 days
• Celebrate quality success	Quality steering committee	7 days

SUMMARY

Regardless of the plan developed to implement TQ in your school district, the plan should contain some fundamental requirements. It should make provisions for exploring the philosophy and principles of TQ to determine whether or not to proceed and how. School people should gain an understanding of the process by studying the leaders in the field. A QS committee should be organized to perform some initial tasks to plan and launch the TQ process, such as selecting a quality coordinator, creating a model, establishing a budget, attending to the guidance system, organizing and establishing a pilot study, and making provisions for education and training. In addition, design teams may be needed to develop instruments for listening to the customer, preparing a quality service measurement system, and creating a recognition and reward program. Once you have designed and implemented your plan, check the steps against the above requirements.

When an implementation plan has been developed and enforced by the QS committee, the next step involves the creation of a TQ model for the school district by the QS committee. This process is discussed in the next chapter.

CHECKLIST FOR MAKING THE TRANSITION TO TOTAL QUALITY

A host of plans can be created to implement TQ in education. The one selected for this book that will facilitate the process is described below:

1. Plan and execute the initial steps for implementing TQ very carefully. Once again, they are as follows:

   - Gaining central school administration commitment.
   - Determining a school organization's readiness for TQ.
   - Creating a strategic vision and guiding principles (the guidance system).
   - Conducting the superintendent's retreat.
   - Involving principals.
   - Initiating early discussions with representatives of unions/associations.

2. Develop a school district's organizational structure for TQ by:

   - Using the existing school organizational structure.
   - Forming a QS committee.
   - Creating a QSS Team.
   - Linking school organization elements.

- Establishing QI teams.
- Initiating QA teams.

3. Assess school organizational readiness for TQ by:
   - Making key considerations.
4. Select an approach to implement TQ by:
   - Implementing TQ on a district-wide level.
   - Identifying methods for selecting pilot schools.
5. Develop a strategy for implementing TQ by:
   - Selecting a top-down or bottom-up approach.
6. Develop an implementation plan.

Chapter Four

Gaining Leadership Commitment

TO TOTAL QUALITY

One of the great lessons of the quality revolution is that leadership is the most important ingredient for launching and sustaining a quality improvement process. If the top dog and his immediate poundmasters do not believe in the process and behave accordingly, it will not happen.

—*Jerry Bowles, et al.*

Central school administrators' recognition of the need for school improvement through quality enhancement, and their willingness to learn more, are the first prerequisites for implementing TQ in education. It is not possible to overstate the importance of the role of central school administrators. Their leadership is crucial during every phase in the development of TQ in a school organization. In fact, as a former superintendent, a professor of education, and a trainer of thousands of administrators, I have found that lack of understanding and involvement, as well as indifference by central school administrators, are frequently the primary reasons for the failure of most school improvement programs, including QI efforts.

To implement TQ in education successfully requires not only a mission, vision, values, quality strategy, and policies, it also requires support such as providing resources of implementation, like time, money, and school people needs. Delegation and lip service are absolutely not enough.

IN THIS CHAPTER, I WILL
DISCUSS THE FOLLOWING:

- Identifying the techniques in which central school administrators can demonstrate support for TQ.

- Describing those activities in which central school administrators can become meaningfully involved in TQ.

- Identifying techniques for changing school leadership style for TQ.

DEMONSTRATING SUPPORT
FOR TOTAL QUALITY

The superintendent of schools and central school administrators can perform a host of activities to demonstrate strong support for TQ. The following represent some of these activities, including approving a budget for TQ, providing adequate time, joining national professional quality associations, organizing a QS committee, conducting total quality stump speeches, retaining a TQ consultant, creating a strategic vision and quality policy, tying recognition to TQ, putting quality first on the board agenda, getting teachers to support TQ in the classroom, and having leadership involvement in TQ activities.

Approve a Budget for TQ

The old adage, "Put your money where your mouth is," remains true today. Nothing sends a stronger signal to school people than the allocation of funds to support the TQ process. In site-based management, the pilot schools across the country received $6,000 to $25,000 per school council from the general budget depending on the size of the school. Most of these funds were needed for education and training purposes.

Provide Adequate Time for Total Quality

In addition to allocating a budget for TQ, a commitment to TQ requires an allotment of time for education and training, conducting quality meetings, visiting benchmarking schools and other organizations, and celebrating quality victories. Not only should the superintendent and central school administrators allot time for school people to engage in TQ activities, they themselves should represent examples to follow. In addition, they should visit, and at times participate in TQ activities being engaged in by their school people.

School administrators must receive required education and training in TQ. Without proper training, they are likely to continue their old ways, achieve the same mediocre results, and nurture the same outmoded attitudes. Not only should the central school administrators attend education and training activities, they should require all school people to do likewise. A key indicator of success is for central school administrators to track the number of school people attending various education and training events. Central school administrators should also recognize and reward school people for pursuing a path of continuous learning through reading, attending workshops and conferences, visiting TQ school districts and other organizations, and engaging in TQ initiative.

Join National Professional Quality Associations

Joining professional associations not only helps establish a network of school districts participating in TQ, it is an opportunity for education and training in the process. This involvement by the superintendent, central school administrators, and principals sends a message of strong personal commitment to TQ. Once you are a member, try for a leadership position.

There are several organizations that are stressing TQ, as indicated below:

- The American Association of School Administrators has organized a TQ network.

- The American Society for Quality Control and the Association for Quality and Participation provide training, publications, and videos on TQ.
- The National Alliance of Business is leading a TQ education project.
- The National Center to Save Our Schools writes grants for school districts interested in TQ, publishes a TQ journal, and provides quality training.

Organize a Quality Steering Committee

A QS committee should be organized to guide and direct the TQ process. It is highly recommended that the superintendent, not his or her designee, chair the committee. This sends a powerful message to school people that the superintendent is a firm believer and supporter of the TQ process.

Conduct Stump Speeches

An effective way to demonstrate a passion for TQ is to deliver five-minute stump speeches, and to require the same for *all* school administrators. In fact, one of the quality indicators for evaluating school administrators should be the number of stump speeches delivered to school people, different community organizations, and groups. Training in how to conduct stump speeches should be provided to school administrators before they are let loose on the community.

Retain a Total Quality Consultant

Implementing the TQ process is much too important, and too complex, to leave all of the training to the staff development department. Excellent TQ consultants who have been certified as team facilitators should also be retained. When considering consultants, use the piece approach, which means retaining consultants to provide pieces of the TQ process. For example, acquire a specialist to provide statistical training, an expert to provide training for the QI team, another to help plan and implement the TQ operation processes, and more. In this way, the school district will be able to capitalize on the strength of each consultant, rather than assuming consultants to be strong in all areas of TQ.

Create a Strategic Vision and Quality Policy

The creation of a strategic vision and quality policy is essentially the responsibility of the superintendent of schools. The vision and policy should be passionately communicated throughout the school and community by the superintendent and others. The superintendent should think of TQ as a religion, and that she or he is a prophet preaching the gospel through the vision, policy, and other elements of the quality guidance system. The principals are the disciples of the superintendents leading the congregation (school people) on the right direction for saving young souls. The more the superintendent and others preach the gospel with fervor and vitality, the more school and community people will get the strong sense of total commitment to TQ.

Tie Recognition to Total Quality

Far too many school districts do not have an adequate recognition program or they recognize school people for the wrong thing. As mentioned in Chapter Three, one effective way the superintendent can demonstrate strong support for TQ is through a recognition program tied to values necessary to maintain and sustain the TQ process.

Put Quality First on a Board Agenda

Request that the board discuss right from the onset of the board meeting the status of quality in the school district. At times, use the board meeting to expose the board and spectators to new quality issues and practices. Invite expert speakers to make brief presentations on quality at board meetings. Request board members to become part of the quality groove. Make certain all of the terms like quality and TQ are spoken at a minimum of two dozen times to demonstrate fanaticism with quality through actions, words, and deeds.

Get Teachers to Support Quality in the Classroom

Early during the school year, a superintendent should conduct a formal meeting with teachers about his or her quality aspirations for the ensuing school year. Request teachers to discuss with students what quality is, what are the types of quality, who is responsible for quality, how quality can be promoted in the classroom, and how students should be rewarded for quality. Purchase a copy of William Glasser's book entitled *Quality Schools* (Harper & Row Publishers, 1990) for each teacher. Inform teachers that several workshops on quality in the classroom will be available early during the year.

Have Leadership Involvement in Total Quality Activities

Although superintendent support is extremely essential to the successful implementation of the TQ process, nothing is more important than involvement by the chief school administrator. Support is often not observed, whereas involvement is. This involvement by the central school administrators must demonstrate strong commitment to TQ, and it must help to build a common TQ language. After all, a common language helps build a TQ culture.

INVOLVING CENTRAL SCHOOL ADMINISTRATORS IN TOTAL QUALITY

There are several ways the superintendent and central school administrators can become meaningfully involved in TQ, as discussed below, including participating in recognition activities, wandering around, serving as a QS committee chairperson, participating on QI teams, conversing with customers, speaking the lingo, establishing a hotline, conducting a superintendent conference, becoming obsessed with quality, and reviewing QI team presentations.

Participate in Recognition Activities

Everyone likes to participate in recognition events, and there are basically three recognition activities in which the superintendent and his or her central school administrators can become important participants. The first is to hold a ceremony for the presentation of certificates to school and community people who successfully complete TQ education and training classes. The second involves the presentation of awards to QI teams that complete QI projects. This activity is also seldom accomplished by school districts, even though site-based management has been implemented by hundreds of them. The third activity is the annual award report when the entire school organization congregates to celebrate those who have met the criteria cited in the district-wide quality recognition program.

Management by Wandering Around

Tom Peters, co-author of the best seller, *In Search of Excellence*, maintains that the superintendent and central administrators should manage by wandering around about 75 percent of their time in schools. I would lower the percentage to 25 percent and gradually work up to 75 percent.

When central school administrators are practicing the philosophy of management by wandering around, they should:

- Meet with all school stakeholders during the course of the year.

- Use this technique to systematically increase their knowledge of the school district, and to stay well-informed.

- Contribute to an atmosphere of caring and trust in the school by allowing people to express themselves openly, and by following through on all conversations.

- Deliberately carry out the following four goals: 1) seek out people to connect; 2) actively listen to them; 3) facilitate their conversation; and, 4) follow through with their concerns about quality issues or anything else.

Central school administrators should seek opportunities to transfer the knowledge they have obtained to other school people. They should perform as a coach by demonstrating commitment through continuous and consistent action. Coaching is an important skill that is imperative in order to effectively implement TQ.

Serve as a Chairperson on the Quality Steering Committee

It is important that the superintendent not be tempted to assign a representative to chair the QS committee. The TQ process is too important for the superintendent not to be actively involved where the activity is taking place. Furthermore, when members of the quality steering committee see the direct involvement of their chief school administrator in TQ, it sends a strong message of support and involvement. As a result, members of the committee also become the superintendent's disciples, who preach the gospel of TQ.

Participate in Quality Improvement Training

The first person to receive any education and training, and therefore, to learn the concepts, tools, and techniques of TQ, is the superintendent of schools, followed by his or her central school administrators. Once armed with this new knowledge, he or she should look for opportunities for all central administrators to portion off a TQ training program. Two elements of education and training in which central school administrators should be well-qualified to teach are awareness sessions and the quality planning elements of TQ.

Serve on Quality Improvement Teams

Another involvement activity in which central school administrators are not prone to participate in is serving on teams that are actively involved in doing things for students. This cannot or should not be tolerated in TQ, because their participation can help to close the quality gap between the school perception and customer needs, requirements, and expectations. In addition, QI teams are more inclined to make the more significant problem-solving quality decision if they consist of cross-functional members. One senior manager in a company actually insisted that all of his managers form a QI team and engage in quality management projects.

Converse With Customers

Talking with customers is an extremely important action for central school administrators in order to promote and participate in TQ. Unfortunately, too few central school administrators involve themselves in talking to *all* of their customers.

If quality means meeting the needs, requirements, and expectations of customers, then it is absolutely imperative for central school administrators to have a clear and current understanding of the customers, and their perception of what they are receiving from the school district. It is wonderful for central school administrators to hear the results of focus groups, interviews, and surveys, but it is greater for them to directly interact with them on a daily basis. Central school administrators should visit customers' homes when possible, speak to them via telephone, and regularly review correspondence from them. After a while, school administrators will have an invaluable personal database of customer perceptions.

Speak the Lingo

As the TQ philosophy becomes inculcated, and the process takes root within the school district, a quality language will evolve. A superintendent who has been fortified with adequate education and training will become quite conversant with the language, words, and phrases, such as internal and external customers, zero defect, cause-and-effect analysis, and root causes. These and numerous other phrases will be spoken throughout the school districts and sites.

It is essential for the central school administrators to speak the quality language to promote and nurture the quality environment. By doing so, central school administrators diminish any barriers among the levels of the school organization. In addition, it facilitates communication and understanding throughout the school district.

Establish a Hotline on Quality

Establish an exclusive telephone hotline on quality so that at a designated day and time, parents and other citizens can contact the superintendent directly and discuss any matters related to quality. In addition, request to appear on television and/or radio to demonstrate a strong support for quality.

Conduct a Superintendent Conference on Quality or Total Quality

Request the quality coordinator to plan an annual conference on quality. Cancel school for the day. Invite community people to the conference. Arrange for business people who are involved in TQ to conduct appropriate workshops on quality. Invite Baldrige National Quality Award winners to address the school and community on topics of quality. Make imprinted T-shirts for a small cost, and either sell these or give them out to participants. Have lunch served at the conference. Invite students to attend the conference and report their quality experiences.

Become Obsessed With Quality Performance

Meet with secretaries and have them develop quality measures, and reach a mutual agreement on quality standards. Insist on quality everyday from all school people, and personally insist that letters, reports, etc., be done over and over until quality standards are reached. Let school people see quality outbursts, but also let them witness quality recognition events. Keep small quality awards available to distribute from time to time when witnessing everyday quality events, such as when a person suggested a quality idea that worked, completed a research study for a quality improvement team, etc. Speak of quality to every person, even though the occasion may not warrant it. The superintendent should demonstrate an obsession with quality by doing odd things, such as purchasing flowers for secretaries or his or her central school administrators during quality month, celebrating the date the school district began the implementation of quality, showing up in school with an imprinted T-shirt with the QI philosophy written on it, and more.

In essence, the superintendent must be possessed by quality. He or she must speak quality, eat quality, sleep quality, think quality, breathe quality, and if necessary, bleed for quality. When he or she walks through the corridors of the central school administrators' office and someone says, "Here comes Dr. Quality," then and only then will he or she have demonstrated a strong leadership commitment to quality.

Review Quality Improvement Team Presentations

The superintendent and central school administrators should make it a point to attend project presentations conducted by either a QI team or QI action team. Attendance at these sessions accomplishes four things:

1.   It demonstrates central level commitment to TQ.
2.   It gives central school administrators an opportunity to evaluate completed projects.
3.   It helps them fully understand how a team reached a solution, and why a particular action was recommended.
4.   It enables the central school administrators to recognize teams that are performing well.

CHANGING SCHOOL LEADERSHIP BEHAVIOR FOR TOTAL QUALITY

Mary I. McWilliams, a quality management consultant located in Avinger, Texas, identifies several interesting techniques to get senior management to participate in TQ. These techniques have applied to education as additional food for thought to get central school administrators involved and participating in TQ. They include the attention phase, the deficiency recognition phase, the proof phase, and the advise and counsel phase.

Attention Phase

The superintendent and other school people must get the attention of central school administrators to nurture their involvement in and support for TQ. Tools that prove useful during this phase are: an analysis of the cost of poor quality, the conduct of a morale survey, an analysis of the customers, and a quality assessments study.

An effective way to bring central school administrators' attention to the need of TQ is to have each one compute the cost of poor quality; that is, to determine the areas of cost with the highest priority. This step will also enable these administrators to determine if the school district is in bankruptcy. For example, a large school district in New Jersey spent around 9 million dollars per year on substitute salaries. When computing the "real" cost of absenteeism, it was determined that it was 117 million dollars, or a little less than half of a 240 million dollar budget. When a central school administrator was told of this, he was surprised. The areas where a central school administrator can determine the cost of poor quality are as follows:

- Student absenteeism (loss of state aid)
- Actual and real cost of school people absenteeism
- Vandalism
- Loss due to student drop-out
- Cost benefit analysis
- Loss due to poor control of cost reserve
- Cost due to waste (energy, food, and supplies)
- Cost due to damage
- Loss due to overloaded inventory

- Student retention program

The conduct of a morale survey is also an effective way to bring central school administrators' attention to the need for TQ. It will help determine the current school district culture, and it will enable the central school administrators to understand what needs to be done to change to a TQ culture.

An analysis of customers by the central school administrators should be conducted to determine their true needs. It should include customer complaint analysis, customer satisfaction surveys, focus groups, and any other appropriate data.

Quality assessments conducted by outside consultants certainly are a sound way to bring central school administrators' attention to the need of TQ. The assessments should begin at the central office level, and proceed to the school level as the total process is being implemented. The assessments should include cost of poor quality, customer needs, requirements, and expectations, human resources, and strategic quality planning. The information should be derived from data included in various reports.

Deficiency Recognition Phase

Central school administrators must understand that their present performance and actions are not good enough. They should encourage visits to TQ school districts and companies, receive TQ articles written by superintendents and other professionals, review TQ videos, read quality-related books, do some benchmarking, participate in quality discussions, and attend TQ conferences and seminars. As a group, central school administrators should visit Baldrige Award winners. A great deal can be learned from these top quality companies and organizations. These visits should be followed with questions and analyses of quality concepts that are helpful for implementing the TQ process. In addition, central school administrators' meetings should be analyzed to determine how much time is spent devoted to TQ issues.

Proof Phase

Central school administrators must be convinced that TQ will work in the school district to perform this feat, select a project, and apply the principles and practices of TQ. The project should not be too difficult that it will take a year or so to complete. It also should not suggest that any process will work. However, before they tackle the project, they should be trained adequately so they have the necessary skills, techniques, and tools to complete the project successfully. This project selection will not educate and train the central school administrators, but it will demonstrate that TQ can work for any school-related problem. Although the superintendent may be obsessed with TQ, some members of his or her immediate staff may need to be convinced of the validity of TQ if they are to become involved and support the process. As a result, the proof project should be carefully selected based on the following:

- What areas of the school district are causing the central school administrator the most pain?

- In what academic areas can the most academic gains be realized?

- Where in the school district can a pilot project be completed in a reasonable period of time?

- What problems of the school district are causing key customers (students, parents, and teachers) the most pain?

Advise and Counsel Phase

The superintendent and other school people must be ready, willing, and able to tell central school administrators what they need to do to support and become involved in the TQ process. At times, the recommendations may be counter to the existing culture. The use of terms such as empowerment, commitment, and delegation are only buzzwords unless they are supported with resources, time, and funds. Too often, principals organize teams to improve the school only to get little or no support from central school administrators. These administrators have been known to sabotage efforts of improvement teams. Central school administrators must take over visible actions, and must improve the quality processes under their control, such as quality deployment and the management systems that guide the operations of the school district.

As stated previously, central school administrators must be educated and trained in the same TQ methods and tools as the rest of the school district. Special central school administrators TQ workshops are not the answer. The best training approach for central school administrators is to attend the workshops that other school people attend.

SUMMARY

To demonstrate a strong commitment to TQ, the superintendent must play the role of an evangelist preaching the gospel of three gurus of quality through the conduct of stump speeches. He or she must be seen and heard in schools, homes, community events, and board meetings, in fact, in any place where people congregate. He or she must be the prime mover, giving school people guidance directions and recognition and rewards for their TQ initiatives. Lastly, he or she must also be a strategic thinker, anticipating and dealing with problems of quality prior to their occurrence, as well as preventing them from disrupting the quality environment.

When the superintendent and central staff have demonstrated commitment and support to TQ, the guidance system should be revisited to determine if any changes should take place to accommodate this new process. This is the subject of the next chapter.

CHECKLIST FOR MAKING THE TRANSITION TO TOTAL QUALITY

The following activities should prove helpful to gain leadership commitment from the superintendent and central school administrators.

1. Develop and execute a plan for the purpose of demonstrating a commitment to TQ.
2. Develop and execute a plan for becoming actively involved in TQ.
3. Develop a five-minute stump speech, rehearse it for inspiration, and present it to teachers at a general assembly.
4. Require all central school administrators to also develop a stump speech, to include in their performance plan to whom they will deliver the stump speech throughout the school year, and to include activities that will further demonstrate their commitment to TQ.

Chapter Five

Creating A Guidance System For Total Quality

Successful managers who carry out ... customer-focused principles are creating a new view of leadership. Today, top corporate leaders have shown what real leaders must do. They personally put the customer first. They promote their companies' visions. They become "students for life," constantly seeking new ways to learn. They believe in and invest in their people. They build customer-focused teams, celebrating successes and encouraging collaboration. And finally, they "lead by example," personifying the organization's purpose.

—Richard C. Whiteley

D r. Deming maintains that school administrators must be concerned with two main problems: those of today and those of tomorrow. An organization that maintains this focus has what he calls constancy of purpose to stay in business. However, for a school district to "stay in business," it must have a guidance system that governs the behavior of its school people on both a short- and long-range basis. This guidance system is a network of aims that spells out the primary reason for the district's and schools' existence and their future direction, and ensures that everyone is working together. Developing a guidance system is an extremely difficult task, because most school people take the guidance system for granted. They have either oversimplified this task, failed to perform it satisfactorily, or completely ignored it. Without a guidance system, the energy level of the school district is multi-focused, has no direction, and is limited to short-range results, and all aspects of the district and schools will not be congruent with each other. Without a guidance system, neither the district nor the schools, departments, and units will ever become what they are capable of becoming.

IN THIS CHAPTER, I WILL COVER THE FOLLOWING:

- Developing a mission statement
- Creating vision statements
- Describing shared values
- Presenting a service strategy
- Developing a quality policy

DEVELOPING A MISSION STATEMENT

One of the most essential strategic decisions that any school district can make is the determination of its mission. A failure to make this decision will leave the district, school, department, and unit without the focal point needed to employ its goals and objectives. School districts do not determine their mission; the customer should make this determination. Thus, effective mission statements always proceed from outside (the customers and the environment) to inside (school administrators or provider response to the needs and desires of students).

The mission statement serves a multitude of purposes. The following appear to be most important:

- It describes the reason for the existence of the school district, school, department, or unit.
- It provides a basis for making the right kind of decisions.
- It serves as a vehicle for measuring success.
- It provides a belief that will foster a school organizational climate, which will produce the instructional program.

- It determines how resources will be allocated.

- It facilitates the task of identifying opportunities and threats that must be addressed.

The mission statement should contain the following key elements, including the nature of the school district, school, department, or unit. Ask yourself questions like: What is the primary purpose or function of the school district, school, department, or unit? Why does the school district exist? What needs in the community or greater society does it satisfy? How are these needs expected to change in the future?

The mission statement should also give a description of the customer. Who are the customers? How well does the school district, school, department, or unit serve the customers? What improvements should be made in meeting customer needs? What is the probability that the school district, school, department, or unit can attract students?

Regardless of the approach used to develop a mission statement, it must include the services and/or product to be provided, and the customers to be served.

There are at least three common types of mission statements, including the standard format approach, the primary and secondary approach, and the grand design approach. All of these should be stated in terms of services and description of the customers. If the customer is *not* designated, the mission statement may encompass too wide a scope, thus depleting limited resources of the district, school, or team.

Standard Format Approach

The most common form of a mission statement usually contains certain elements, like beginning with a description of the entity (school district, school, department, or unit), such as the Apex School District; or you could specify the act the entity is responsible for carrying out by indicating: "The Unnatural School District will direct, support and participate in the development and administration of the total quality (TQ) process

You should also indicate the customer(s) to be served by the unit, such as: The Apex School District will direct, support, and participate in the development and administration of the TQ process. Its internal customers are students and teachers. Its external customers are parents, citizens, businesses, industries, colleges, and universities.

Primary and Secondary Approach

The second form of a mission statement involves citing the primary and secondary mission of the school district or school as illustrated here:

The primary mission of the Apex School District is to enable all students within the school to become more than they ever hoped to be through a TQ process. This will be done by providing them with top quality staff and top quality products so that they will be proud and capable citizens.

The secondary mission of the Apex School District is to engage in benchmarking in order to search for, and capitalize, on the best practices so that we are better able to meet our primary mission.

Grand Design Approach

The grand design approach to preparing the mission statement involves a general statement about the quality thrust of the school district and specific statements regarding the stakeholder, school people, students, providers, community, and governments.

The following is an example of the mission statement using the grand design:

The mission of the Apex School District is to provide our customers with the best education possible as compared to our contiguous school districts. More specifically, the school district shall endeavor:

1. To provide students with top quality services and products at reasonable cost to the community.

2. To consider stakeholders' varied interests when effectuating change in the school district.

3. To provide school people with a top quality working life, regardless of their position in the school system, including the opportunity for solving unit, school, and district problems.

4. To be perceived by providers as a school district that is appreciative of their products and services.

5. To actively support the community in order to improve its people's quality of life, and to assist in the improvement of the community.

6. To convince the governments in which the school district operates to give constructive support to our TQ process.

The preparation of a mission statement is probably the second most important task a leader can perform. The *first* most important task is to manage the district, school, department, or unit in such a manner that the mission is fully realized. Important guidelines for preparing the mission statement are as follows:

1. The mission statement should be developed by a cross section of school people and other stakeholders of the school district.

2. It should be prepared after a lengthy discussion has taken place.

3. A consensus should be reached concerning the contents of the mission statement.

4. Enough time should be allotted to disseminate a copy of the mission statement, and to clarify it throughout the district, school, or team by discussing each of its key elements.

5. Be prepared to make minor revisions, if warranted.

6. Whenever possible, use a consultant to facilitate the preparation of the mission statement.

7. In TQ, the mission statement may be developed for the school district as a whole, the school, the department, the unit, the team, and the subteam.

CREATING A VISION

The second element of the guidance system is creation of a vision. A vision is the deepest expression of what a school district or school desires. This declaration of a desired future creates the conditions for producing an aligned school district or school. It is the interaction about the vision that helps to connect the district or school with school and community people in a way that matters. Only then can the school and community support the school district's or school's efforts. Although a vision can be a source of conflict, in most cases it is a source of connecting and pulling forth in a united effort.

What is meant by a vision? Basically a vision is a person's mental image of the future, based on a collection of information, knowledge, ideas, aspirations, dreams, dangers, and opportunities.

Creating a vision is a two-stage operation. The first part is the intuitive imagining of a possible desired achievement. The second part is the most difficult, yet crucial aspect of planning: converting the intuitive vision into an action plan. These two aspects of creating a vision must be carried out alternately, with the right, or creative side of the brain thinking of an ideal to help realize the desired achievement, and the left, or analytical, side of the brain determining the concrete implications of the intuitive vision.

The vision of a leader is not simply a vague idea of a desired end, nor is it a clear picture of a single aspect of a district or a school. It is an operating model of all aspects of the school organization, as well as each school that is being created, and the actual steps taken that are necessary to make that model a reality. To pursue greatness requires much time building and testing the mental mode of existence. The ability to visualize the steps from an idea to realization is one of the most important jobs of a district and school.

The traits of visionary leaders are identified in the book *Creating Excellence* (New American Library, 1984) by Craig R. Hickman and Michael A. Silva. They use the work of Abraham Zalenik of the Harvard Business School to identify traits of visionary leaders. The ten traits are as follows:

1. Be able to search for knowledge, ideas, concepts, and ways of thinking until a clear vision crystallizes.
2. Be keen at articulating the vision into an easy-to-grasp philosophy that integrates strategic direction with the values of the school.
3. Be adept at motivating all school people to embrace the vision by providing constant encouragement, and by performing as a role model.
4. Be able to relate to all customers in a warm, supportive, and expressive way, always communicating to others that "We are a family. What affects one affects all of us."
5. Be adroit at keeping in contact with all customers at every level of the district and school in an attempt to understand their concerns and the impact of the vision on them.
6. Be able to translate the vision so that everyone is able to relate it to his or her own individual interests, concerns, and position.
7. Be astute at remaining at the core of the action so as to be the primary source for shaping the vision.
8. Be able to evaluate the progress of the school district or school in terms of the degree to which the vision has been actualized.
9. Be adept at focusing on the major strengths of the school district or school in an effort to centralize the vision.
10. Be cunning in seeking ways to improve, augment, or further develop the vision of the school district or school by carefully monitoring changes within and outside of the school environments.

Under centralized management, a vision is developed and articulated for the entire school district by the superintendent. With TQ, every school serves as a miniature school district. Each school must create and communicate its own vision. Therefore, TQ requires three types of visionary statements: the strategic vision, the superintendent's vision, and the school vision.

The Strategic Vision

A strategic vision is the mental image of the future direction of a school district based on a thorough analysis of the internal and external environments. It is broad in scope, and covers a period of five years or more. The remaining visions are created as a stepping stone to reach the strategic vision. The strategic vision is usually one sentence, such as: "To enable our students to become more than they ever hoped to be through total quality."

The Superintendent Vision

When the superintendent has completed his or her final version of the strategic vision, he or she develops a superintendent/school district vision to realize the strategic vision. The following is a complete example of a superintendent/school district vision statement:

"What must we do to enable our students to become more than they hoped to be? In performance of our strategic vision, we must become a great district; not an excellent school district, but a great district. Our commitment will reflect our greatness in everything we say and do in our members and in our parents. We will strive to achieve greatness first by realizing our philosophy. For example, by creating a strong and healthy culture that bonds our people together with a common purpose helps students become more than they ever hoped to be. No doubt this vision will require more money. However, we will explore other ways to supplement our budget. These might take the form of encouraging business to adopt schools, entering into a partnership arrangement, or establishing non-profit organizations to raise funds to support our move to greatness. If we think creatively, I am certain we will find ways to raise the money we need.

"Second, we will restructure the entire school district into quality improvement (QI) teams. For example, all departments, units, and schools will be reorganized into teams. My intent in doing this is to give everybody—every teacher, every secretary, every clerk, every custodian, every student, every parent, and every citizen—an opportunity to become involved in this district's decision-making process. In essence, I will decentralize our school district. What we have accomplished through centralization has produced some gains; however, the gains I want to realize will call for a concrete effort on all of our parts. Each one of you will be empowered. I expect staff management to be replaced by self-management. I expect most decisions to be made by consensus. I expect QI teams to study their needs and their aspirations to pursue projects, and to solve problems that will enable us not to achieve excellence, but greatness. I want a transformation to take place within our schools. To take a cue from Dr. Deming, I want to give birth to a new religion—a total quality (TQ) religion.

"Next, we will decentralize the budgetary process so the team will determine where best to spend the funds to better educate our students. For instance, if the team feels that it should implement zero-based budgeting and start from scratch to arrive at its budget, so be it. If the team feels that less money should be spent for school people and more money for instructional aids, so be it. If the team wants to adopt a staff attendance improvement plan to reduce absenteeism, so that the savings can be carried over to the ensuing school year, so be it. The only thing I want from this team is to justify its expenditures.

"We will also need to train and retrain. When I say that our people are our greatest resource, I am going to demonstrate to you that I will put my money where my mouth is. No longer will we spend more money to maintain our vehicles than we do to maintain the people that are employed in our schools. I will require that all of our people undergo a minimum of thirty-six hours of training each year. I expect to increase this requirement over the next three years. I will go to the board and request that one percent of the salary allocation in the budget be earmarked for training and development. I will require school administrators to attend the training session of our teachers as well as those specifically designed for them. Our school district will truly be a learning institution for both of our students and all of our school people."

"The key factors that will determine if my vision will become a reality are:

- My strong determination to make our schools great.

- The empowerment of teachers.

- Setting superior service standards and not settling for anything less.

- Going beyond excellence, and pursuing TQ.

- Implementing a comprehensive training and development program.

- Insisting that our school administrators treat our teachers with dignity and respect, and involve them in the decision-making process."

"Finally, I will do whatever it takes to bring my vision to fruition. You should all understand that I don't expect this vision to be implemented fully for three years. However, I am prepared to teach and preach my vision in the schools, in the homes, in the churches, in the stores, and in the community, so there is no misunderstanding as to where I want to take us. We are going to be great, because we are great. However, we have a tremendous job before us."

When the superintendent has completed his or her school district's vision, a cross section of school and community people is organized into a task force. The superintendent's visionary statement is used as a springboard for soul searching, discussing, modifying, and informal understanding of the superintendent's vision. To do this, the task force member must review the visionary statement and ponder the following questions:

- Is the visionary statement realistic?
- How long will it take to realize the vision?
- Are resources available?
- What evidence is there that it will work?
- How much will it cost?
- Is the leader really committed to the visionary statement?
- Does the leader have the staff necessary to realize the vision?
- Is the school district or school committed to the vision?
- What obstacles will impede the realization of the vision?
- Is the vision appropriate for the school district?
- Is the leader capable of realizing the vision?
- Is the superintendent able to translate the vision so school people will embrace the vision?

Once these, and perhaps other, questions have been considered when reviewing and discussing the visionary statements, the superintendent should be requested to appear before the community to defend these visionary statements by clarifying and modifying them, if warranted. After the defense of both the visionary and strategic statements of the school district, a plan should be developed to disseminate and clarify these visionary statements to the board and all school people.

The School Vision

When the strategic vision has been completed, approved by the board, disseminated, and articulated throughout the school district and community, the next step requires that all schools create their own vision. This involves reviewing pertinent information. Each school must review the strategic vision, the information pertaining to their respective schools, plus other information that reflects conditions within and without the school.

When sufficient information has been collected and digested, the school should ponder the following questions for introspection and projection:

- What does our customer want? Do they value what we do for them? Can we enhance our values? How should we change for the future?

- What can we do to become the best Total Quality school in the country?

- What can we do better than any other school in the United States?

- Why have we succeeded or failed in the past? Do we really understand the reasons for our success or failure? Are we being honest with ourselves?

- If we could rewrite our school history, what would we change?

- What are other districts doing to restructure their schools for TQ?

- How can we use the frustration and disappointment of our customer as learning experiences to improve our schools?

- What is the major strength of our principal? What is her major weakness?

- How committed are central school administrators to Total Quality?

- How do we handle situations in which our customer lets us down?

- Do we have a committed Board of Education and Superintendent?

- What can the school do to maximize the number of students going to college?

- Why do any students fail, and what can be done to minimize failures?

- What kind of training will we need today to enable us to become the best we can become? What kind of training will we need in the future? How should the curriculum be changed to fortify students for the future?

- What does the school do well? What does the school do poorly? How can the school improve? What constrictions keep the school from improving?

- What is the school's potential? Where could the school be in five or ten years?

- What does our school do worse than any other school in the United States? How can we use this situation as an opportunity? What support will we need?

- How would you describe your school using an analogy?

- What are other schools doing to improve their instructional programs?

- Are we delivering what customers want? What evidence do we have?

- What can the school do to enable its students to be more than they ever hoped to be?

- How can we attract other students to our school?

- What can be done to help students prepare for the future?

- How does the school treat the majority of its students? How should the school treat them?

When the school has answered these questions, key visionary areas need to be identified. Key visionary areas are highly selective visionary statements that depict the future direction of the school and must be realized in order for it to become what it aspires to be. These key visionary statements are usually arrived at by using brainstorming or the nominal group process.

The total number of key visionary areas is equal to the vision. This means that the results of the introspection of the past, and projection into the future, must lead to those crucial and essential issues and activities that describe a reference point in the future to which all efforts of the school and community must be directed. This does not mean that other areas may be neglected; rather this is what the team should be concentrating its efforts on. Design teams should be established to deal with any other areas. Each statement is an expression of hope, desire, and aspiration. However, it is not enough just to create a vision, not even a vision of excellence. What you should be striving for is a vision of greatness. A vision of greatness demands that you hold nothing back; that you set no limitations; that you push faith with everything you have; that you eliminate caution and reservation; and that you believe in the future.

The following are some examples of key visionary statements:

- Function as a synergistic team in which everyone feels responsible for the success of the team.

- Develop, implement, and continuously improve on a strategic curriculum.

When using either brainstorming or the nominal group process to generate key visionary statements, the problem should be stated similarly to the following:

Describe in single sentences those key visionary statements you think and feel should define the future direction of our school.

In order to realize the vision, each key visionary statement has to be linked to a program strategy. A program strategy is a series of long-term action plans designed to guide human efforts in realizing a key visionary area. Below is a program strategy for the key visionary area: Function as a synergistic team in which everyone feels responsible for the success of the team. The program strategy is:

1. The team will interview all candidates so each member shares responsibility in the selection process. The key basis upon which teachers and administrators will be recruited is that their personality and character are consonant with the shared values and TQ philosophy of the school.

2. All school people are required to undergo a minimum of forty-five hours of training sessions per year in TQ update, planning, problem solving, and meeting management; and sixty hours of training per year in technical skills. All school people will attend most training events as a group.

3. All school people will be evaluated based on how well each one has contributed to the success of TQ. All school people will also evaluate all support staff, including the superintendent, in terms of how well they supported the efforts of the school.

4. A QI plan will be developed by the QI team, presented and discussed with the school as a whole, and mutually agreed to by both parties.

DESCRIBING SHARED VALUES

A district or school aspiring to become a TQ system must clarify its mission, create a vision, and identify shared values. When values are not stated or shared, the district and school find it difficult to unify individual components. As a result, each operates as a separate entity, creating conflicts and disunity among its segments.

Values are the fundamental and common beliefs that unite a team, integrating its work efforts, guiding its actions, and channeling its energies so as to bring fulfillment to all members and to the school system. To accomplish this, it is necessary to develop a value statement at the district and school levels. More specifically, values:

- Provide godliness for governing the behavior of administrators, teachers, and others within the school system.
- Provide a sense of direction for those associated with the district and the schools.

- Are the basis for guiding school people's decisions and actions.

- Affect performance of school people in a positive manner.

- Help school people perform better (because they are influenced by the substance of each statement).

- Communicate to others what is expected from the district and school.

Some general guidelines for preparing the district and school shared values statements are:

- Include only belief statements.

- Review the statements for clarity, impact, and accuracy.

- Limit each statement to effective matters (attitudes, values, beliefs). Avoid behavioral and cognitive matters.

- Use a directive to construct values statements, regardless of the approach selected.

Once the superintendent's value statement has been developed, it is presented to each central school administrator to study prior to a meeting that will take place during a designated weekend off of school grounds.During this meeting, each values statement is discussed, clarified, defended, and/or modified until a consensus is reached between the superintendent and central school administrators. The nominal group process may be used as a method for arriving at an integrated superintendent's and central school administrators' values statement.

The school district's shared values statement is global in nature, and is used as an umbrella for each school to create its own value statements. Its purpose is to:

- Describe how the district should be managed.

- Identify the values, beliefs, expectations, and attitudes of the superintendent.

- Be used as a basis for synchronizing the values of the central school administrators with the superintendent.

- Provide guidance and direction for managing school people of the district.
- Forecast where the district should be headed.
- Provide a springboard for schools to create shared value statements.

The preparation of the school shared value statements is as follows:

- The team requests its members, facilitators, community people, and a consultant to serve on its shared values task force.
- The task force arranges the nominal group process and other techniques to arrive at a semifinal shared value statement.
- The task force discusses the semifinal shared value statement with designated school and community people to get their input.
- Based on this input, the statement is modified and/or revised. The entire school family is requested to appear at a meeting to receive, review, and discuss the final document. Minor adjustments are then made.
- Once the generated list of indicators for each values statement has been completed, each indicator is used as a topic for training in a series of ten- to fifteen- minute workshops conducted over a period of several months.
- Districts and schools should include value statements for both teachers and students. If value statements indicate how people are to be treated in school, this applies to how school administrators should treat teachers, and how teachers should treat students.
- When all of the activities have been completed, the district and schools are in a state of readiness to determine if school administrators and teachers walk like they talk. This is determined through challenging each value statement on a yearly basis, and taking appropriate action when warranted.

There are perhaps several dozen ways to develop shared values statements, including the simple statement approach, the action-oriented approach, the quality standard approach, and the whereas approach.

Simple Statement Approach

The simple statement approach is probably the most common method through which school districts prepare shared value statements, and is the least prepared by practitioners. It consists of two steps. The first is to identify a list of shared value statements. Teamwork is an example of a value. Next, define each core value, such as "teamwork and cooperation are essential." However, I don't recommend this method because the terms teamwork and cooperation mean different things to different people, and they are difficult to measure.

Action-Oriented Approach

Perhaps the best method to declare a shared value statement is the action-oriented approach. There are two basic steps to this approach. First, meet and mutually agree on a set of TQ shared values, such as "research, facts, and data are better than hunches and guesses."

Next, reach mutual agreement on all appropriate action necessary to support the shared value, as demonstrated below:

- Research, facts, and data are better than hunches and guesses.
- Base all decisions on research.
- Train team members to follow fact-based problem-solving techniques.
- Provide diagnostic support, and help teams locate needed data.

I prefer this action-oriented method over the others because it identifies activities mutually agreed on by school people to engage in to support the values. It therefore minimizes guesswork. In addition, each shared value can be assessed pe-

riodically to determine the extent to which they are being inculcated throughout either the district or the school.

Quality Standard Method

An effective method of creating shared values is to attach
standards of quality to each value. There are four steps for
creating shared values using the quality standard methods.
First, identify single core value terms to perform this task, and
reach a consensus on key value terms that represent the school
district's quality focus, like caring, respect, integrity, empowerment, and intimacy.

The next step involves describing each term with no more
than two to four words, such as:

Caring—
1. Reach out.
2. Be friendly.
3. Care for each other.

For the third step, now that the core value has been briefly
described, use short descriptive statements to indicate how
each will be carried out. For example:

Caring—
1. Reach out. Welcome all irate parents appearing in school
   for an audience. Acknowledge their presence. Make eye
   contact and smile. Introduce yourself in a pleasant tone of
   voice. State your name and your position. Whenever possible, use the parent's name to address him and/or her.
   Above all, engage in active listening by paraphrasing what
   the parent(s) said. Try to reach a solution to the problem.
   Be attentive, genuine, and positive.

Finally, it is not sufficient to list core values. Each year, a
process must be put in place to determine the degree to which

the core values are being inculcated in the district or school. Some techniques for assessing core values are as follows:

1. Conduct a general session with the school as a whole and use the values and quality standards for discussion purposes.
2. Request that those monitoring the values assess the extent to which the values are being carried out.
3. Request that the QI team perform an assessment.

Whereas Approach

Another effective approach to create shared value statements is to describe the values, then further change the values with therefore statements. There are three steps to this process. First, use consensus to arrive at a list of shared values to depict the district or school quality focus, such as, "quality is our number-one concern."

Second, precede the sample value statement with a "We believe" or another appropriate phrase, such as "We believe quality is our number-one concern."

Finally, complete the "We believe" values statement with "therefore," followed by a statement further clarifying the value statement, such as "We believe quality is our number-one concern; therefore, quality is everyone's responsibility."

Some districts and schools may desire to proceed further with this correctly written statement and amplify the words "quality is everyone's responsibility." To do this, brainstorm or use the nominal group process to generate evaluation indicators for the word "expectations." Such a list may resemble the following, using the stem statement, All school people demonstrate a responsibility for quality when they ...:

1.... either as individuals or teams engage in activities to improve performance on a continuous basis.
2.... attend a minimum of sixty hours of education and training on statistics, problem solving, and meeting management.

3.... as individuals, provide a minimum of five suggestions per year that actually improve school performance.

PRESENTING A SERVICE STRATEGY

Some organizations are known to develop a service strategy. A service strategy is a super-ordinate goal designed to declare what should be accomplished, how it will have a significant quality impact on the school district, and when it should be done. It is basically a guide to help all school people make decisions and to act on them at all levels of the school organization. For example, a service strategy should answer these three basic questions:

1. What is the school district's unique contribution?
2. Who are the customers?
3. What core or key values of the school district should the customers perceive?

To complete the service strategy statement, use the following framework:

We are giving notice to the public at large that the Apex School District is committed to the total quality process, which is designed to produce a zero-defect, and to continuously make improvements in all units of the school organization.

The service strategy should be one of the multiple means to measure the TQ process.

DEVELOPING A QUALITY POLICY

When the superintendent is firmly committed to TQ, he or she must develop a policy statement and communicate it to all school people. This act is intended to achieve and demonstrate that this superintendent is committed to TQ as a concept and as a goal. Sometimes the superintendent will develop the policy statement. At other times, he or she will organize a design team or request the quality coordinator to prepare the policy statement. Once the policy statement is developed, the superintendent should require all central school administrators to stick with it, to live it, to breath it, and to protect it in order to demonstrate central school administrators' support and commitment.

The following are four steps for preparing the quality policy statement:

1. Review and analyze quality policies of other quality-oriented school districts and companies.
2. Identify the requirements for a quality policy.
3. Draft and discuss the quality policy with central school administrators, union/association officials, movers and shakers, and other appropriate stakeholders.
4. Familiarize yourself with the quality policy to demonstrate that central school administrators are committed to the quality process.

A quality statement should be brief and easily comprehendible by all school people. It should contain the following elements as a minimum: quality standards, a customer-focus, and a provision for continuous improvement.

The following are examples of continuous improvement policies:

The Apex School District will consistently provide TQ services and products that meet and exceed our customers' requirements and expectations.

Here is an example of the quality pledge approach:

I, (Superintendent's name), pledge that the Apex School District places total quality (TQ) services and products above all else because customer loyalty and exceeding their expectations are our foremost concern. TQ means everybody is responsible for providing quality in everything they do. Quality means meeting customer needs, requirements, and expectations the first time and every time, and we recognize that customers exist both within and outside the school district.

I further pledge that all school people will receive adequate education and training in the principles and practices of TQ, and will be involved in meeting the school district's quality goals. I will see to it that the financial resources necessary to carry out this policy will be made available, so help me God.

_____

Superintendent of schools
Apex School District

_____

Date

Here is an example of the agreement approach:

The Apex School District intends to become the best school district in the state within five years, and to be recognized as such by our school people, providers, students, parents, and other customers. To achieve this goal, we must adopt a customer-driven focus of meeting and exceeding the needs, requirements, and expectations of our internal and external customers every time. We fully endorse the goal and make the following commitment:

- We will adequately educate and train all of our school people in the principles and practices of TQ.

- We will constantly support all school administrators, directors, and supervisors as they involve their school people in the process to improve service and product quality beyond the expectations of their respective customers

- We will specifically encourage and support a full empowerment of our school people; involve parents; increase tolerance of risk-taking and failure; and recognize and reward all contributions made to improve quality efforts.

Superintendent of schools

Date

I, (Principal's name), as principal of the (Name of school), endorse the goal of the Apex School District to become the best school in the state by serving every internal and external customer beyond their expectations every time. Accordingly, I make the following commitments:

- I will make every opportunity to become educated and trained in the principles and practices of TQ.

- I will assist every school in the district to create its guidance system and conduct five-minute stump speeches throughout the school year preaching the gospel of our quest for greatness.

- I will encourage all of our school people to generate and execute a number of ideas that significantly improve service and product quality with a goal of serving every customer beyond their expectations.

- I will champion the empowerment of all school people to aggressively pursue greatness through educating, training, and creating a day-to-day school environment to support our quality goal.

Signed by principal

Date

The first point of the agreement outlines what the central school administrators are willing to do on a school district-wide level to support the principals, directors, and supervisors in advancing the TQ process. The second portion of the agreement outlines what principals are willing to do on a school level to support the TQ process.

Each principal receives two copies of the agreement. The upper portion is signed by the superintendent. Each principal is requested to sign both copies and return these to the superintendent, who will place the parchment in a plaque, and return it to the principal.

SUMMARY

One of the most essential tasks for a school district in implementing a TQ process is the creation of a guidance system to govern the behavior and attitudes of all school people, including students. Far too many school districts create a "paper guidance system," one that is created by assigning a school administrator to this task, inserting it in the board policy manual, and forgetting about it. To properly implement TQ, the guidance system must be created by and mutually agreed to by a cross section of school and community people, disseminated throughout the school and community, and vigorously enforced through words, deeds, and actions.

When the guidance system has been updated, the next major move toward TQ is for the QS committee to create a district-wide model for implementing TQ, which is the subject of the next chapter.

CHECKLIST FOR MAKING THE TRANSITION TO TOTAL QUALITY

The following list of activities have been designed to enable you to construct a guidance system to govern the behavior and attitudes of your school people:

1. Develop a mission statement for the school district and each school, department, and team.

2. Create and communicate a strategic vision, and use this statement for each school to develop their own vision statement. Defend the strategic vision before customers.
3. Prepare core shared values and measure them on an annual basis.
4. Develop and communicate a strategic vision for TQ on a school- and community-wide basis. Get customers to support the service strategy.
5. Write a quality statement for those principles and practices that are necessary to launch, maintain, and evaluate TQ.

Chapter Six

Organizing For Total Quality

... Structuring for quality means that we are building a parallel organization structure, not a new one. Most organizational effectiveness experts agree that many organizations are far too complex and multilayered today to even begin to tolerate added organization community. The parallel quality organization structure is simple and begins to send an important signal to the rest of the company, a signal which communicates that we are aligning ourselves for something new.

—Thomas H. Berry

Developing an organizational structure that will institute, sustain, and facilitate expansion of the quality improvement effort is an essential element for success. The structure is the vehicle for focusing the energy and resources of the school organization towards one common goal—continuous improvement of the products and services it provides to the customer.

Successful school districts tailor the structure so that it maximizes strong points and accommodates their unique mission, culture, and approach for improving quality. This accounts for some of the differences in the way organizational charts are drawn, and for variations in the nomenclature used to describe the TQ school organization. In spite of the differences, several common practices emerge that merit examination and illustration.

IN THIS CHAPTER, I WILL FOCUS ON THE FOLLOWING:

- Creating a TQ model
- Establishing a quality steering (QS) committee
- Selecting a quality coordinator
- Creating a quality service support (QSS) team
- Establishing quality improvement (QI) teams
- Organizing quality action (QA) teams
- Selecting quality facilitators/process observers
- Describing functions of school administrators

CREATING A TOTAL QUALITY MODEL

Although there are some variations on the same theme, a typical TQ model consists of the following components as illustrated in Figure 6.1.

FIGURE 6.1
Total Quality Model

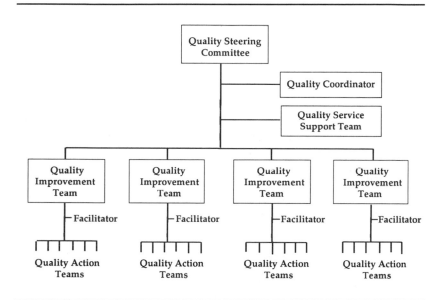

Virtually every organization that has successfully introduced TQ has formed a QS committee during the early stages
of implementation. The first critical responsibility of this committee is to plan the TQ process so that success is inevitable.
This will require the proper structure and a deep-level commitment to the process by each member of the QS committee.
During the selection process, care must be taken to ensure that
all service and support areas are represented.

Many school districts find it advantageous to overlay the
TQ school organization onto the existing management structure. This allows the school district to use the existing lines of
authority and communication to foster the QI efforts while
avoiding major disruption in the school organization.

Rather than requiring a major revamping of the school district, the TQ process can improve the effectiveness of the structure in place. For example, cross-functional teams that identify
customer requirements in each step of a process learn how the

process of each unit impacts on the quality of the next school's, department's, or unit's performance.

The advantage of a QS committee is:

- It helps the school district stay focused on pursuing the same goals, rather than having schools, departments, and units working at cross purposes.

- It fosters increased teamwork and decreased competition.

- It improves communication throughout the school district, and enhances understanding of how all the pieces fit.

- It improves the school district's ability to replicate programs, processes, and ideas, and to standardize solutions that have applicability to process in schools, departments, and units of the school district.

If a QS committee is not organized to guide and direct the TQ process, certain problems will occur, including:

- A common mechanism linking the committee will not exist.

- QI teams and leaders will not receive proper guidance.

- QI team members will complain that the time and effort expended by members seems out of proportion to the impact they are having.

- QI teams will forget that they are supposed to represent the entire school, and that others have a stake in what they are doing.

- Accountability for performance, goals, objectives, effective communication networking, and/or action plans will not be established among QI team members.

- The overall plan for rewarding successes of QI team activities will not be established.

- Failures of TQ will not be perceived as opportunities for school quality enhancement.

- Principals and QI teams will not be clear about their roles. The QI team leader or principal will develop too strong a sense of process ownership.

Although school districts can implement TQ without a QS committee, implementation problems experienced by several school districts are convincing evidence that such a committee enhances the effectiveness of the quality process. For example, sometimes the superintendent is slow in understanding the powerful effect of TQ on students in the school district, and is not ready to implement the process. Individual classes or schools may implement TQ without the direction of a QS committee.

The membership of the QS committee is comprised of individuals selected from a variety of levels within the school organization so that every position is represented. However, each school district that establishes such a committee should do so by considering its own individual needs as well as the political realities. The membership usually ranges between fifteen and twenty-four members. The committee should not be so large as to make it unwieldy and slow, nor should it be too small to make it ineffective in hearing different views, and in taking advantage of the varied experiences in the school district.

The QS committee is chaired either by the superintendent or his or her representative, or is co-chaired by the superintendent and the president of the unions/associations. In education, membership in the committee usually comes from a cross section of school and community people. In manufacturing, industry, and service organizations, membership is usually comprised exclusively of top management.

An example of members of a QS committee is as follows:

- Superintendent of schools
- Assistant superintendent of business and assistant superintendent for human resources
- Two union officials
- Two community business people

- Three parents
- Two principals (QI team leaders)
- Coordinator of quality
- Two students
- Three teachers
- Three civil service people

Because the QS committee plays such an important role in the installation of TQ, it is highly recommended that a charter or component description be prepared to spell out authority, functions, membership composition, and the responsibilities mentioned earlier.

Authority of the Quality Steering Committee

To enable the QS committee to become an official decision-making body for TQ, the superintendent or designee must prepare a charter and give the committee the power and authority to exercise judicious control over the planning, implementation, maintenance, and improvement of TQ. The person designated to respond on behalf of the QS committee is known as the quality coordinator. This charter should be approved by the board of education. For instance, to establish a QS committee, the superintendent usually selects a design team to decide on members of the committee, prepare the charter, arrive at a budget, and make other recommendations to get the committee operating and running.

In order to execute the charter, the superintendent must chair or appoint a designee to chair the QS committee, and empower it to function as an official body to guide and to direct the TQ process. The committee will function by carrying out the following fourteen steps:

1. The chairperson prepares and distributes and agenda to the QS committee members for each meeting prior to the time of the meeting. Any person who wishes an item included on the agenda will submit the topic and subject

matter in writing to the chairperson prior to the preparation of the agenda. Other persons who desire committee consideration of a topic will submit the topic and subject matter to the principal or immediate supervisor; the school person will then determine the advisability of submitting the item to the chairperson.

2. Counsel the superintendent and other central school administrators in order to reach decisions on policy and general operating matters pertaining to the TQ process.

3. Determine the philosophy, goals, and objectives of the TQ process, and guide the development and operations of the school organization toward this accomplishment.

4. Formulate or approve policies, procedures, programs, and plans for execution by the quality coordinator.

5. In the unavoidable absence of any member from a QS committee meeting, an alternate is appointed by that member to represent and act for him or her.

6. Voting within the committee is to be in person at any duly called meeting, at any meeting when all members are present, or by mail.

7. All matters are decided by a consensus of those present.

8. A quorum constitutes 50 percent of the membership.

9. The QS committee has among its membership community people. These members make criticism of, suggest changes in, and advise with respect to policies, procedures, plans, programs, personnel, and other activities regarding the TQ process.

10. The QS committee and the individual members keep themselves as informed as possible concerning all activities of the QI efforts to the end that they may advise the chairperson and quality coordinator as intelligently as possible.

11. The chairperson assigns individual members of the QS committee to investigate certain areas. Members report back to the committee at the time designated by the chairperson.

12. It is expected that any subjects brought up at the meeting are evaluated by the chairperson for appropriateness for committee consideration or discussion. When the subject matter is not sufficiently advisory or of general interest to the committee, the chairperson in his or her capacity coordinates the particular functions involved at a later time.

13. One member of the QS committee is appointed secretary by the chairperson. The secretary prepares notes on the committee's discussions and recommendations and distributes them to each member.

    The secretary is to properly record items still pending because of insufficient information. These items are recorded in the minutes for follow-up. Then the member responsible for the execution of this particular matter is alerted to the necessity of procuring data for the next meeting, or will at least report at the next meeting on how the problem has been taken care of. The secretary sends notice of the time and place of each meeting to members of the QS committee, and at least one week prior to the meeting, arranges to have the agenda for the meeting sent to all members.

14. Give final approval of periodic reports to the superintendent.

The primary responsibility of the QS committee, as deigned by the superintendent, is to create a TQ process that will have a measurable impact on the operations of the school organization. The QS committee is responsible for planning, conducting, and evaluating all TQ activities to ensure the success of the TQ process. The commitment of time by the membership will be heavy. It usually calls for weekly meetings for a period of two months or more. This is in addition to the time needed for reading, thinking, and discussions outside of meetings. Once TQ is defined and launched, the time required by the QS committee members will be substantially reduced. It will be limited to staying abreast of the process in the school district, keeping up with developments and new trends in TQ, taking part in recognition events, attending monthly meetings, conducting speaking engagements, and more.

The QS committee is also responsible to the superintendent of schools for planning, conducting, and directing the TQ process. Its customers are the superintendent if she or he is not a member of the steering committee or the board of education.

The committee exists to manage the change process when new quality-oriented behavior modes are fully inculcated throughout the school organization. It is involved in planning, monitoring progress, and evaluating the change process itself. Its specific responsibilities include:

1. Developing quality policies and procedures to guide and direct TQ.
2. Identifying quality areas that need improvement.
3. Becoming involved in quality planning and improvement.
4. Providing direction and guidance for the QI teams.
5. Developing decisions or proposals in respect to the operations of the TQ process.
6. Developing TQ processes including procedures and practices
7. Determining program philosophy, goals, and objectives.
8. Implementing the pilot project and providing continuous consultation.
9. Evaluating the effectiveness of TQ.
10. Preparing process reports, annual plans, and other records.
11. Providing direction and guidance to the quality coordinator.
12. Reconciling conflicts, interests, or viewpoints regarding TQ.
13. Preparing the budget to foster TQ.
14. Developing, disseminating, and clarifying quality strategic plans to operate TQ.
15. Recruiting a highly competent quality coordinator and facilitators.

16. Approving the implementation plan.
17. Promoting TQ.
18. Approving, maintaining, and amending the policies and procedures of the recognition and reward program.
19. Approving quality strategic plans and operational plans.
20. Approving measurement and evaluation of the program.
21. Approving vertical and horizontal expansion of the process.
22. Reviewing and evaluating the quality coordinator.
23. Reviewing, monitoring, and evaluating the impact of the TQ process on the school organization.
24. Including TQ as an integral component of the school organization.
25. Pursuing administration support on all levels.
26. Conducting an effective training program in order to provide an awareness session, and in-depth training in subject matters related to total quality.
27. Approving the job descriptions of the quality coordinator.

Selecting a Quality Coordinator

Another function of the QS committee it to select a qualified quality coordinator whose primary function is to make it easy for the QI teams to perform their function. He or she is crucial to the success of TQ. The coordinator is, or should be, a "process" consultant rather than an "expert" consultant. He or she must help the team leader to develop the operation process by which the team can assess itself, its functions, its method of operating, and its need for and ability to change with the changing times and conditions. The coordinator does not solve problems for the team, but helps it solve problems by making it aware of its own operation process, and the manner in which that process affects the performance of the team.

The following fourteen points represent the criteria for selecting a quality coordinator who is responsible for the overall operations of all TQ efforts.

1. Be familiar with all levels of the school organization.
2. Be adept in verbal and written communication skills.
3. Possess leadership ability, and participate in the decision-making process.
4. Be experienced and successful in training a facilitator, team leaders, and members.
5. Have previous skills in dealing effectively with human relations problems.
6. Possess the ability to get others to actively support the program.
7. Possess the ability to deal effectively with school people problems.
8. Be sensitive to the needs of others.
9. Possess the ability to foresee problems before they occur, and to deal with them effectively when they do occur.
10. Maintain employment in the school district for a while.
11. Determine who is self-secured and able to confront the status quo.
12. Determine who has a strong belief in participative management.
13. Determine who are the team players and builders.
14. Determine who is credible.

One of the first acts a quality coordinator should perform is the preparation of a tentative description of his or her roles and responsibilities. This recommendation is based on the theory that in order to develop such a document, he or she will most likely have to review the literature, talk to specialists in the field, visit and observe other QS committees in action, confer with other coordinators, and complete a host of other activities in order to determine the major roles and responsibilities for his or her position. As a result, a more in-depth picture will have emerged concerning what the quality coordinator should and must do in order to facilitate TQ. These twenty-one responsibilities include:

1. Becoming thoroughly trained in an established and certifiable facilitator's training TQ process.
2. Preparing and instituting a quality implementation plan.
3. Serving on the QS committee and assisting it in formulating strategic quality planning to affect the program.
4. Helping select the necessary school and community people to the staff and the pilot project.
5. Recommending enactment of new or modified quality policy and guidelines relating to TQ.
6. Ascertaining the availability of resources to operate QI team meetings.
7. Interpreting and following established quality goals, objectives, guidelines, policies, and procedures.
8. Ensuring accurate and timely reports for the QS committee as a basis for sound decision making.
9. Developing guidelines to ensure union officials' acceptance of the process.
10. Forecasting anticipated problems, evaluating their significance, and recommending possible corrective action.
11. Functioning as an advisor, coach, and counselor for team leaders.
12. Reporting and recommending action to the QS committee and team leaders.
13. Identifying the conditions that are necessary for change to take place, and those other conditions that will facilitate the change process.
14. Fostering and ensuring, through appropriate guidelines and directions, the continuous and harmonious working relationships with the union.
15. Initiating prompt and complete follow-up on all problems or potential problems pertaining to the program, and keeping the QS committee informed of program progress.
16. Assisting the QS committee in budgeting the process.
17. Observing the performance of team leaders in meetings, and meeting with them to provide feedback.

18. Assuming the leadership role to advance TQ.

19. Providing for and authorizing training programs to ensure a high level of skill among team leaders and members.

20. Recommending and coordinating the activities of outside consultants, whose retention is deemed necessary to establish, maintain, and implement the TQ program.

21. Communicating with central school administrators, the QS committee, and others by frequent visits, correspondence, and periodic issuance of bulletins and monthly progress reports.

Organizing a Quality Service Support Team

The QSS team's primary role is that of an internal consultant team. Because quality should be blended in every activity initiated in the school district, directors and supervisors of various specialties should be organized into a QSS team, not only to provide their expertise in specific subject areas, but also in quality. These directors and supervisors must be talented and respected people who possess not only excellent specialty skills, but excellent consulting skills, TQ knowledge, and organizational development abilities. This team is organized to support continuous improvement. As a result, this team becomes a vital district-wide quality resource responsible to the QS committee. Although all directors and supervisors are not required to be members of this team, a representative from each specialty should be. However, all directors and supervisors should be a member of the QSS team.

The QSS team's purpose is to directly support the development, implementation, and enhancement of the TQ process, and to provide consulting, education, and training services to school QI and QA teams for the effective implementation of the TQ process. The QSS department is also responsible for communicating, coordinating, and reporting results and progress of the TQ process. A district-wide quality facilitator or coordinator may lead this department. QSS customers are QI and QA teams and the QS committee.

There are twelve responsibilities for the QSS team:

1. Serving as an internal consultant for quality teams.
2. Conducting TQ awareness and orientation sessions.
3. Helping in the preparation of the quality service measurement system.
4. Providing leadership in benchmarking.
5. Preparing and conducting surveys.
6. Preparing a TQ manual.
7. Publishing a TQ newsletter.
8. Spearheading conduct of an TQ annual conference.
9. Training members in the TQ process.
10. Assisting in facilitating team meetings.
11. Acting as a troubleshooter for teams.
12. Providing assistance in detecting and closing performance gaps.

Organizing Quality Improvement Teams

The fourth element of the QI process model involves the creation of QI teams for each school, department, or unit. An individual school, such as a large urban high school, may have several QI teams; one for the instructional program, another for secretarial staff, etc. On the other hand, a school may have one QI team, but several QA teams: one for solving s discipline problem, one for solving the cost of poor quality, one for solving a teaching problem, etc.

A QI team should limit its membership to eight to twelve members, each serving a three-year period. Since TQ is a process by which administrators are responsible for correcting the school system through controlling variations in the system, the principal should be the leader of the QI team; however, this depends on the principal and his or her relationship with teachers.

QI teams are responsible to the QS committee. Its customers are students, parents, teachers, communities, colleges, universities, and industries.

QI teams exist to divert all TQ activities in their respective schools. They investigate quality problems using problem-solving processes and analytical tools. They also measure quality, and establish quality standards.

The QI team's twenty-three responsibilities are:

1. Developing a mission, vision, and shared values.
2. Selecting TQ improvement projects.
3. Conducting QI meetings.
4. Investigating quality initiatives.
5. Developing a quality accountability matrix.
6. Developing a TQ implementation plan.
7. Forming QI/QA teams.
8. Making arrangements for TQ training.
9. Participating in a TQ annual conference.
10. Preparing QI plans.
11. Detecting and closing performance gaps.
12. Evaluating service support.
13. Inculcating TQ principles and practices throughout the school.
14. Conducting various techniques to collect information on customers.
15. Establishing a quality service measurement system.
16. Improving quality standards.
17. Celebrating quality achievement.
18. Assessing TQ culture.
19. Visiting Baldrige Award winners and TQ school districts.
20. Instituting a student quality team.
21. Creating a suggestion program.
22. Engaging in benchmarking.
23. Investigating and resolving customer complaints.

Once you have organized for district-wide TQ, each QI team needs to begin the QI project selection and action team formation process. Each QI team should be directly involved in this extremely important activity. If good projects are selected, either by the team itself, the principal, or the QS committee, the teams performing them will feel meaningfully involved, and the results realized will make a major contribution to the school reaching greatness. Success in selecting good projects will motivate school people and parents to achieve additional positive results. Poorly selected projects, however, can frustrate team members and diminish their enthusiasm for TQ. A QI project is a task designed to gain an enduring breakthrough or outstanding result that realizes improvement of a process, product, or service.

There are three types of QI projects, including the problem-solving projects, the implementation project, and the research project.

A problem-solving project is a planned undertaking to analyze a problem, determine its root causes, solve, and prevent it from recurring. For example, transcripts are not being properly completed. An effective test for spotting an appropriate QI problem-solving project is to ask: What is the problem? Incomplete transcripts project identifies a problem that a team can review to find the root causes. No solution is presented in the statement of the project.

The implementation project is an undertaking designed to complete a task; for example, the preparation of an action plan to implement TQ. In this project, the problem and root causes are not subject to examination and discovery. The solution is assumed.

A research project is an undertaking designed to collect information, determine the facts, and render a conclusion. For example, why are parents complaining about the attitudes of some teachers? To study this situation, information will have to be collected and analyzed, and a conclusion reached.

Once the QI team decides on a project, it must go through a cycle of communication and coordination of all of the activities necessary to produce an effective TQ process.

The QI team reviews the school situation, receives ideas from its members, the staff, or from the QSS Team, and determines what kind of project is warranted to deal with this situation. Once a decision is made, it communicates its intent to the QS committee, which may or may not provide advice and/or support and approval or disapproval. When approval is given, the QI team decides how it will complete the project itself, or if it will activate a QA team. If it decides to complete the project, it will do whatever is necessary to do so, and then go before the school as a whole to either get a consensus, majority vote, or to consult and/or inform. Sometimes valuable input from the school as a whole may necessitate modifying either solution on the implementation plan. Once the project has been completed, it is communicated to the QS committee. If the TQ team gives the project to a QA team, it is required to develop a mission and a role description, seek its approval from the QI team, and seek the necessary training to complete its charge. When the QA team completes its project, it must make a presentation before the QI team for approval. Once the project is approved, it goes before the school as a whole for either consensus, majority vote, consultation and/or information, and then to the QS committee. The cycle is completed for each project. However, this process may vary.

Establishing Quality Action Teams

Depending on the size of the school or site, a QI team may decide to form QA teams within the school or unit. These are mini-QI teams that are responsible to their QI teams, and are required to function in the same manner. That is, they will develop their own mission and responsibilities statement and quality implementation plan, and arrange for appropriate training, etc. A QI team may form a permanent QA team, perhaps in the area of budget, or curriculum and instruction. Usually, however, QA teams are temporary teams, and as soon as their projects are completed, the teams are dismantled.

The QA teams exist to support the quality efforts of QI teams. They either perform research, solve problems, or implement solutions on behalf of the QI team.

QA teams carry out assignments designated by the QI team. These assignments may consist of the following:

1. Investigating a customer complaint and solving the problem.
2. Conducting a focus group.
3. Conducting interviews.
4. Collecting and analyzing data.
5. Solving a specific problem.
   - Conducting a quality audit
   - Developing an assessment instrument
   - Preparing a control chart to correct a process
6. Conducting the Delphi technique.
7. Preparing an implementation plan.
8. Conducting a presentation.
9. Conducting a survey.
10. Exploring some opportunities.
11. Developing a stakeholder analysis.
12. Preparing a customer value package.
13. Acting as a "mystery customer" to evaluate a procedure.
14. Doing other things as designated by the QI team or principal.

Selecting and Training Facilitators

One of the many functions of the steering committee is to make certain there are a sufficient number of facilitators to assist the QI teams to operationalize TQ. These facilitators can either be full- or part-time school people who have an interest in facilitating the process. Sometimes, principals are called on to facilitate QI teams in schools other than their own. If teachers are selected to be facilitators, funds must be allocated to pay for substitutes while they are facilitating team meetings.

The responsibility of facilitators are as follows:

1. Attend team meetings as neutral observers to facilitate the operation process.
2. Maintain a log on all teams activities.
3. Prepare progress reports on teams.
4. Coach and assist team leaders prior to and after meetings to improve their performance.
6. Intervene in team meetings to keep members on track.
7. Assist in training team members.
8. Clarify his or her role and responsibilities to team members.
9. Keep the quality coordinator informed.
10. Review difficulties and problems encountered, and measures used to eliminate them.
11. Assist in exporting the TQ process.
12. Conduct improvement meetings with team members.
13. Assist QA teams to carry out their charge.
14. Prevent burnout of team members.

Identifying Functions of School Administrators

The following represent indicators of the commitment from administrators that is necessary for the successful maintenance of the TQ process:

1. Provide time for facilitators, team leaders, and members to become fortified with knowledge and training related to the TQ process.
2. Appear for a minimum of twenty hours of training on school-based management.
3. Provide timely feedback on problems and difficulties relating to TQ.

4. Promote TQ.
5. Provide for recognition and rewards.
6. Attend QS committee meetings and QI team meetings.
7. Support TQ through words, deeds, and actions.

SUMMARY

A major steps for the steering committee is to determine the needs of the school district, and to create a TQ model. This model should contain, at a minimum, a person to carry out its policies and procedures, a district-wide team to provide support to both the QS committee and each school, QI teams and mini-teams for each school, and facilitators to assist teams to operationalize the TQ process.

Once the TQ model has been developed, the school district should establish a quality service measurement system to guide teaching and service performance of all school people and students.

CHECKLIST FOR MAKING THE TRANSITION TO TOTAL QUALITY

Organizing for TQ is not a difficult process. In fact, it is a creative and fun endeavor. Follow these procedures to do so:

1. Brainstorm all of the organizational needs of the school districts. Use this information to accomplish the next step.
2. Use the information gained in this chapter to illustrate and describe your school district TQ model. Consider the following:
   a. QS committee
   b. Quality coordinator
   c. QSS teams
   d. QI teams
   e. QA teams
   f. Quality facilitators (district-wide and for each school)

Chapter Seven

Establishing A Quality Service Measurement System

*A commitment to service quality without a commitment to stand-
ards and measurement would be a dedication to lip service, not
customer service. Only with customer-focused standards and customer-based satisfaction measurements can you create and manage
dynamic, information-based service delivery systems that can be
tuned and refined to changing customer expectations.*

—Ron Zemke

Presently, there are two thoughts that pervade America's
public schools on how to best provide quality performance. The prevailing thought is that quality improvement
properly begins inside the school organization with the focus
on improving the degree to which school people meet standards identified by the school administration. The other thought
indicates that quality improvement begins with the customer's
evaluation of quality itself, and only when the two voices meet
and mutually agree will there by a truer depiction of quality
performance and service. When it comes to providing quality
service in public education, unlike industry, customers are not
the only ones determining quality. It must be a joint consensus
effort, because of the professional expertise of the educators.

Customers do not have all the knowledge about what their needs, requirements, and expectations are. In fact, in some instances, customers do not know what their needs should be. Educators, too, have knowledge about customer needs, requirements, and expectations. Only when the two parties can sit down together and reach a consensus on customers' demands will there be valid needs, requirements, and expectations.

As an aside, although customers and providers were discussed in the first chapter, some attention is given to it in this chapter, too. In every community, there are a multitude of customers. No school district can exceed to greatness by trying to be all things to all people. Some of the questions school people should consider when identifying their principal customers are? Are parents the principal customers? What about local citizens? Is the largest business in the school district the principal customer? Is the university the principal customer? Is a community group, like the community action committee, the principal customer? Are teachers principal customers? Are two or more of their stakeholders the principal customers? Or is the billionaire who lives in the community the principal customer? Careful attention must be given to identifying the principal customers or the school district may be using the wrong base for developing a quality service measurement system.

Superior quality service is when the customers and school district mutually agree to the service characteristics, measures, and standards, and when the customer says so. The only true and reliable measurement of quality service assessment is the customers' most recent experience with the school district, and their level of satisfaction with their experience.

IN THIS CHAPTER, I WILL
DISCUSS THE FOLLOWING:

- Defining a quality service measurement system
- Identifying the components of a quality service measurement system

- Measuring individual and group performance

QUALITY SERVICE MEASUREMENT SYSTEM

A quality service measurement system is a process of listening to the customer to identify service areas, characteristics, measurements, and standards, and to evaluate efforts to enhance customer satisfaction.

Ron Zemke, author of *The Service Edge* (The Penguin Group, 1990), identifies several pointers to create a top-notch measurement feedback system. The author state: Measurement can be a confusing area, primarily because of the statistical arcanery and psychobabble the measurement experts shape about their craft. There are some statistical niceties to observe, but must involve sampling techniques making sure you survey enough people and in the right way."

When well-designed, a service strategy can be an invaluable quality-measurement guide. For instance, "Our promise is to build a zero-defect school district and to continuously make improvements so that all the students and people who service them can become more and do more than they ever hoped." In other words, the school will strive operationally to reach a level of zero defect and to continuously make improvements, which are both measurable standards.

The service strategy also suggests other less obvious measurements. To continuously make improvements is an internal measure that addresses the questions of who should make these improvements, and how many and what kinds of improvements should be made.

Another point is to measure quality frequently. School districts have a lot of improvement to make in this area. Some organizations measure their performance on a monthly basis; others do so every sixty to ninety days. Domino's Pizza formally measures its performance on a weekly basis. The reason for frequency in measuring performance is the need for current information on the customer.

Ask customer-based questions. Request information on the customer's experience ("What happened to you as a result of your experience in this district, school, classroom?"), and perception ("How do you feel about what happened to you?").

Ask pertinent questions. Dwell only on questions school people can deal with. Focus on people-regulated processes, not machines that school people may not be in a position to change.

Acquire data that relates to groups as well as to individuals. The clerk who answers the telephone should know how the entire clerical staff is perceived by school administrators.

Include full coverage. The quality service measurement system should be all-encompassing; that is, it should not only include service areas for the curriculum, but also other areas, such as the following:

- Food service
- Transportation
- Instructional service
- Public relations
- Facility
- Special programs
- Financial service
- Security service
- Maintenance and custodial
- Health service
- Research and evaluation

Identify areas that need improvement. Collect information on school districts that have excelled in these areas and visit them. Collect information to imitate their programs, procedures, and practices with or without modifications. Collect quantitative and qualitative data. An effective quality service measurement system collects objective and subjective information about the customers.

Display the results by demonstrating information on the customers. One effective way to do this is to require each school to collect data to compute a satisfaction index for parents, students, and teachers. Make certain the results are school-people friendly. Display the results in averages and ratios rather than in weighted index scores. Results that state "The receptionist was rated as cheerful and helpful by 92 percent" are more comprehensible than "The school received a 4.5 and a 10-factor weighted average score quality and appreciation index."

Make certain results are credible. If school people are involved in the collection of the data and are informed of the results, they are more likely to use the information. If, on the other hand, the information received from the central administration office is filled with statistics, or gives the impression that the results are abstract, customers may tend to discard or discount it. To make the data credible, some organizations have been known to let the unit collect, compile, and post the data.

Use the results. School people will use the results on the customer if the information is widely discussed, and is used for problem-solving purposes, and for upgrading quality standards. Merely posting an abstract of the results will not activate much effort to use the information.

The quality service measurement system must be based on customer input. Customers' perception of quality is the only perception that counts. A system that does not incorporate customer feedback is flawed.

The most effective quality service measurement system is one that will capture data on an individual level, and that will also provide for the aggregation of data at the operating school district, school, department, and unit levels. The best way to ensure accountability on an individual level is to measure service at that level. Measuring service at either the school or unit level is also valuable, because it can be used to make a comparison among similar school organizational groups, and it can be used to nurture cooperation among these groups. Favorable outcomes of group measurement should be publicized in the school organization, and tied to the reward and recognition program. The more positive the quality service measurement system, and the reward and recognition program, and the more committed of the educational leadership, the more likely it is that the measurement system will lead to favorable results.

Measuring the service performance of individuals and groups can be accomplished using many of the techniques discussed previously in this book.

IMPROVE QUALITY THROUGH AN EFFECTIVE FEEDBACK SYSTEM

The primary purpose of an effective quality service measurement system is to collect information about customers so that school people can use it to meet and exceed the school district's quality standards. When the feedback system is ineffective, it is usually because the information collected is being used incorrectly. When this occurs, it is no longer a feedback system, but a problem.

Karen Brethow, an industrial psychologist, identifies six questions to ponder when establishing a quality service measurement system. They are:

1. Is the information used to belittle, punish, or degrade school people?
2. Does the information have value for the school people receiving it?
3. Is the information timely; that is, is the information too late for school people to act on?
4. Is the feedback about something the school people receiving it can neither change nor affect?
5. Is the feedback about the wrong thing?
6. Is the information difficult to collect and record?

To achieve greatness in the public schools in the United States, school people must continuously and carefully listen to their customers. They must understand what customers are really saying as it applies to the business of serving them, and then respond proactively and creatively to what they are saying.

There are basically four reasons to listen to customers. First, you must understand the customers' moments of truth and determine their perceptions as to how well or how poorly the school district is serving them. Second, you need to stay attuned to the changing needs, requirements, and expectations. Third, you have to hear of unexpected ideas customers and those who work with them can bring to the sounding table. Fourth, to listen carefully to customers is an invaluable way to involve the customer in the quest for greatness.

For example, a new superintendent in New Jersey decided to engage his staff in a strategic planning process. However, prior to the planning, he decided to restructure the school district around a school of choice plan in which any parent would have the opportunity to send their children to any school in the school district. This superintendent intended to listen to the customer through the strategic planning process. However, he failed to do so, and the board refused to back the school of choice plan. He probably would have been more successful if he had used the strategic planning process as a forum to get the participants to accept his plan. New superintendents usually make this mistake by trying to introduce new programs and ideas without first listening to the customer.

There is no best way to listen to customers. In addition, there is no such thing as paying too much attention to customer needs, ideas, and opinions. The following are various ways to listen to customers, including the face-to-face interview, comment and complaint analysis, customer advisory panels, focus groups, customer hotlines, mutual education, mail surveys, and research.

Face-to-face Interview

The simplest way to listen to customers is across the table, beside, or one-on-one, and ask them what they want, need, and expect from their schools. The face-to-face interview is also an excellent opportunity for the customers to hear what the school district can and cannot do for them.

For instance, in an effort to listen to customers, as superintendent of schools, I organized a "You Are People" program in which once a month on a Sunday, "key families" were requested to hold dialogue sessions in their homes whereby parents and other community people could attend with teachers and school administrators to listen to their concerns. Names of community people who voiced a concern, need, or idea were taken, and received feedback either through a telephone call, letter, or visitation. When planning for the following school years, information from these sessions was appropriately considered in the planning process. A minimum of 3,000 school and community people met during these meetings. Many of them otherwise seldom visited their children's school.

Comment and Complaint Analysis

Every effective TQ school organization should maintain customer comment and complaint files. Comments and complaints are used strictly as a paper trail to track the relationship between customers and the school district. A technique should also be devised to keep a record of problem resolutions.

Some crafty superintendents go a step further by encouraging school people to use this raw information to see themselves from the viewpoint of the customer. Other comments from letters, phone calls, comment cards, and follow-up satisfaction surveys can provide a source for customer perception of the school district.

Customer Advisory Panels

Customers need not be painful to listen to. A few companies have organized a panel of inquisitive, dissatisfied, critical, and sometimes hostile customers who they could interview, and with whom they would sometimes play devil's advocate.

In one of the best-run companies in the United States, three different panels of customers are organized to provide input on the company's products and services. School districts should emulate this practice.

Mutual Education

Workshops at which both the customer and provider attend together are a good source for listening to the customer. This is particularly true if the workshop is on the quality service measurement system.

Mail Surveys

Developing an appropriate survey to acquire information on customer needs, requirements, and expectations has been an effective instrument for a few school districts to get feedback from customers. However, the problem is only a few school districts survey the needs of customers via the mail. Mailing surveys have very little if any value unless school people appropriately act on the data.

For example, the Edmonton (Canada) School District in Edmonton, Canada, mails out 20,000 surveys to its customers' homes. If a parent fails to mail back the survey, either the home is visited or a telephone call is made to interview the parent to complete the survey. Each year, the response to the survey has been around 98 percent.

Focus Groups

Establish a group of not more than twelve internal or external customers. Use a qualified facilitator/interviewer to conduct a forum with this group to generate discussion, ideas, and feedback on the service and products of the school district. To conduct a focus group, do the following:

1. Prepare the questions and distribute them in advance.
2. Determine how many and what customers to invite.
3. Design a plan for analyzing the results.
4. Conduct the discussion.

Customer Hotlines

Establish a customer hotline so that customers can connect with school people to answer questions on school problems. Some school districts have made use of an 800-number, but have not used it effectively to collect and track information on the satisfaction or dissatisfaction of their customers. This method works well for both internal and external customers. Central school administrators can be assigned to spend time on incoming service, complaint, and information calls. It gives them an anonymous, status-free contact with customers that helps them to better understand their problems with the school district.

Research

Traditional research to determine the needs, requirements, and expectations of customers consists of focus groups, conducting surveys, and service audits. In some situations, such research often involves bringing in a third party to do the unbiased listening. Although school districts seldom engage in market research, perhaps it is high time that they did. The most important thing market researchers can do is provide the ability to sample customers broadly and fairly, and to conduct a formal meeting with both customers and suppliers to present their findings.

COMPONENTS OF A QUALITY SERVICE MEASUREMENT SYSTEM

Without knowing what quality is and how to measure it, a school district cannot be expected to effectively implement TQ. Knowledge and a common understanding of quality and quality areas, characteristics, measures, and standards is absolutely necessary to obtain district-wide acceptance, commitment, and responsibility for TQ. The full benefits of TQ in education cannot be readily realized unless the quality service measurement system is adequately addressed and mastered. Figure 7.1 illustrates all of the components of the quality service measurement system. It describes quality service areas, identifies what service characteristics are relevant to the customer, matches quality service measurements for those service characteristics, and establishes standards for each quality measure. Also included as a part of the system are measuring performance and increasing customer satisfaction.

FIGURE 7.1
The Quality Service Measurement System

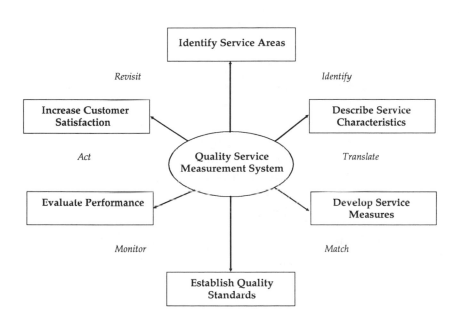

Source: Richard C. H. Chua. *A Customer-Driven Approach for Measuring Service Quality.* ASQC, Nashville, TN, May 18-20, 1992, pp. 1195-1201.

Quality Service Areas

Quality service areas are identified as those functions that are necessary and crucial to the survival and growth of the school district, school, department, or unit. Although these functions are usually decided by the school district, they should be jointly developed by the customer and the school district. Quality service areas can be identified through the following means:

- Using those service areas that presently exist and adding and detracting from them.
- Retaining an outside consultant/trainer to identify them.
- Using focus groups to help generate them.
- Acquiring those of other school districts, and using them as a base to arrive at those appropriate for the school district.

The following are some examples of quality service areas that were generated by a joint committee of parents, teachers, students, and school administrators using the nominal group process:

- Instructional services
- Curriculum
- Supervision
- Guidance counseling
- Health services
- Information
- Use of technology
- Resources
- Interpersonal relations
- Systems analysis

Some school districts may deem it necessary to break down these areas further. This is acceptable. The important point is to describe a complete set of quality service areas to give customers (students) a comprehensive and complete education.

There are three steps to selecting quality service areas as discussed below:

1. Use a flipchart to generate, either through brainstorming or nominal group process, in order to identify all principal internal and external customers of the school district, school, department, or unit in which services or products are delivered. Prioritize this list. For a discussion of internal and external customers, refer to Chapter One.

2. Use the nominal group process to list and prioritize all the services or products the school district, school, department, or unit provide for its principal customers. Review the list and select the vital few activities that relate most closely to achieving the school district, school, department, or unit's mission. Some items on the list may need to be combined.

3. Once the list of services has been identified and prioritized, select one or two to focus on.

   Example:

Internal Customers

Students
Teachers

External Customers

Parents
Community
Society
Business and industry
Colleges and universities

Example: *Prioritized Services for Students*

- Instructional service
- Health service
- Counseling
- Guidance
- Psychological services

- Physical education

- Leadership

QUALITY SERVICE CHARACTERISTICS

The key to developing quality service characteristics is the willingness of school people to actively listen to the customer, and to use that input to jointly develop or redevelop the quality service areas, characteristics, measures, and standards.

It is extremely important that correct service characteristics be identified in terms of what customers want and consider important. The significance of this step cannot be overemphasized, because implementing the rest of the quality service measurement system without actively listening to customers' needs, requirements, and expectations would be useless.

How should quality service characteristics be selected? Should they be selected by customers? Should they be determined by providers (school administrators and teachers)? Or should they be selected by both providers and customers? The preferred method is that they be determined by both customers and providers.

There are several options open to arrive at a collection of quality service characteristics, as identified below:

1. Any one of the sources can be used unchanged or revised.
2. Ideas can be obtained from each of the sources to create other characteristics.
3. Seek other sources.

Figure 7.2 identifies five different sources to use for food-for-thought for a joint committee of school and community people to arrive at a complete set of service quality characteristics.

FIGURE 7.2
Instruments for Deciding Quality Characteristics

SERVQUAL Method	Customer Value Package	Key Results Areas	SCANS Report	Effective School Correlates
• Functional characteristics and performance	• School environment	• Student learning and growth	• Allocate time	• Clear and sound mission
• Response time	• Aesthetic	• Financial resources	• Allocate money	• School-site management
• Ease of access	• Interpersonal	• Physical resources	• Allocate materials and financial resources	• Leadership
• Tangibles	• Procedural	• Innovations	• Allocate human resources	• Staff stability
• Reliability, consistency	• Deliverable	• Community involvement and relations	• Acquire and evaluate information	• Curriculum articulation and organization
• Diagnosis, response, and recovery	• Financial	• Organizational management	• Organize and maintain information	• Staff development
• Empathy, consideration	• Information	• Performance evaluation and training	• Interpersonal and committee information	• Parental involvement and support
• Assurance		• Instructional purpose and services	• Use computers to process information	• School-wide recognition of academic services
• Positive results			• Participation as a member of a team	• Maximized learning time
			• Teach others	• District support
			• Service clients/customers	• Collaborative planning and collegial relationships
			• Exercise leadership	• Sense of community
			• Negotiations	• Clear goals and high expectations
			• Work out cultural diversity	• Order and discipline
			• Understand systems	
			• Monitor and correct performance	
			• Improve and design systems	
			• Select technology	
			• Apply technology to task	
			• Maintain troubleshooting team members	

SERVQUAL Instrument Method

A method school districts should carefully consider when deciding on a framework for establishing a quality measurement system is the use of the SERVQUAL instrument. In 1983, a formal research report was conducted by Marketing Science Institute in Cambridge, Massachusetts, which initiated a major study of service quality by three professors from Texas A&M University. Their findings were published under the title, *A Conceptual Model of Service Quality and Its Implications for Future Research*. Because so little was known about how quality was perceived by customers either receiving or providing service,the researchers began by conducting a series of customer focus group interviews and extensive interviews. Although none of the customers were school-related (they were from retail, banking, credit cards, security brokerage firms, and product repairs and maintenance), much of the research is valid for educational purposes. The researchers uncovered four fundamental and universal characteristics of good services.

First, most services are *intangible* because they are performance rather than objects. As a result, they cannot be measured, tested, or verified for quality in advance of sales. For example, when a teacher is hired, it is difficult to know in advance how well he or she can teach, and inevitably, how well the students will turn out.

Second, services in most instances are *heterogeneous*. As a result, the quality will vary from provider to provider, from customer to customer, and from day to day. For example, a principal's behavior may vary from teacher to teacher, and an individual teacher may not exhibit the same behavior as another.

Third, *production* is inseparable from its *consumption*. For example, a teacher that teaches students algebra is providing instructional service while the student is consuming the instructions. The success of the student, or quality, depends on how well the teacher communicates the instructions to students, and on how well the students comprehend the instructions, as well as on the students' desire to learn.

Four, services are *perishable*. Services cannot be inventoried: saved and sold later. An empty seat in the classroom has lost its value forever. As a result, this characteristic makes it difficult for a school to manage supply and demand.

The researchers also determined that a customer's experience of quality service can be determined on five quality dimensions, including result, process, conformity, interaction, and emotion.

The quality category refers to the "what" in terms of the delivery of the service or product. The functional characteristics and performance include customization/standardization, and compatibility with other services.

Quality in the process refers to the delivery of the service or product in terms of response time (promptness and cycle time), ease of access (convenient location and time, cafeteria lines not too long, and customer-friendly), and tangibles (premises/environment, decor, uniforms, costumes, comfort, cleanliness, luxury, technology, equipment, supplies).

Conformity refers to the delivery of the service or product in terms of reliability and consistency, including:

- Results as implied or promised

- Everything functional

- Punctuality

- Accurate and timely information

Quality of interaction relates to the human interaction—diagnosis, responsiveness, and recovery—that takes place during the delivery of the service or product, including:

- Listening, availability, understanding

- Adapted reopens, problem-solving

- Explanation, communication, education

- Global treatment, follow-up

It also refers to empathy and consideration involving:

- Courtesy, respect, tact, signs of recognition, use of names
- The customer is important; a guest not a tourist
- Good faith is recognized

The emotional quality category refers to the assurance and positive experience received by the customers in the delivery of the service or product. The assurance refers to:

- Trust, reassurance, minimum risk and discord, safety, guarantee
- Explanations, preparation, education
- Quality treatment, follow up
- Guarantee of result

The positive experience refers to:

- Spontaneity
- Convivial, at ease, part of the group
- Autonomy, opportunity to contribute, to control the situation

Customer Value Package Method

Some school districts may find the customer value package an excellent guide to begin establishing a quality measurement system. The eight descriptions cover the full spectrum of quality, and can be applied to education. A value package can be prepared for each customer, and subsequently verified by them.

A customer value package is the combination of tangibles, intangibles, experiences, and outcomes designed to acquire the customer's approval. In the book entitled, *The Only Thing That Matters* (Harper Business, 1991), Karl Albrecht describes that "the customer's entire experience determines his or her perception of quality." As a result, perception is determined by the district's or school's "product," processes, and practices as they are compared to the customer's expectations. Thus, quality is the measure of the customer's satisfaction with the total experience, not just the delivery of a product or service.

The challenge for school districts today is to understand and arrange the customer's total experience in order to make it a satisfying experience. Therefore, they must be able to deliver to customers a total experience of value. One way to do this is by producing a customer value package. The following are eight components of such:

1. School environment is the physical setting in which learning takes place. It could be the physical plant, the classroom, the community, the library, etc.
2. Aesthetic is the direct sensory experience of the customer. It can include sights, sounds, smells, feelings, discomforts, physical sensations, aesthetic features, and the visual or psychological ambience of the school environment. The appearance of the people who work in the school is also included in this category.
3. Interpersonal is the interaction between the customers and providers and customers as a part of the total experience. The interaction process includes friendliness, courtesy, helpfulness, physical appearance, and competence in performing a task.
4. Procedural is the experience the customer receives in getting the information needed to receive the service. This may include waiting, explaining the need, completing forms, providing information, or receiving manipulation or treatments.
6. Deliverable is anything that is physically submitted to the customer during the service. This would include books, supplies, and food delivered to students.
7. Financial includes what or how parents pay for their children's service and product experiences. In many instances, this would be obvious; in others, not so obvious. For example, if schools are allowed to purchase their support service from either support area specialists inside the district or from consultants outside the district, this would require

two types of transactions, because in the former case, this would only be a paper transaction, whereas in the latter, there would be a money transaction.

8. Informational involves the acquisition of the information needed to function as a customer. For students, this could mean instruction in the classroom. For parents, it could mean translating the report card. For teachers, it could mean reviewing a catalog of training events.

Once a customer's value package has been created using the above framework, the next step involves evaluating how well it delivers the value elements.

Key Results Analysis Method

If the school district has already put in place a strategic planning process, it probably has already identified key results areas (KRA). Even if KRA have not been defined, some school districts may opt for this method for creating a quality measurement system. KRA are critical operations of the school district that must be performed to ensure the survival and growth of the school district. Although KRAs differ from school district to school district, the following is a list regarding public education from an urban school district.

- Student learning and growth
- Financial resources
- Physical resources
- Innovations
- Community involvement and relations
- Organizational management
- Performance evaluation and training
- Instructional programs and services

KRAs are affected by every decision maker and consequently must be considered in the quality strategic and operational planning process. There are also guidelines for directing performance so that a well-coordinated effort will be exerted by all school people to meet the vision of the school district. When KRAs are used in the Total Quality Process, each area must be viewed as interrelated components that function together to comprise the quality service measurement system.

Tangibles are the observable part of the service offered to customers, such as facilities, equipment, and appearance of the providers. Customers tend to associate tangibles with the service received. For example, a parent who sends her children to school where there is graffiti spread around the building, boisterous students loitering in the corridors, and untidy classrooms, will not have the same impression as a parent whose child goes to a school with no graffiti, orderly students, and impeccable corridors.

One way to survey an impression of quality service is to look like a quality school district. This means paying attention to details and being considerate and acting on the tangibles.

No TQ process in education is complete unless a direct attempt is made through quality measurements to improve student academic learning and growth. Learning refers here to the modification and/or change in student behavior in the cognitive domain. Growth refers to changes in the affective and psychomotor domains.

In the area of student learning and growth, the district selecting this quality service measurement system may benchmark its performance against the contiguous school districts. The school district would also track student learning by a number of different variables, such as stanine, percentile, etc.

To set goals without planning for financing is like trying to operate a vehicle without fuel. In education, financial planning is usually thought of as a component of operational or tactical planning. This is far from the truth. Quality measurements must be devised on a long-term basis to expend those funds in the most efficient manner.

Physical resources, such as capital facilities, equipment, and machines, are too important to be excluded from the quality service measurement system.

Quality measure must be set to improve on every critical area of the school organization. It can no longer be assumed that school people will innovate to improve performance results.

Quality measure may involve the community in the educational process and keep the public-at-large informed of the various operations of the school organization.

To become and remain effective, a school district must establish quality measures to improve the operation of the school district through positive administrative leadership and organizational structure.

Performance evaluation is one area in education in which quality measure is seldom established. Staff evaluation must be continuously planned and carefully executed. An important component of quality measure is training. The success of each of these two activities depends upon the other.

Quality measures should be established for:

- modifying the existing program, which may involve changing procedures, abilities, products, skills, or services; and/or,

- changing the current program or substituting a new one, which may necessitate the acquisition of new skills, products, and services.

Regardless of the approach selected, quality measures must be set to effect instructional improvements in either programs or services.

Secretary's Commission on Achieving Necessary Skills (SCANS) Report

Some school districts may find the SCAN report an informative guide to help produce their quality service measurement system. The SCAN report includes resources, information, interpersonal, systems, and technology.

For resources, would need to select relevant, goal-related activities, rank them in order of importance, allocate time to activities, and understand, prepare, and follow schedules.

Further, would need to use or prepare budgets, including cost and revenue forecasts, keep detailed records to track budget performance, and make appropriate adjustments.

Resources include materials and facility resources. Students would need to acquire, store, and distribute materials, supplies, parts, equipments, space, or final products in order to make the best use of them.

Finally, allocate human resources by assessing knowledge and skills, and distributing work accordingly; evaluating performance, and providing feedback.

Students need to acquire and evaluate information. Identify the need for data, obtain it from existing sources or creates it, and evaluate its relevance and accuracy.

Further, organize and maintain information by processing written or computerized records and other forms of information in a systematic fashion.

Interpret and communicate information by selecting and analyzing the results to others using oral, written, graphic, pictorial, or multi-media methods.

Finally, use computers to process information.

Participate as a member of a team. Work cooperatively with others and contribute to the group with ideas, suggestions, and efforts.

Students should also exercise leadership. Communicate their thoughts, feelings, and ideas to justify a position, and encourage, persuade, convince, or otherwise motivate an individual or group, including responsibly challenging existing procedures, policies, or authority.

Work toward an agreement that may involve exchanging specific resources or resolving divergent interests.

Work with cultural diversity—with men and women and with a variety of ethnic, social, or educational backgrounds.

Students should know how social, organizational, and technological systems work, and operate effectively within them.

Monitor and correct performance. Distinguish trends, predict impact of actions on system operations, diagnose deviations in the function of a system/organization, and take necessary action to correct performance.

Also, make suggestions to modify existing systems to improve products or services, and develop new or alternative systems.

Judge which set of procedures, tools, or machines, including computers and their programs, will produce the desired results.

Understand the overall intent and the proper procedures for setting up and operating machines, including computers and their programming systems.

Finally, maintain and troubleshoot technology by preventing, identifying, or solving problems in machines, computers, and other technologies.

Effective School Correlates

Those school districts that have implemented many of the effective school correlates (indicators) may find it convenient to use these research-based indices of effective schools as one source for creating their quality service measurement system. The following describes these correlates:

1. School-site management
   - Autonomy for each school
   - Emphasis on school culture
   - Implementation of innovation
2. Leadership
   - Supportive principal
   - Instructional leadership by the principal
3. Staff stability
   - Maintain staff togetherness
   - Coherent and ongoing school personality
4. Curriculum articulation and organization elementary level
   - Acquire basic and complex skills

- Skill-focused curriculum
- Skills conducted across grade levels
- Planned and purposeful diet of courses
- Required courses

5. Staff development
- Collaborative planning
- Collegial relationships
- Attitude training
- Behavioral training
- Training in new skills and techniques

6. Parental involvement and support
- Informed of school goals
- Participate in decision making

7. School-wide recognition of academic success
- Appropriate use of symbols and ceremonies to honor academic achievement.
- Students adapt norms and values appreciating academic achievement
- School culture reflects emphasis in academic achievement

8. Maximized learning time
- Greater part of school day devoted to academic subjects
- Classroom free of disruption
- Teachers trained in classroom management

9. District support
- Specialized assistance to teachers
- Guidance and help in role by district office

10. Collaborative planning and collegial relationships
- Void of barriers

- Use of consensus decision-making
- Feeling of unity and community

11. Sense of community
    - Teachers contribute to reduce alienation
    - Appropriate use of ceremony symbols, rules, etc.
    - Community spirit

12. Clear goals and high expectations
    - Clearly defined purpose
    - Focus on vital few tasks
    - High expectations
    - Mutually agreed-upon goals
    - Continual monitoring of student performance

13. Order and discipline
    - Discipline is maintained
    - Clear and measurable rules for governing student behavior
    - Secure and safe school environment

Benchmarking Method

Another effective method school districts should consider to measure quality is to study what the best are doing and capitalize on their successes. This process is known as benchmarking. Xerox has pioneered the use of benchmarking as a competitive strategy; that is, studying the attributes of the best companies in the world, and adopting them as their standards. Xerox defines benchmarking as "the continuous process of measuring products, services, and practices against the company's toughest competitors and against companies recognized as industry leaders." The following are steps for benchmarking:

Identify the Problems

Identify the problems; that is, what is to be benchmarked. A quality improvement (QI) team selects a product, a service, a process, or a production, and sometimes a level of customer satisfaction. There are a host of problem areas to choose from to determine where the benchmark is to take place. For example, is there a problem with at-risk students? What new technology is being used in the human resources department? Are secretaries responding to parents in a congenial manner? Is the performance evaluation program as good as it should be? These, and hundreds, perhaps thousands of problems can be solved by locating district or other organizations that have succeeded in these problem areas, and learn from them.

Identify Benchmarking Partners

Identify appropriate exemplary school districts or organizations. Benchmarking partners can be either other units within the school district, other school organizations, private or parochial schools, industrial, or manufacturing organizations that are judged to be the leaders in the areas to be benchmarked. Start with the Malcolm Baldridge National Quality Award winners. They include Motorola, Xerox, Milliken and Company, Federal Express, Cadillac Motor Car Division of General Motors, and IBM in Rochester, Minnesota.

Determine Measurement Method

Determine data collection method and collect data. The team determines what measurements will be used in the benchmarking process. Prior to the visitation, one organization did the following:

1. Identified specific objectives to be realized through the observation.
2. Required team members to read related book and articles and tested them on what they learned.

3. Studied and thoroughly discussed its own problems to determine performance gaps.
4. Generated a list of questions to be brought to the visiting organization for responses.

Conduct the Visit to the Organization

Organize a team of interested school and community people to make the visit. Team members may be assigned to specific aspects of the area being studied.
   During the visitation:

- Bring along a gift for the host organization. This will demonstrate appreciation for the visitation.

- Inform the host of the problem presently being experienced by the school district or school.

- Prior to the visit, prepare a written list of questions and assign individual questions to designated team members.

- Be on time for the meeting, and do not overstay the welcome.

- Ask questions.

- Praise the host organization, and demonstrate appreciation of what is seen even though it may not be related to the visit. Avoid criticizing the host or bragging.

- Look for areas and items pertinent to the visit, but stay alert for other ideas that may be useful when returning to the school district.

Conduct a Debriefing Session

One of the most essential steps to benchmarking is the debriefing session. Some practitioners recommend that there be a debriefing session before as well as after the visit. There are three requirements for debriefing:
   1. The team should capture and discuss first impressions.

2. The team should focus on what was observed and learned. (Specific discoveries can help the school district.)
3. Each team member should prepare a written report.

Communicate Benchmark Findings and Recommendations

Once the written reports have been submitted to the team leader, the information is analyzed and synthesized, and a final report is discussed with the team membership. A consensus final report is submitted to either the superintendent, the QS committee, or the QI team indicating methodology, findings, and program strategies for approval.

Implement the Changes

Once approval has been obtained, the information is communicated to those school people who will be responsible for implementing the strategies. The team submits final recommendations on what changes must be made based on the benchmark finding, develops an action plan, and establishes objectives and measurable quality standards.

Communicate Findings to the District

Communicate the findings throughout the school district. Require team members to make speeches about the findings, give awareness sessions, create a video on the benchmarking findings and prepare an article for the district's newsletter or local newspaper.

Monitor progress

Once the action plan has been implemented, data on the new performance level should be collected, and studies and adjustments made. If the objective or any phase of the plan is not being met, a need may exist for a QA team to investigate the situation.

Show Appreciation

Communicate to the host organization what was learned. Later on, indicate steps taken to implement what was learned during the visitation and any difficulties that were experienced. Keep in touch with the host organization so that if new problems should show up, it can be contacted for guidance and assistance.

Recalibrate Benchmarks

From time to time, reevaluate and update the benchmarks to make certain they are based on current performance data.

When quality measures have been identified, the next important step for establishing a quality service measurement system is to match these measures to standard which will be the basis for evaluating performance.

IDENTIFYING SERVICE AREAS

A service area is an operation or activity designed to fulfill needs, requirements and expectations of customers. There are several ways to identify service areas as cited below:

- Ask customers.
- Engage in brainstorming.
- Collect those of other school districts.
- Use a consultant.

The following are some service areas of a school district:

- Instructional service
- Maintenance
- Custodial service
- Payroll
- Transportation

DETERMINING QUALITY
SERVICE CHARACTERISTICS

Quality service characteristics are defined as descriptive statements of services and products that are required to be performed by the provider to accommodate the needs, requirements, and expectations of customers.

The recommended ways or methods to identify service characteristics that are relevant to the customer includes the following:

- Customer surveys

- Interviews

- Use of scenarios

- Focus groups

- Others identified in this book

There is no best method to identify service characteristics; perhaps the better method would be to use a combination of the methods. The important point is to identify "correct" characteristics — those that the customers think are important. The instruments cited in this chapter should be used as a springboard to assist you.

The following quality service characteristics were designed for the service area of instruction using the SERVQUAL instrument:

Service Area	Service Characteristics
Instructional service	Participate as teams
	Evaluate information
	Exercise leadership
	Empathy and consideration

DESCRIBING SERVICE MEASURES

When quality service characteristics have been identified for customers, the next step involves translating those characteristics into clear measurable terms. This translation is critical because they must be valid and reliable. Validity if defined by responding to the query: Does the school district measure what it thinks it is measuring? The emphasis is on what is being measured.

Once the service area and characteristics have been determined, the next step involves developing quality measures for service characteristics. There are four steps to this.

Analyze Each Quality Service Characteristic

The school district, school, department, or unit should organize a design team to thoroughly analyze each service characteristic and identify those measures that should accompany that specific service characteristic. The best way to do this is to use a stem statement. The following is an example of how the quality measures were developed for the quality characteristic of instructional service.

Start the process of instruction by....:

1. Beginning and using warm-ups.
2. Presenting the lesson.
3. Dividing the lesson into multiple chunks.
4. Using transition to prevent boredom.
5. Using technology as one transition.
6. Grouping students for cooperative learning.
7. Summarizing frequently throughout the lesson.
8. Using games to make learning fun.
9. Reaching agreement on acceptable levels of quality.
10. Making use of homework.

Refine the List Into Acceptable Quality Measures

When refining the list into acceptable measures, make certain they are valid and reliable, and organize a team to ensure that they are. In addition, they should be written in measurable terms, as indicated below:

Service Area	Service Characteristic	Quality Measures
Instructional service	Teaching performance	Number of warm ups Services per lesson Length of presentation Number of chunks Number of transitions Use of technology Grouping variety Number of summaries Number of games to make learning fun Acceptable level of quality Homework assignment

Conduct a Trial Run

Once specific quality standards have been matched with each quality measure, the school district, school, department, or unit should conduct a trial run of the process to determine if it produces the results expected. If not, the quality characteristic, as well as each measure, should be examined to determine if they should be reused. Again, each measure should be examined for validity and reliability. Consideration should also be given to the sequence of the quality measures, and whether or not additional measures should be included in the process being measured.

ESTABLISHING STANDARDS FOR EACH QUALITY MEASURE

Once each quality measure has been established, quality service standards must be established. These quality service standards should be based on the needs, requirements, and expectations of customers and potential customers. Standards should be clearly written and matched to each quality measure, and should be well understood and committed to by all school

people. When quality service standards have been clearly identified, quantified, qualified, accepted, and written down, they
provide a systematic and orderly basis for interaction and
analysis, and a solid foundation for performance expectations.
They facilitate maximum individual and group achievement
and self-realization, and enhance the probability that performance will meet the customers' expectations.

Quality service standards are statement conditions that
will exist when a task is satisfactorily achieved. These standards are the basis for evaluation of a completed task, and
should be realistic, feasible, specific, and of ample number to
ensure accomplishment.

Once the appropriate research has been completed and
analyzed, quality service standards should be developed in
terms of what customers expect. Another way to view quality
service standards is that they should answer the questions
"What?" and "How often?" "What?" refers to the required
service behavior and "How often?" relates to the frequency
with which it is expected. For example, the "What?" of a quality
service standard might specify that "The teacher must follow
up on all assignments given to students with additional
thought-provoking questions."

Another quality service standard might include asking all
questions prior to calling on a student. Call the students by
their last name, preceded with their title, and thank the students for responding either right or wrong. In this situation,
the answer to "How often?" would be "In every classroom
encounter with students." Well-defined quality service standards will reflect what the customer expects that research has
identified as important.

Setting quality service standards defines what customers
expect from the service or product in a way that the provider
can fully understand. Quality service standards should be negotiated between the principal and QI team to make certain
that the final standards are credible, achievable, and worthwhile. When quality standards are negotiated, there is a sense
of belonging; that "We are all in this together."

An effective way to build a TQ process using quality service standards is by starting with a goal of zero defect or zero errors, then later refining those quality standards to a level less than zero defect or zero errors. School people should be encouraged to shoot for zero defect, but should be allowed to reach a level a little less than zero defect without having it affect their reward and recognition.

Quality service standards are quality measurement tools used to control the achievement of performance. They should be viewed as signals that indicate when the task has been satisfactorily achieved. As such, the following ten-step procedure is recommended to properly establish, implement, and fully utilize quality standards in TQ.

1. Quality service standards must be based on research, because they will be of little use unless they reflect customers' most important expectations. If they are based on assumptions and are incorrect, they will lead school people in the wrong direction, causing them to overlook or de-emphasize that which is most important for customers.

2. Quality service standards should precede training, because the heart of training and development should be to give school people the skills, knowledge, training, and inspiration to meet, exceed, and upgrade quality standards.

3. School people who are going to be affected by a task should agree on the measurement system and quality service standards that will be explored to evaluate performance results.

4. Quality service standards for a task should be complete, and include the entire area being controlled.

5. The period covered by the standard should correspond to that being evaluated. Some activities are evaluated more frequently than others.

6. Quality service standards should be related to the most significant things being undertaken in any area of activity. One successful technique is to identify five or six of the

most important things (quality service standards) that will indicate whether these things are done well.

7. Quality service standards should be reviewed and revised when a method or activity has changed significantly. Quality service standard costs should be consistent with the value of the measurement.

8. The frequency with which standards are compared varies depending upon the degree to which performance has been successful.

9. Quality service standards should at all times be indices of the accomplishment of the measurement. However, they should be revised as quickly, as often, and as drastically as necessary to keep pace with changing times and conditions. Any proposed changes should be agreed on by those expected by the measurement.

10. Quality service standards should be validated by using past experience and performance for preparing each statement.

There are an indefinite number of measurable factors that can be used as quality service standards. All individuals and QI teams must determine what standard will best serve their individual purposes.

For each quality measure established in the preceding step, quality performance standards must be identified. A quality standard is a very specific level of performance that satisfies either a need, requirement, or expectation. Quality standards should be established based on the demands of customers and potential customers. There are a variety of ways to determine measures as to what level of performance are considered minimum standards. One way is to conduct focus groups and individual interviews with customers. Another way is to benchmark each quality measure against those school districts that are considered to be the best in the nation.

- Establishing well-conceived quality standards cannot be overemphasized. When quality service standards are well entrenched in TQ, certain benefits will be accrued, not only for the QI team, but for the entire school organization. Some of these benefits are:

- Quality service standards enhance the probability that each task will be achieved to the satisfaction of the customer.

- Each set of quality service standards becomes a plan of action, as well as the basis for measuring the accomplishment of a task.

- Self-appraisal is facilitated, and motivation is improved.

- When quality service standards have been arrived at in a team setting, the members begin to understand the relationship of measurement to standards, with a resultant positive effect on the entire school district.

- Quality service standards can act as a means of continuous and constant reassessment methods and results.

- Quality service standards can help pinpoint problems that are hindering progress.

- Correctly written quality service standards form a common base of expectations for the entire school community.

- Once the complete list of quality service standards is developed, it can become the basis for recruiting school people.

- Preparing job descriptions to guide performance.

- Written quality standards establish a goal toward which all school people can direct their efforts.

The following is an organized way to display quality measures and standards:

Quality Measures	Quality Service Standards
1.1 Number of warm ups per lesson	1.11 Minimum of two topical or social per lesson
2.1 Length of presentation	2.11 All presentations are kept within twenty minutes
3.1 Number of chunks	3.11 Multiple use of fifteen-, ten-, five-, two-minute chunks per lesson
4.1 Number of transitions	4.11 Minimum of five transitions
5.1 Use of technology	5.11 Minimum use of two technologies per lesson
6.1 Grouping variety	6.11 Minimum of three groupings per advice are made per lesson
7.1 Number of summations	7.11 Minimum of four summations per lesson
8.1 Number of techniques to make learning fun	8.11 Minimum of three techniques used throughout lesson
9.1 Acceptable level of quality	9.11 All students attain a minimum quality standard of 90 percent
	9.12 Students not attaining minimum quality levels are provided with three opportunities to meet standards
10.1 Number of homework assignments	10.11 Minimum of three per week

Quality service standards can become the most viable force in the TQ process. When skillfully used as guides, motivators, and indices for measuring performance, they are invaluable. They should not be used for punitive purposes, but rather to help school people achieve their personal goals as they work toward school goals. Although standards should be used in a firm and consistent manner, allowances should be made if circumstances beyond human control prevent the achievement.

Principals should rely on their own judgment when balancing quality service standards with human consideration, because they are solely responsible and accountable for performance results of their respective schools.

Why Quality May Deviate From Standards

There are three basic reasons performance might deviate from the preset quality service standards. These include uncertainties, unusual events, and human factors.

Uncertainties are events that have a reasonable likelihood of occurring. They may be internal events, such as absenteeism, accidents, or strikes. External situations may involve meetings, legislative reviews, or routine correspondence.

Unusual events are not likely to occur, but could and would adversely affect school performance. These events might include the death of an administrator, a budget cut, a personnel freeze, or an epidemic.

One or more human factors may cause drastic performance deviation from preset quality standards. Human factors usually fall into two categories:

1. Honest error, which occurs due to a variety of reasons even though the individual responsible is a capable and competent school person.
2. Incompetence, which results due to gross negligence, ignorance, or inability to perform.

Whenever there is a distinct deviation in performance, the reasons indicated above should be explored to determine if a single or multiple cause is responsible for the discrepancy. Appropriate steps should be taken to ensure that the task will be obtained.

Formulating Quality Service Standards

There are several approaches to developing quality service standards. Usually they involve an individual or team. These include the individual, joint, and team approaches.

In the individual approach, the school person who will be affected by the quality service standards should be the first person to draft them. The rationale for this action is that no one knows more about the job than the person performing the task. In addition, when an individual has ownership of a standard, a greater value is placed on it, and achievement is more likely.

The ideal approach to setting quality service standards is the joint approach, in which both the school person and principal participate in the process. There are several ways in which this can be done:

1. Quality service standards are set by both parties through discussion.
2. A list of quality service standards for each task is discussed by the parties concerned.
3. A list, prepared by the principal, is subject to joint discussion and acceptance.
4. A list is prepared simultaneously, but independently, by both the school person, principal, and parents, and then discussed and mutually accepted.

Although there are several ways to perform the team approach, the usual method is to assemble a QI team to identify appropriate quality service standards for each measurement. The QI team then submits the drafted list to, and discusses it with the principal. Together they agree on changes and additions.

Writing Quality Standards

Quality service standards should be clear. They should be written so there is no misunderstanding nor misinterpretation of the precise meaning. They should also be short and to the point. They must also convey observable behavior, be practical and obtainable, and should correspond to the desired measures.

The following guidelines should be kept in mind when quality standards are being matched to quality measurements:

- Quality standards must be planned and negotiated by appropriate school people, including customers.
- They should progress toward zero defects.
- They should be stated clearly and in writing.
- They should satisfy customers' need requirements and expectations.
- They should be manageable and comprehendible.
- They must be supported by school administrators and supervisors.
- Deviating from quality service standards is not acceptable.
- Outdated quality service standards should be deleted.
- They must be communicated effectively and continuously.
- They should be continuously improved.
- They should be measurable and attainable.
- They should truthfully reflect customers' needs, requirements, and expectations.
- They should be in the control of the school person or team establishing them.

Measuring service quality should become a part of the overall service quality strategy of the school district. The school administration should establish a comprehensive quality review process where plans for preventive, as well as corrective action can be established and implemented. There obviously would include training and improving performance on critical key quality measures.

Research and experience have indicated that customer satisfaction is a function of gaps between expectations and performance. If performance exceeds expectation, then the customer is satisfied. However, if performance falls below expectations, the customer is dissatisfied.

When quality service standards have been established, they must have measured performance against service standards regularly, and formally and informally. Measurement and feedback are crucial to continuously make quality improvements. Evaluating performance can be accomplished by using any of the tools stated in this chapter, such as focus groups and surveys. A combination of feedback approaches should be used to obtain feedback from customers. It should be stressed, however, that the evaluation items on the customer survey should be indicative of the critical service characteristics. Figure 7.3 illustrates an effective example to obtain feedback or customer expectations and perceptions.

School administrators should include as a part of a broader service strategy a recognition and reward program for outstanding quality performance. In fact, the performance evaluation process and recognition and reward process should be tied to the quality service measurement system.

FIGURE 7.3
Customer Service Expectations and Perceptions

	Strongly Agree						Strongly Disagree
Expectation Statements:							
1. Classroom instruction should begin with a warm-up	7	6	5	4	3	2	1
2. All lectures/presentations should not exceed 20 minutes	7	6	5	4	3	2	1
3. All lessons should consist of multiple chunks	7	6	5	4	3	2	1
4. All lessons should contain transitions	7	6	5	4	3	2	1
5. Technology should be used in all lessons	7	6	5	4	3	2	1
6. A variety of group procedures should be used	7	6	5	4	3	2	1
Perception Statement:							
1. Classroom instruction begins with a warm-up	7	6	5	4	3	2	1
2. Teacher's lectures/presentations are limited to 20 minutes	7	6	5	4	3	2	1
3. Lessons are divided into multiple chunks	7	6	5	4	3	2	1
4. Transitions are used throughout the lesson	7	6	5	4	3	2	1
6. Variety of group procedures are used throughout the lesson	7	6	5	4	3	2	1

SUMMARY

Listening to the customer is paramount if TQ is going to be viewed as a process that separates it from countless other processes that have not produced great school districts. There are numerous techniques that can be used by school districts to listen to customers. These include focus groups, surveys, interviews, "mystery parents," complaint cards, customer panels, and visiting customers.

The quality service measurement system is one of the key components of total quality. It should be done with care, making certain that it contains specific outcomes expected of both teachers, support people, and students, and that is covers five to ten years in the future. Minimum required components of the measurement system consist of service areas, quality service characteristics, measurements, and standards. If your measurement system does not include all of these components, I suggest that you modify it.

Once the quality service measurement system if in place, the next step involves detecting and closing any performance gaps. This will be discussed in Chapter 8.

CHECKPOINTS FOR MAKING THE TRANSITION TO TQ

The following are guidelines to assist you to establish a comprehensive quality service measurement system:

1. Develop a service strategy for the school district.
2. Master the various techniques to listen to the customers—all customers.
3. Acquire the quality service measurement system of other school districts, and use it as a basis for developing one for your own school district.
4. Understand that the quality service measurement system must formally be decided by the school district and customers so that TQ can only be determined by the customers.
5. Recognize TQ on individual and group levels.
6. Use feedback as a method for validating the TQ efforts.
7. Each succeeding component of the quality service measuring system must feed on the preceding components.
8. Understand that the best customer is the one who is never satisfied.

Chapter Eight

Detecting And Closing Service Performance Gaps

The service quality challenge boils down to closing the gap between the service that customers expect and the service that they perceive is delivered. It sounds so simple, but in fact, it is not simple at all. The good news is that service quality is definable and measurable. Service quality does have a handle that we can grab and hold. Without definition, the service quality journey is destined to be an aimless wandering in a desert of good intentions.

—Leonard L. Berry, et al.

Measuring performance in traditional school management is one-dimensional; that is, performance is measured from the point of what presently exists and what is desired. The distance between the two points is known as the performance gap, and is the basis upon which all performance efforts are exerted. In addition, performance is viewed in terms of what school administrators perceive to be the needs of customers. On the other hand, in school districts that have implemented TQ, measuring performance is multidimensional; that is, performance should be measured from five different, but interrelated gaps.

Gap one is not knowing what the customers expect. Gap two is the wrong service quality standards. Gap three is the service performance gap. Gap four is when promises do not match delivery of services. Gap five is when customer expectations don't match some people's perceptions.

IN THIS CHAPTER, I WILL DISCUSS THE FOLLOWING:

- Identifying the five performance gaps

- Describing how to close the performance gaps

SERVICE PERFORMANCE GAPS AND SOLUTIONS

The following is a discussion of various service performance gaps, which is illustrated under Figure 8.1. I have identified the problems that caused these performance gaps (there are probably others), and described some corrective ways to eliminate them. Although initially you may find dealing with so many performance gaps confusing, with time and experience, you and other school people will find this task easy and quite a creative endeavor.

Problems Causing Gap 1A—Lack of Research on Customers

Research is not coordinated often enough to generate current information about what students and parents want. The school district does not conduct focus groups and a variety of other research methods to gather information on quality service to deliver to students and parents. School administrators neither understand and utilize research findings on students and parents, nor meet with them often enough to learn what is on their minds.

FIGURE 8.1
Potential Performance gaps in Total Quality

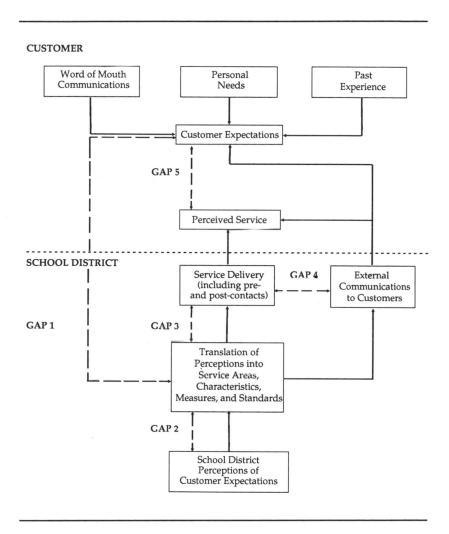

Source: Valarie A. Zethamel, A. Parasvramam, and Leonard L. Berry. *Delivering Quality Service.* New York: The Free Press, 1990, p. 46.

Closing Gap 1A—Research Customer Expectations

Determining what customers expect is crucial to providing quality service. Even if the school district is small and has limited resources to conduct research, there are a variety of ways to explore what customers expect from the school district to close the gap. Even though some of these methods have already been mentioned elsewhere in this book, I would like to discuss them again here briefly.

Use customer complaints strategically. Although listening to customer complaints is not sufficient to understand customer expectations, it can become part of a large research process of staying in touch with customers. It can provide important information about "spots of poor quality" in the service system. If compiled, analyzed, and fed back to school people who can correct the gap or problems, complaints can become an inexpensive and continuous service for adjusting the service system.

Research what other school districts are doing

Research internal customers such as teachers, which can be a useful and efficient way to obtain information about students and parents. One way to perform this feat is to conduct a method called the interview design technique to collect a wealth of information about customers' expectations from either students or parents.

Create customer panels, which school districts can organize to represent large segments of customers. The panel can convene three or four times a year to discuss school district services or products.

A research trend that is gaining popularity in service organizations is the transaction-based customer survey in which customers are surveyed immediately after a particular service about their satisfaction. This type of research is easy to perform, and provides school administrators with current information about customers.

Engage in comprehensive customer expectation studies. Some companies such as Met Life use surveys, focus group interviews, and SERVQUAL to monitor the expectations and perceptions of their customers. Customer expectations may change over time due to more knowledgeable customers, different interests, etc. To stay in touch with customers, school districts should allocate sufficient funds in the general budget to establish and maintain comprehensive research studies on customer expectations.

Problems Causing Gap 1B—Inconsistent Policies and Procedures

Policies and procedures for serving customers are inconsistent throughout the school district. School administrators, directors, and supervisors have significant autonomy in procedures and policies.

Closing Gap 1B—Increase Interaction Between School Administrators and Customers

School administrators must spend time in and out of schools interacting with customers to gain an increased understanding and appreciation of their needs, requirements, and expectations. The best way to do this is to implement a formal program for encouraging informal interaction information. For example, several years ago, the superintendent of Cherry Creek School District in Colorado conducted a class in the high school to stay close to students. In addition, he insisted that all central school administrators do the same.

Direct interaction with customers is the best way to really know customers, and to appreciate their needs and expectations.

Problems Causing Gap 1C—Poor Upward Communication

School administrators do not encourage suggestions from teachers and students concerning quality service. No formal or informal opportunities exist for teachers to communicate with central school administrators. Further, central school administrators do not have face-to-face contact with teachers or students.

Closing Gap 1C—Improving Upward Communication From Teachers to Central School Administrators

Upward information provides central school administrators with information and activities about how the TQ journey is proceeding. Formal information includes reports of quality problems, exceptions in quality service delivery, special causes of variations, etc. Informal information includes discussions between teachers and central school administrators, management by wandering around, etc. A variety of approaches should be implemented to achieve upward communication.

Problems Causing Gap 1D— Excessive Hierarchical Levels Between Teachers, Students, and Central School Administrators

Too many hierarchical levels separate central school administrators from teachers and students.

Closing Gap 1D—Reducing the Number of Hierarchical Levels

Tom Peters maintains that no organization should exceed five hierarchical levels. However, in some urban school organizations, there are sometimes more than twenty five levels. However, school superintendents are recognizing the value of reducing the number of layers, and are teaching central school administrators to focus on both internal customers (teachers and students) and external customers (parents) so they can become sensitive to their needs, requirements, and expectations.

Problems Causing 2A—Lack of School Administration Commitment to Quality

Resources are not adequately committed to either schools, departments, or units to improve quality service. Internal programs do not exist for improving quality service to customers. School people are not properly recognized and rewarded to improve quality of service. Reaching long-range goals and short-range objectives are more important than delivering quality service customers. School administrators are not committed to provide service quality to customers.

Closing Gap 2A—Gaining School Administrators' Commitment to Quality Service

Delivering quality service requires committed and supportive leadership for the central management team. Without this commitment, quality service simply will not happen. Teachers and principals do not commit to improving quality service without strong leadership from the superintendent and his or her team. If the superintendent and his or her staff is the key to setting service standards to deliver quality, then the principal's commitment is the key to making those standards work. If principals are not committed because they feel TQ is just another fad, they may not put forth their best effort to make the process work. To build school administration commitment to quality service, more education, quality experience, and training will be needed. In many cases, it has been determined that there is a relationship between knowledge, training, and commitment; that is, the more education, training, and experience they have with a process, the more they are inclined to become committed to the process.

Problems Causing Gap 2B—School Administration Perception of Infeasibility of Meeting Customers' Needs

The school district does not have the necessary capability to meet customer requirements. Customer expectations cannot be met without creating a financial burden on the school district. Schools, departments, and units are unable to meet customer expectations. Resources are unavailable to deliver the level of service that the customer demands. And, policies and procedures need to be revised to meet customer needs.

Closing Gap 2B—Creating a Belief That Customer Expectations Can Be Met

Assure school administrators and other school people that it is all right to fail. The important thing is to take the risk to do the right thing for the customer. In addition, be open to innovation, and be receptive to different and better ways of doing business in education. Not only school administrators, but everyone must have the perception that almost anything the customer needs and expects can be met. It may require a transformation. If it does, Dr. Deming's paper on the System of Profound Knowledge should be studied and mastered by all school administrators and school people.

Problems Causing Gap 2C—Inadequate Standardization of Task Systems

Standardizations are not in place to improve operating procedures so that consistent quality service is provided.

Closing Gap 2C—Standardize Service Deliver

Standardization of service delivery can take three forms:

1. substitution of hard technology for personal contact and human efforts;
2. improvement in service process or soft technology; and,
3. combinations of these two methods.

Hard technology involves simplifying and improving customer service by handling routine, repetitive tasks and transactions. Hard technology is useful in standard settings, and includes information databases, automated transition, and scheduling and delivery systems.

Soft technology involves standardizing some aspects of a service process. An excellent example of standardizing service process is the teaching process. This is done by breaking down the teaching or instructional process into discrete elements (teaching service characteristics), providing measurements to these characteristics, setting performance standards, and devising ways for engaging the system. Once the system is operating, a control chart can be devised to determine if the process is within statistical control; if not, the system is corrected.

Problems Causing Gap 2D—Lack of Goal Settings

Service quality goals are set based on school people perceptions of customer needs, requirements and expectations. The school district is not clear as to what it desires to accomplish. And the school district does not measure its performance in meeting its quality service goals.

Closing Gap 2D—Setting Service Quality Goals

Effective quality service goals have some basic characteristics as described below:

Service quality goals should be customer-oriented. They must be designed to meet customer needs, requirements, and expectations. To perform this feat, all research data on the customer should be creatively analyzed to determine what is important to the customer—and setting quality goals follow.

Service quality goals should specify that these goals be defined in specific ways that all school people are able to understand what they are being asked to deliver. In addition, they should be measurable, challenging, and realistic. They should not be vague.

Service quality goals should be accepted by all school people. School people will perform to quality standards consistently only if they understand and accept the goals. This is one of the reasons why quality standards should be negotiated.

Improved quality standards will lead to resistance, resent-ment, absenteeism, and a number of other negative side effects.

Service quality standards should be matched to critical service characteristics. It is impossible for school people to de-liver all of the service characteristics of a job. It is essential for quality characteristics to be prioritized so that most of the focus can be provided to vital few critical characteristics that are responsible for major portions of the service to be delivered.

Service quality should be challenging and realistic. Several studies indicate that school people perform at their highest level when goals are challenging and realistic. If they are not, school people well get little reinforcement for attaining them. However, when goals are not realistic; school people may be-come frustrated by not being able to attain them.

Problems Causing Gap 3A—Role Ambiguity

School administrators do not provide accurate information to school people concerning service instruction, board policies, procedures, and performance assessment. School people do not understand any of the services and products offered by the school district. School people are not able to stay abreast of changes that affect their job. School people are not properly trained to interact effectively with customers. School adminis-trators do not communicate school district vision, quality goals, and expectations often enough to school people. Finally, school people do not understand what school administrators expect from them, and how to accommodate those expecta-tions.

Closing Gap 3A—Provide Role Clarity

Four tools can be used to clarify roles to school people: com-munication, feedback, confidence, and competence. First, school people need accurate information about their role in the school district. They need specific and frequent communica-tion from central school administration and principals about what they are expected to do. They need to know goals, strategies, objectives, and the guidance system of the school district. They need to know current and complete information about the service and products of the school district. And, they need to know the customers and their needs, requirements, and expectations. They need to know how well they are performing compared to the standards and expectations of school administrators. Feedback provides reinforcement when school people perform well, and provides an opportunity for correcting performance when they do not perform well.

They need to feel confident and competitive in their jobs. School districts can close this gap quite often just by improving their emphasis on training. As a result, school people should receive the following:

- Technical training in the various aspects of the service they provide.

- Interpersonal training to deal with sometimes demanding, dissatisfied, and angry parents and/or other colleagues.

- Training in knowing the customer. The more teachers know about customer perception, expectations, and problems, the better they are able to serve them.

Problems Causing Gap 3B—Role Conflict

Role conflict problems usually occur when teachers feel frustrated, because they cannot satisfy all the demands of their students; when school administrators emphasize student achievement over learning; when school administrators demand quantity over quality; when too many demands are imposed on teachers; when there is excessive paperwork or internal road blocks; or there is excessive contact with too many customers.

Closing Gap 3B—Eliminating Role Conflict

Role conflict can have a negative effect on school people satisfaction and performance, and can increase absenteeism and turnover. When a school district defines service roles and standards in terms of customer needs, requirements, and expectations, role conflict is automatically minimized. One way to do this is to involve school people in the quality standards setting process. Role conflict can also be minimized under the following conditions:

1. A quality measurement system is used that focuses on the customer, as well as internal efficiency goals.
2. School people are trained in priority setting and time management.
3. Frequent breaks are given.

Problems Causing Gap 3C—Poor
Supervisory Control System

School people do not know what aspects of their jobs will be stressed most in evaluating performance. School people are not evaluated in terms of how well they interact with customers. Exemplary school people are not more likely to be rewarded than other school people. School people who make a special effort to service customers are not recognized or rewarded. Further, school people do not feel appreciated for their contribution toward quality service.

Closing Gap 3C—Measuring and
Rewarding Service Performance

Implement a behavioral control system to keep tabs on school people performance. One technique could involve interviewing customers in terms of how individual teachers treat parents who contact them via phone.

Teachers should also be monitored and recognized for everyday performance. In fact, the quality service measurement system should be tied to appropriate recognition and reward.

Problems Causing Gap 3D—Lack of Control

School people spend time in their jobs trying to resolve problems over which they have little or no control. School people are not given freedom to make individual decisions to satisfy customer needs. School people are not encouraged to learn new ways to improve their service to customers. School people are required to obtain approval from another school, department, or unit. School people are not personally involved and committed to the school district.Some school people compete more than they cooperate with other school people when servicing customers. And, school people are not encouraged to work together as a team to provide quality service to customers.

Closing Gap 3D—Empowering School People

Empowering school people means several things, as indicated below:

1. Giving all school people decision-making power.
2. Granting teachers the authority to make important decisions about serving students and parents.
3. Creating new and effective approaches to solving customer problems.
4. Replacing tight structures with looser structures to deal with customers.
5. Providing school people with timely information to make important decisions.

Problems Causing Gap 4A—Inadequate Horizontal Communication

Internal customers (teachers) have not had contact with the public relations office. Internal customers were not aware of the external communications before they occurred. The public relations office did not discuss with internal customers the level of service that can occur by the school district. Further, the public relations office used only one of the communications solely to make the superintendent look good.

Closing Gap 4A—Improve Horizontal Communication

When the school district creates public relations documents that depict its quality service, it must truthfully and accurately reflect actual quality service that the school district is providing the customer. Coordination among the schools, departments, and units is essential.

To close this gap depends upon the honesty and integrity of the person writing the communique. To deal with these problems effectively, the school district deals with quality dimensions and features that are most important to customers (i.e., student achievement), accurately reflects what customers actually receive in quality service delivery, and assists customers in understanding their roles in performing the service.

Other techniques to close this gap should involve the following steps:

1. Request input or opinions from those delivering the quality service by monitoring the service encounter.
2. Prior to publicizing the public relations communique, let providers preview the information.
3. Involve the providers of the quality service in the preparation of the public relations document.

Problems Causing Gap 4B—Difference in Policies and Procedures

If school administrators have a great deal of autonomy in development procedures and policies, customers may not receive the same level of service quality in another school. Therefore, what they expect and receive from one school may be different from what is delivered in another school.

Closing Gap 4B—Providing Consistent Quality Service Across Schools, Departments, and Units

If customers are to receive consistent quality service across schools, departments, and units, then the school district must develop a mechanism for ensuring uniformity. True, the curriculum is one vehicle for doing so; however, others are needed, such as the following:

1. Standard operating policies or procedures.
2. Quality manual.
3. Quality strategic planning.
4. School quality improvement plans.
5. Special guidelines.
6. School district's guidance system.
7. Strong training programs (everybody is trained in the same contents and in the same way).
8. Setting quality service goals, and letting each school, district, and unit establish the means to achieve these goals.

Problems Causing Gap 4C—Propensity to Promise Too Much

Because of increasing pressure from the board of education or superintendent, some school districts may feel the need to overpromise. To accomplish this, they may oversell the school district. The greater the extent to which the public relations office feels pressure to make the school district look good, the greater the school district's propensity to overpromise.

For example, I received a copy of an annual report of a superintendent in a large urban school district in Texas. The report was well-designed and described all the "good things" that were happening for students. In fact, I used that same annual report to request participants in the workshop to visit the school district. What a mistake that was. A subsequent visit to that school district revealed a multitude of problems with parents and teachers. Obviously, the public relations person who prepared the annual report for the superintendent failed to communicate to other departments and units of the school district to get their input.

Closing Gap 4C—Developing Appropriate and Effective Communication About Service Quality

Appropriate and effective communication begins with an understanding of the aspects of quality service that are important to customers. These communiques should be reliable in terms of what the school districts can provide to students. They should be honest in selling the school district, and should be cleared by the superintendent of schools who will be distributing them to customers.

Closing Gap 5 will exist when all the other performance gaps have been closed.

SUMMARY

Measuring performance in a school district is usually one-dimensional; that is, performance is measured from the point of a performance gap in terms of what is the present performance level and what is desired. In TQ, measuring performance is multidimensional; that is, performance is measured in terms of several gaps of dimensions. Schools, teams, and individual performance will be based on the quality service measurement system. As a result, the measurement system should be well planned, projected over a period of five to ten years, and should contain all of the elements addressed in this chapter.

The next chapter discusses how to implement TQ in the classroom.

CHECKPOINTS FOR MAKING THE TRANSITION TO TOTAL QUALITY

Gap closing requires careful detection, keen analysis, and a systematic approach. The following steps should help to perform this task:

1. Check out performance gaps in sequential order.
2. Determine the root causes of each gap.
3. Use the Shewhart/Deming Plan-Do-Check-Act cycle or some other method to close the gaps.
4. Review the system to determine why any performance was "above plan," and use that information to improve the system.

Chapter Nine

Implementing Total Quality In The Classroom

... Dr. Deming's ideas can be brought undisturbed into our schools so that the present elitist system, in which just a few students are involved in high quality work, will be replaced by a system in which almost all students have the experience.

—*William Glasser, M.D.*

As educators and parents, we should not be satisfied with excellent schools. Excellence refers to the best traditional school administration, principles, and practices that have produced some positive results in our schools. However, these traditional principles and practices are no longer adequate to accommodate the needs of our students. The school environment has changed drastically, and so have our students. What is required is a transformational change. The only well-thought out, field-tested alternative available today for us to elevate from excellent to *great* schools is to begin the journey to TQ. The journey toward achieving greatness in schools is predicated not by merely implementing it on a district-wide or school level, but also on a classroom level. It is at this level that the transformation must take hold, thereby transforming the teachers and students, along with parents. It is also at this level where school administrators find it very difficult to relate TQ principles and practices for classroom use.

IN THIS CHAPTER, I WILL DELINEATE THE FOLLOWING:

- Selecting appropriate TQ principles for classroom observance

- Understanding the System of Profound Knowledge as it relates to the classroom

- Teaching classroom use of the Shewhart/Deming Plan-Do-Check-Act cycle

- Identifying TQ expectations of principals, teachers, and students

- Discussing Dr. Deming's Triangle of Interaction

- Identifying classroom activities for implementing TQ

SELECTING APPROPRIATE TOTAL QUALITY PRINCIPLES

The first step for implementing TQ in the classroom involves reviewing the principles of the three gurus of quality mentioned in Chapter One, Drs. Deming, Juran, and Crosby, and selecting those principles that are appropriate for classroom observance. Some revisions may be necessary. I have chosen the following principles for your review:

1. Make it clear that teachers are committed to quality (Dr. Crosby).
2. Create constancy of purpose toward improvement of service and product (Dr. Deming).
3. Drive out fear to maximize student efforts (Dr. Deming).
4. Raise the quality awareness and personal concern of all students (Dr. Crosby).
5. Replace competition with cooperation (Dr. Deming).

6. Cease dependence on grades and ranking. Require statistical evidence of quality (Dr. Deming) instead.

7. Organize to attain quality (Dr. Juran).

8. Train teachers to actively carry out their part of the quality improvement process (Dr. Crosby).

9. Encourage students to communicate to teachers the obstacles they face in attaining quality improvement (Dr. Crosby).

10. Report classroom quality progress (Dr. Juran).

11. Recognize and appreciate students for their quality initiatives (Dr. Crosby).

12. Do it all over again to demonstrate that quality improvement never ends (Dr. Deming).

Some school districts may wish to confine themselves to the principles of a specific guru, such as Dr. Deming. This is certainly all right; however, are you certain that all your beliefs about TQ should be covered by a single set of TQ principles? For example, Dr. Deming's principles are devoid of recognition; Dr. Juran's principles are devoid of commitment (although implied); and Dr. Crosby's principles are devoid of constancy of purpose. In essence, you should study each set of principles carefully before developing your own or adopting one specific set.

The principles, techniques, and activities of TQ are to be integrated with everything the teacher does in the classroom. For example, according to Theresa May Hicks, an elementary school teacher who practices Dr. Deming's philosophy in the classroom: The System of Profound Knowledge can be taught with social students, science, math, etc. The Shewhart/Deming cycle can be taught to students to produce a product in social studies, to write a report, etc. The fish bowl diagram can be used to help students to see the relationship between cause and effect; between what they do and its effect. In fact, TQ principles and practices can be used in conjunction with any academic subject matter to make learning fun and enjoyable.

Make it clear to students where the teacher stands on quality. The first action that must take place is to produce a TQ classroom for students to understand what quality is; who is responsible for quality; what is expected of students in a TQ classroom; and how students can produce quality.

Talk to students about quality not only as it pertains to school, but also as it pertains to their personal lives. During this meeting with students, the teacher should demonstrate a deep passion for TQ. Through his or her words, actions, and deeds, students should get the sense that the quality of their lives are interwoven and bent on how well they embrace the TQ concept and pursue the quality journey. The teacher should discuss the following:

- What is quality?
- Who are customers and providers?
- Who are internal and external customers?
- Who are internal and external providers?
- What do students have to do to put forth quality work?
- What are learning characteristics, measures, and standards?
- What does it take to have a quality experience?
- Who defines quality?
- How is quality traditionally defined?
- Where does quality happen?
- Who should produce quality?
- Why should students be convinced about quality?
- How does a class implement quality?
- What are the activities of quality?
- What are the different ways to produce quality?
- What role do teams play in quality?
- Why are teams essential for improving processes?
- Why is team building important?

- Discuss the role of team leaders and members.

- Discuss how the team will solve problems.

After the teacher demonstrates a strong commitment to TQ, the next step involves the creation of a mission, vision, and shared values statements. Techniques to develop each are described below.

Prepare a Mission Statement

First, indicate to students that a mission statement identifies the aim or purpose of the class; that is, Why does the class exist? Whom does it serve? Engage students in a discussion of questions, such as: Why are you here? What are you trying to do? What does it mean to you to do well? What does the teacher have to do so you can do well? How will we know if we are doing it well together?

Ask students to independently write their versions of the class mission on a sheet of paper.

Go around the room looking for excellent examples of student-prepared mission statements, and request them to write their creations on a flipchart sheet or blackboard.

Discuss each mission statement. Ask students to decide on the best two examples. Use the examples to reach a consensus on a mission statement acceptable to the classroom.

Communicate the mission statement by reaching an agreement on how it should be communicated (i.e., printed on school stationery?, etc.)

Create a Vision Statement

Indicate to students that it is insufficient just to prepare a mission statement, and that a vision statement must also be prepared and communicated. Explain that a vision statement identifies the future direction of the classroom; that is, the vision statement describes what the classroom wants to become.

Ask students to take a pencil or crayon and a sheet of paper, and to draw a picture of how their classroom should look in the future.

Ask students to respond to the following statement to write a vision statement: My parents want our class to prepare me for the future by ...

Ask students to imagine that they are journalists, and have been assigned the responsibility of writing an article. They are to describe the successes the classroom will have achieved at a future time (five or ten years from the present).

Ask students to think about what they value most about the classroom. Then, have them list five ways to complete the following stem statement: In our classroom, we really care about ...

Once the above steps have been completed, develop a worksheet as described below to discover key items that should be associated with the vision statement. For instance, use a five-whys worksheet to illuminate the vision statement, such as:

- Why should our class implement TQ? Because TQ makes learning fun and enjoyable.

- Why does TQ make learning fun and enjoyable? Because emphasis is on continuous improvement, cooperation, quality effort, and no failure.

- Why is the emphasis on continuous improvement, cooperation, quality effort, and no failure? Because every student is given an opportunity to be more productive.

- Why is every student given an opportunity to be more productive? Because school should be designed to maximize learning on the part of every student in school.

- Why should school be designed to maximize learning on the part of every student? So that every student can become more than they ever hoped to be.

Use all that has been discussed, and assign a group of students to draft a vision statement. Discuss the draft version of the vision statement with the entire class and agree on a final version.

Create a Shared Values Statement

Now that the mission and vision statements have been completely spelled out, the next step involves preparing a shared values statement for students, teachers, and principals. Shared values statements in essence describe specific behaviors desired from students, teachers, and the principal. This can be carried out simply by having students brainstorm those beliefs they feel are important to ensure a smoothly operating TQ classroom.

The following stem statement is an example of one that can be used to generate acceptable behavior in a TQ classroom: How should students conduct themselves in a TQ classroom? This statement can also be used with minor revisions to generate acceptable beliefs for both teachers and principal.

Drive Out Fear in the Classroom

Discuss with students the term fear. Ask them to describe what happens to them emotionally when they are fearful. Tell of an incident when the teacher experienced fear either in school, at home, or in some other situation. Also discuss what he or she did to dissolve that fear. In an effort to reduce fear in the classroom, request students to generate a list of practices that produce fear. Depict these items by producing a Pareto chart. In addition, consider the following other activities to reduce fear in the classroom.

Request students to conduct a force field analysis to identify the major forces to reduce fear in the classroom. Ask students to execute a cause-and-effect analysis to identify the major causes of fear in the classroom, and to perform another to eliminate those causes. Have students produce a list of activities through brainstorming to make learning fun and enjoyable.

Create Quality Awareness

Raise the quality awareness and personal concern of all students in the classroom by implementing the following activities:

- On the first day of the week, convene a meeting of all students and discuss where each individual and the class are in terms of quality.

- Use appropriate quality terminology throughout the school day everyday, and expect students to do the same.

- Prepare T-shirts with "quality" imprinted on them for students.

- Send quality progress reports home with students.

- Invite Malcolm Baldrige National Quality Award winners in to talk quality to students.

- Train parents to embrace quality philosophy, principles, and practices.

- Celebrate quality victories.

- Nurture a classroom environment whereby every student demonstrates a genuine concern for each other.

- Be on-call for all students twenty-four hours a day.

Replace Competition With Cooperation

Schools are set up to be competitive for both teachers and students. Explain to students what competition produces. Indicate the following:

- A victim is required.

- Results will produce a winner and a loser.

- It places blame on others.

- Change is resisted.

- Self-esteem is affected.

Ask students to identify examples of competition, such as the following:

- merit program for teachers;
- tracking of students;
- competing for grades;
- teacher evaluation;
- ranking of schools; and
- ranking of classes.

Inform students that when they compete, some fear is realized, even by those who are winners, because they are fearful of losing. Emphasize that everybody within a system is interrelated; what happens to one component has an effect on another. In fact, the Theory of Systems implies that in a win-lose situation, there are no winners. Everybody loses.

Cooperation should replace competition. TQ requires the formulation of teams to work on projects in which results are shared, and each team member's success is linked to another. Cooperation is engaged when the following is instituted:

- peer tutoring;
- cooperative learning;
- articulation between junior and senior high school;
- mentoring (when an experimental teacher assists a new teacher needing assistance);
- learning groups;
- teacher-administrator planning;
- team teaching; and
- network system.

Change Focus of the Grading System

Meet with parents to explain improved techniques of evaluating student learning and growth with less of an emphasis on traditional testing and grading and more on statistical evidence and authentic testing. Reach an agreement to either replace the traditional testing and grading with authentic testing and statistical evidence, or use both with the former on an experimental basis. Consider the following:

- Eliminate Fs and Ds.
- Eliminate all grades and establish a B for minimum quality acceptance.
- Agree on minimum standards such as eighty and increase that standard on an annual basis.
- Give students A-pluses for extra work.
- Solve a problem.
- Use a video portfolio.
- Evaluate work based on five indices, but without a failing index.
- Design a proposal and mock-up.
- Assemble a portfolio.

Organize to Attain Quality

Organize the classroom for quality by first organizing quality improvement teams of students, and turning them loose on the classroom or school to locate and solve problems.

Create cooperative learning teams to facilitate the learning process from time to time.

Identify problems by creating and initiating a variety of ways to listen to the customers.

Use the teacher as a facilitator, coach, problem solver, manager, mentor, or chief executive officer to arouse and maintain the quality interest of students.

Organize one or more QI teams to work on either classroom or school problems. Require students to meet and manage their quality meetings similar to how quality improvement teams conduct their meetings. At times, the team may need the service of other students from within or without the school. In certain situations, an adult school person may need to be on the team. The teacher should serve as a facilitator.

Familiarize teams with the three different projects in which they will work on throughout the school year:

- Research project (to collect data
- Problem-solving project (to arrive at a solution)
- Implementation project (to implement the solution to problems)

Require all teams to develop a set of rules or guidelines with associated consequences to monitor the rules that are broken in their teams. Instruct students to maintain a histogram with each infraction receiving a colored dot corresponding to the rule. The left axis should be labeled "number of broken rules," and the right axis should be labeled, "date."

Teach students how to use consensus to arrive at team decisions.

Encourage teams to search for opportunities to initiate quality improvement, to innovate, and to grow.

Encourage teams (as a group) to prepare a newsletter summarizing progress toward achieving either the mission or vision.

Promote team learning. The teacher should choose at random one team member to demonstrate what he or she has learned. Advocate the team on that basis.

Assign complementary roles by requesting one team member to record items, another to encourage full participation, another to be a devil's advocate to challenge common views, and the fourth to observe and provide feedback to help the team reflect on how well it is operating.

Encourage the team to devise and publicize their own name and symbol.

Encourage teams to unite with other teams to contribute to each other's successes.

Strengthen the teams' skills at evaluating alternatives by assessing each alternative on four criteria:

- The tangible gains and losses for the team or class
- The tangible gains and losses for the customer

- Intangible gains and losses in the self-approval of team members and other students
- Intangible gains and losses in the self-approval of teachers, school administrators, and parents

Require teams to develop a balance sheet. On one side of the balance sheet the team identifies the tangible gains and losses for the class and school, and on the other side, the intangible consequences. They then rate each item on a scale from one to ten, and from no importance to extreme importance, and then discuss them.

Train Teachers to Implement Total Quality

The effectiveness of the class and student as teams is predicated on how committed and fortified with knowledge and know-how the teachers are in implementing TQ in the classroom. Teachers must be educated and trained in the following areas:

- History of quality;
- Drs. Deming, Juran, and Crosby and their quality principles;
- The System of Profound Knowledge;
- Shewhart/Deming Plan-Do-Check-Act cycle;
- Dr. Deming's Triangle of Interaction;
- Basis of quality improvement concepts;
- Scientific approach;
- Decision-making tools;
- Cooperative learning;
- Team-building skills;
- Consensus;
- Strategies for integrating course of study with quality concepts;
- Program strategies;

- Customers and providers interface; and
- Cooperative learning;

Encourage Students to Communicate With Teachers

From time to time, students will be faced with a number of obstacles that may prevent them from attaining quality. Initially, students should generate through brainstorming a list of obstacles that will hamper their attempts to achieve quality, and they should develop a strategy for preventing them. Periodically throughout the school year, the teacher should convene an obstacle meeting, and discuss with students those problems, either in schools or at home, that prevent them from producing quality. It may also be an excellent idea to establish a suggestion program in the classroom or school whereby students, parents, and teachers can contribute problems and ideas. Early in the school year, have them generate through brainstorming a list of obstacles that may hamper their attempts to achieve quality, and develop a strategy for removing these obstacles.

Report Classroom Quality Progress

Even though the teacher may be the only person implementing TQ in the school, he or she should make it a point to communicate TQ results either on an individual, classroom, or school level. This should not be an opportunity for the teacher to brag that his or her students are using statistics, but to engage school people in a conversation as to what her or his students did the previous year (before quality initiatives), and what is being accomplished this year. Perhaps the best way to approach this is to involve the principal and students in these exercises.

The following are a number of other activities to report student quality efforts:

- Invite Baldrige winners to the class and have the students show off their quality initiatives.

- Assist the class to produce a quality newsletter using the Shewhart/Deming cycle, and distribute it throughout the school district.
- Invite local newspapers to visit the classroom to report on the students' quality efforts.
- Schedule students to go to community groups to present their quality initiatives.

Recognize and Appreciate Students

Although Dr. Deming is not much for recognizing quality efforts, the other two gurus are. However, the recognition and reward programs in TQ in education must change to include the following:

1. Don't have anymore losers. The 1 to 2 percent who are winning and are recognized for their achievement in school in the traditional approach are abandoned for 100 percent winners in the TQ approach.
2. Establish a peer-to-peer award. This award is activated by a student when another student desires to recognize that peer with an award. A process is initiated by the teacher to enable the student to do so.
3. Create quality recognition activities. All members of quality teams are given T-shirts or sweaters with the imprint of "Unnatural Elementary School Quality Team." Food is served as a celebration event when some extraordinary feat of quality is performed.
4. Team efforts are recognized, as well as individual efforts.
5. Recognize and reward parents for their quality efforts also.
6. Give students an opportunity to attend board meetings to give a presentation on quality.
7. Invite teachers, students, and parents to attend presentations given by quality teams.
8. Give students certificates for completing training in quality.

9. Establish a quality recognition program whereby students are given quality booklets. Whenever a student produces something of quality, the teacher stamps the booklet. At the end of the term, students turn in their booklets and receive prizes for the number of stamps of quality received by them.

10. Take the class to a Baldrige National Quality Award-winning company and have the recipients "talk quality."

TQ is a continuous process. Get other teachers and students turned on to quality. Request to appear at a meeting of the board of education to get the members excited about quality. Further, locate a teacher to help him of her become a champion of quality. Educate and train the principal to adopt the principles and practices of quality. Finally, get parents involved in the quality movement. Give them T-shirts with the imprint "I am a quality mother/father helping to produce a quality child. Join me."

THE SYSTEM OF PROFOUND KNOWLEDGE

In order to make the transformation to TQ in the classroom, both teachers and students must make the journey. Dr. Deming maintains that the journey must be guided by a System of Profound Knowledge, and that the teacher must become the leader. Everything accomplished by the teacher for students (classroom management, teaching strategies, curriculum and instruction, etc.) is done with the notion that the primary purpose of TQ in the classroom is to educate students about the System of Profound Knowledge. As discussed in Chapter Two, the system has four interrelated parts or components: theory of systems, theory of variation, theory of knowledge, and theory of psychology.

Theory of Systems

Explain to students the relationship between process and system. Indicate that a process is the grouping in sequence of all the tasks required to produce something. Give a personal example, such as the number of tasks a student must accomplish when he or she arises in the morning to go to school. Ask them to identify some processes in school and at their homes.

Once you feel that students are aware of processes, introduce them to a system. Indicate to them that if a series of related tasks can be called a process, then a group of interrelated processes can then be seen as a system. For example, a school system includes all the people in the school performing numerous tasks to educate students. Give students some examples of thought-provoking systems, and ask them to explain how the following are systems: a vacation, wildlife, and a book.

Inform students that a system includes the following:

- It must have an aim or purpose.

- The aim must be clear to everyone in the system.

- All parts or components must be interconnected and interrelated.

- All parts or components cooperate rather than compete.

Tell the class that you are going to introduce them to a new word. Cite the syllables of the word optimization. See if any of the students can define the word. If not, define the word for them.

Optimization is defined as a process of orchestrating the efforts of all components toward the achievement of a single aim. Indicate to students that a system that is not optimized is at suboptimization level. To reinforce comprehension of the term, ask students questions such as the following:

- How is a system optimized?

- What can you do to optimize the education you are receiving?

- What are problems that can cause suboptimization of a system?

- Can a system be optimized if one component is not achieving its aim? Why?

- Why is competition harmful to a system?

Theory of Variation

Teachers should introduce the concept of variation to students by explaining that everything—all systems, processes, people, performers, products, etc.—vary over time. Explain that whenever a problem occurs in a system, it is due to either a common or a special cause. A problem due to a large number of small sources of variation results in a large number of defects or mistakes due to common causes. The sum of these common causes determines the variation of the system, and therefore its limits and capabilities.

On the other hand, special causes of variation are not due to the system. They occur because of specific circumstances. For example, a delay in delivery of textbooks to the school may be a special cause of why a large number of students did not pass the course. Discuss the two types of mistakes people make when analyzing such variation, and explain the following:

1. People sometimes mistake the cause of variation as being special, when in fact the variation is caused by the system (common cause).

2. People sometimes mistake the cause of variation as being common, when in fact it is special in nature, and should be analyzed further and eliminated.

   - Discuss with students the following questions on variation:

   - What two steps can be taken when dealing with a stable system (common cause)?

   - What steps should be taken to deal with special causes that are above control limits? Below control limits?

   - Why is it important for students to comprehend the theory of variation?

   - Is it fair to blame people for variations in the system? Why, or why not?

- Identify when you are confronted with a common or special cause of a system? What do you do about it?

- Request students to identify steps that can be taken to eliminate special causes that fall below the control limits. Explain that understanding the Theory of Variation is important, because most of our problems rest not in the people, but in the system in which the people are involved. Therefore, charting whether or not the problem is within or without the system is important in order to solve system problems.

Engage students in the following activities to reinforce their learning of variation in the system. Have students play jacks and record how many jacks a student catches every time he or she drops the ball while playing the game. Depict the vertical axis with a scale of 0 to 5 and the horizontal axis with a scale of 0 to 20.

Have a student jump rope twenty separate times before missing a jump. In this case, the horizontal axis would be numbered 0 to 20 to indicate the number of repetitions.

Encourage students to determine what can be done to improve the process if the fault lies within the process or outside the process.

Theory of Knowledge

Indicate to students that according to Myron Tribus, a consultant on quality, quality education has four dimensions: knowledge, know-how, wisdom, and character.

Explain that the first dimension of a quality education is knowledge that enables students to understand what they learn, and how to relate it to other things that they learned. Indicate that knowledge provides them with the ability to generalize from their experience.

The second dimension of a quality education is know-how. Know-how enables students to put to work the knowledge that they have learned. Although knowledge can be gained from many sources, such as reading, listening, and discussion, know-how can only be acquired through doing.

The third dimension of quality education is wisdom. This is the ability of students to understand what is important and what is not important. Indicate that wisdom enables students to establish priorities, and helps them to determine what is worthy of their focused attention.

The fourth dimension of quality education is character. Students should be taught to see character as a combination of knowledge, know-how, and wisdom, coupled with motivation. Ask students to relate the four dimensions of quality education to a process. Some examples of questions are as follows:

- Are the dimensions interrelated?
- What would happen if one component was missing?
- What is the product?
- What is the cumulative effect?
- Identify a special cause that could impact this process.

Theory of Psychology

Explain the Theory of Psychology to students by indicating that in order to help them to understand themselves and people, they must appreciate how people differ and behave. They must understand that people learn differently and at different speeds, have similar and dissimilar likes and dislikes, and have different needs and expectations.

Some of the theories students should be introduced to are the theory of personal goal fulfillment, the theory of expectancy, the theory of human zones, and the theory of human addictions.

Inform students that all human beings fulfill their personal goals before fulfilling other people's goals. Ask them to explain this theory to you, and to cite when it occurred for them. Tell them that if they are not sensitive to the needs of others, and do not integrate their goals with those of others, people will think they are selfish.

Explain the theory of expectancy to students by asking them to define the term expectancy. Emphasize that if they want something bad enough, they will need to have high expectations for it. Indicate that "you get what you expect."

All human beings have three zones: the goal of acceptance; the goal of indifference; and the goal of rejection.

Usually, to get people to accept anything, their zone of acceptance has to be increased, causing a corresponding decrease in the zone of rejection. To widen the zone of acceptance, other theories may need to be applied appropriately. For example, you may need to entice them with something they hold valuable to encourage them to widen their zone of acceptance.

All human beings are endowed with three basic addictions: security, sensation, and power. The security addiction is related to food, shelter, clothing, or whatever you equate with your personal security. The sensation addiction is concerned with finding happiness in school and in life by providing you with more and better measurable sensations and activities. The power addiction is concerned with dominating people and situations, and increasing your prestige, wealth, status, and pride, in addition to other subtle forms of manipulation and control.

When initiating change, all three addictions must be taken into consideration, particularly the security addiction. Thoroughly discuss these theories with students. Bring this discussion up to date from time to time. There are a number of theories of psychology that are appropriate for the teacher to discuss with students. These can be found in any book on psychology.

THE SHEWHART/DEMING
PLAN-DO-CHECK-ACT CYCLE

Teach students the Shewhart/Deming Plan-Do-Check-Act cycle or scientific planning model, as illustrated under Figure 9.1 and as described below.

FIGURE 9.1
Shewhart/Deming Cycle

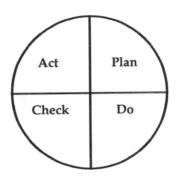

PLAN:
1. Identify the problem or opportunity for improvement; define it as a process to be improved (usually a single objective will suffice).
2. Find the possible reasons (causes of variation) for the problem or situation. Determine only major causes.
3. Analyze the major causes to determine the effect they have on the process in order to ascertain the major causes.

DO:
4. Take corrective action of the process by developing a well-thought out plan with clear objectives.

CHECK:
5. Evaluate the impact of the corrective action, and compare results to objectives. If improvement results, proceed with steps six and seven; if not, go back to step one, and continue the process.
6. Standardize; otherwise, go back to step two.

ACT:

7. Standardize the proposed change to prevent problems from recurring, and plan the next improvement initiative.

There are a variety of ways in which teachers can use the Shewhart/Deming cycle in the classroom. The following are a few examples:

- Request teams of students to interview either a teacher or principal to determine the most pressing problems confronting the school, and solve these.

- Ask students to request that their parents to give them a problem around the house that has not been solved, and solve it using the Shewhart/Deming cycle.

- Use appropriate course content, and request students to produce a product using the Shewhart/Deming cycle.

- Ask students to plan a vacation with their families using the Shewhart/Deming cycle.

- Request the class to use the Shewhart/Deming cycle to develop a school conference on TQ.

- Ask students to develop a plan for implementing TQ in the school using the Shewhart/Deming cycle. Show the plan to the principal and get his or her reaction. If approved, give the plan to teachers and students for their comments and suggestions. Create a flowchart for the plan.

- Request students to develop a comprehensive plan using the Shewhart/Deming cycle to research information on what parents' needs, requirements, and expectations are concerning the school.

DR. DEMING'S TRIANGLE OF INTERACTION

Dr. Deming maintains that neither the creation nor the testing of a product and how it will perform or be accepted are sufficient to describe it as quality. He says that quality can only be measured by the interaction among these participants, as shown in Figure 9.2 and discussed below.

FIGURE 9.2
Dr. Deming's Triangle of Interaction

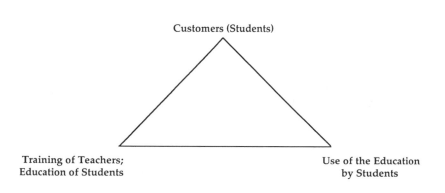

The top of the vertex of the triangle refers to the product; that is, the education received by the student, testing of the education in actual use, and steps taken by students to improve or enhance their education.

The right vertex of the triangle refers not only to the way the student makes use of his or her education, but what he or she thinks about the education they have received.

The left vertex of the triangle refers to the actual education received by students; additional education engaged in by students to enhance their knowledge; additional assistance given to students when they experienced difficulty in grasping topics; what subject matter is available to them; as well as the training received by teachers.

According to Dr. Deming, a student can receive the best education in the country, but if he or she uses that education for destructive means, then he or she has not received a quality education.

Explain Dr. Deming's Triangle of Interaction by doing the following seven steps:

1. Request students to arrive at a list of "bad" and "good" uses of the knowledge they gain from education.
2. Request students to generate a list of ways in which they can use their education now and in the future.
3. Have students use the nominal group process to silently generate a list to identify ways in which they can improve their education.
4. Ask students to see if there are ways in which they can "take care" of their learning.
5. Request students to suggest ways the teacher can continue his or her education, even though he or she has finished formal education.
6. Ask students to relate Dr. Deming's Triangle of Interaction to their experiences in the classroom.
7. Use Dr. Deming's interaction triangle to demonstrate how it can be put to use to operate the classroom as a small business.

IDENTIFYING ACTIVITIES FOR IMPLEMENTING TOTAL QUALITY IN THE CLASSROOM

There are a countless number of activities that can be used to implement the principles and practices of TQ in the classroom, while at the same time making learning fun. The following are the three basic steps for accomplishing this feat:

1. Fortify the teacher with knowledge and experience in the various tools, such as brainstorming, fishbone diagram, force-field analysis, etc.
2. When the teacher feels comfortable with the knowledge and experience she or he has received in using the various tools in TQ, she or he should look for opportunities to use the tools in the classroom to reinforce and make the learning process fun.
3. Teach TQ tools to students, with or without integrating them into classroom work, starting with the easiest tool, such as brainstorming, and ending with the control chart.

The following are some activities that can be used to strengthen student use of TQ tools:

- Drive out fear in the classroom by having students brainstorm ideas, select the top six to nine, and develop an action plan or the Shewhart/Deming cycle to drive out the fearful activities.

- Determine why students are not doing homework in a timely manner by having them do a cause-and-effect analysis to determine the major causes, and eliminate these by performing the Shewhart/Deming cycle.

- Ask students to assess the teaching process using a control chart to ascertain why a large number of students are not passing a particular course or subject.

- Have students track student lateness to class using a run chart.

- Ask students to use force-field analysis to identify the main reasons why parents are not involved in their children's homework.

- Request students to use cause-and-effect analysis to determine the root causes for students who are experiencing difficulty passing a course.

- Give students experience in developing the Pareto chart by having them prioritize problems in the classroom or school.

- Ask students to conduct an analysis to determine problems affecting the reputation of the school.

- Request students to measure the effect of a process change using a histogram.

- Ask students to determine the relationship between time spent on a task and student achievement. (Is there a relationship between the time students spend on learning and level of achievement?)

- Request the class to conduct the nominal group process to generate and prioritize a list of things that destroy quality.

- Have students collect information on problems, either in the classroom or school, and show them the many ways the information can be illustrated in charts and graphs.

- Ask students to develop a fishbone diagram to determine why there has been a loss of or increase in joy in learning.

- Request students to develop a flowchart regarding brushing their teeth.

- Ask each student to develop a flowchart on a process of their own choosing.

- Request students to develop a flowchart to conduct a quality improvement meeting.

- Ask mini-teams of students to use the nominal group process to develop a fishbone diagram to determine the cause of discipline problems in the school, without prior explanation of the nominal group process.

- Explain to students three behavioral life styles as they pertain to the classroom. Delineate win-win, win-lose, and lose-lose styles, and give some examples of these. Indicate that the orientation needed to make TQ work in a classroom is win-win. This means that everyone—individuals and the school system—benefit from advancing TQ. Stress that this means that all students in the class have a clear understanding of what they can do to support and contribute to nurturing not only their own success, but also that of the class and school.

- Ask students to create a master list of what win-win would mean to the class. Begin by asking the class to break down into small groups or teams and brainstorm: "What does win-win mean for our class in finding quality services and products?" Record responses on a flipchart sheet for all to see. The master list should contain from one to twenty-five key actions.

When the master list has been completed, the teacher should ask the class if they are really committed to this list, and if they will take every action listed to support the win-win requirements. Ask each student to sign his or her name on the master list, indicating support for building a TQ classroom through win-win requirements.

The class should schedule another meeting within sixty to ninety days to reinforce their commitment to win-win relationships. Situations or actions in which win-win is not working should be discussed and reworked.

SUMMARY

To reach greatness, school districts must develop and implement a plan to integrate the principles and practices of TQ in the classroom. Only when we are able to perform this feat will we be attempting to reach greatness. The methods, techniques, principles, and practices we use to do this will vary from school district to school district. The important point is to be guided by either the philosophy of Drs. Deming, Juran, or Crosby, and use the Seven Deadly Sins, Thirteen Obstacles, and the System of Profound Knowledge of Deming to complete the transformation.

CHECKLIST FOR MAKING THE TRANSITION TO TOTAL QUALITY

The following activities have been designed to facilitate the implementation of TQ in the classroom:

1. Review the principles of quality of the three gurus and select those that you think are appropriate for the class-room.

2. Draw an illustration of the System of Profound Knowledge and post it in classrooms. Request that teachers refer to this illustration throughout the school year and incorporate it into coursework.

3. Illustrate the Shewhart/Deming cycle, and fortify all students with the procedure. Make certain the cycle is used by teachers and students.

4. Generate a code of behavior for principals, teachers, and students, and have the parties sign it.

5. Request teachers to discuss at length, the participants in the Triangle of Interaction.

6. Have teachers meet as a group and develop appropriate TQ activities to incorporate in the classroom.

Chapter Ten

Educating And Training For Total Quality

Enthusiasm is like rain. If it does not start at the top, you will never find it at the bottom. To keep creating that enthusiasm, senior executives should be first in line for service training and education.

—Leonard L. Berry, et al.

The planning and implementation of a comprehensive training and education program is the heart and soul of a good TQ process. However, this is easier said than done. Most school districts in the United States fail to provide the necessary funds to sufficiently maintain their school people through an adequate education and training process. It is not uncommon to hear school administrators who attempt to install TQ say, "We implemented TQ without increasing the budget." TQ requires more education and training than most processes, because the training is all-encompassing. That is, every level of the school organization will need some education and training in the principles and practices of quality improvement, because school people will have to be retrained and receive advanced training when the program has blossomed.

IN THIS CHAPTER, I WILL DISCUSS THE FOLLOWING:

- Defining training
- Citing benefits of education and training
- Implementing an education and training program
- Planning the TQ training process
- Phasing TQ throughout the school district
- Focusing on TQ training
- Managing TQ training
- Augmenting the formal TQ training
- Evaluating TQ training

DEFINING TRAINING

Training is an organized human growth and development activity designed to improve team members' skills and abilities to perform the various functions and activities of TQ management.

The primary purpose of the education and training program associated with TQ is to change or modify the behavior of school and community members in order to improve their individual knowledge, skills, and attitudes regarding the implementation, maintenance, and evaluation of the TQ process.

Knowledge training provides team members and others with the necessary information to function. This may mean writing vision, mission, or shared values statements; it may mean reading guidelines, parameters, and conditions associated with quality; or it may mean computing statistical data in order to put data into a useful form. Sometimes, it may mean that additional specialized knowledge will have to be acquired to perform a function.

Team leaders, members, and facilitators will be required to perform a variety of functions, but will often have only the minimal skills to do so. It is the responsibility of the school district to provide sufficient training in strategic planning, the

Shewhart/Deming Plan-Do-Check-Act cycle, quality improvement planning, and problem solving to enable school and community people to perform their respective roles and responsibilities. In addition, teachers must receive skills training in their area of certification in order to stay current of changing times and conditions.

Attitude training reflects the expectations and philosophies expected of all school people associated with the TQ process. To a large extent, the leadership style and behavior of the superintendent, facilitator, team leaders, and other administrators and supervisors will affect the attitudes of team members. Attitude training in TQ is essential on a school basis and school organization perspective where team members will receive attitude training. This will help them reach:

- an understanding and appreciation of the philosophy of the TQ process;
- obedience to the culture of the school organization;
- assessment of the climate of the school organization; and
- an evaluation of the leadership style of school administrators and supervisors.

Attitude training is best performed through the role model behavior of the principal. The single most important factor in attitude training is how the principal treats team members. If the principal is people-sensitive, then the attitudes of team members will be positive. Change the undesirable behavior of a principal, and there will be resultant attitude changes in team members.

Attitudes are difficult to change, and to do so will usually take a great deal of time. In some instances, the damage created by the principal may have been so injurious to the climate of the school work environment that it may be necessary to position the principal elsewhere in the school organization where he or she will be more effective.

CITING THE BENEFITS OF
EDUCATION AND TRAINING

The implementation of a comprehensive education and training program carries with it a number of benefits for the school organization, school, principal, and school people.

For the school organization, it provides a minimum of teacher turnover, improved quality and productivity, more effective long-range planning, and increased potential for meeting future quality needs.

For the school, it provides better cooperation among team members, competent teacher force, better morale, improved use of team members' skills, more goal-oriented team members, joint problem solving/situation improvement, and increased respect and dignity.

For the principal, it provides a more stable and productive team, improved self-esteem and greater personal satisfaction, increased team morale and productivity, more effective leadership, fewer problems, and easily solved problems.

For school people, it provides multiple opportunities to increase capabilities and skills by performing a variety of jobs and functions, greater work satisfaction, opportunities for personal growth, and more unity among team members.

In an effort to maximize any investment made in the education and training program, the following guidelines should be implemented:

- Begin with a training needs analysis, and use the results to implement a training and development program.

- Begin with quality education and training initiatives by involving the central administration in the TQ process from the onset.

- Require that quality be integrated into every skill knowledge activity provided by the school district.

- Implement education and training from the top down, making certain every level communicates what transpired during the session of the previous upper level.

- Insist that quality education and training be placed on the agenda of weekly meetings.

- Use a variety of education and training approaches.

- Build education and training opportunities into staff meetings.

Attitudes are difficult to change, and will usually take a great deal of time. In some instances, the damage created by the principal may have been so injurious to the climate of the school work environment, that it may be necessary to position the principal elsewhere in the school organization, where he or she will be harmless.

PLANNING THE TOTAL QUALITY TRAINING PROCESS

All successful TQ practitioners report that systematic and planned deployment of TQ training was critical to their success, and that the deployment of training was tied directly to their TQ plan. The following outlines some of the important characteristics of such plans, including training, funding, job skills, assignments, scheduling, and participating.

Training as an Essential Component of Total Quality

Many traditional school districts treat training as a separate support function that is not a part of everyday mission-related operations. In contrast, all successful TQ school districts I contacted report that TQ training is an integral component of their TQ efforts, and they plan accordingly. The specific implementation needs of the school district—where the initial TQ focus will be, the schedule for phasing TQ throughout the school district, the existing mix of TQ knowledge and skills—determine the focus, form, timing, and targets of TQ training. As suggested above, school districts beginning TQ should first develop a comprehensive quality strategic plan to guide TQ implementation, and to make TQ training an integral component of that strategy. They should conduct an inventory of TQ-related skills and knowledge that already exist, and project needed training as a consequence of the TQ implementation strategy.

Funding for Total Quality Training

TQ practitioners generally agree that training is indispensable to any successful TQ effort. TQ generates fundamental changes in the way school districts are managed, including the respective roles of school people. Because training is the primary way school districts introduce all school people to the basic concepts and tools of TQ, successful TQ school districts invariably report that they assign a high priority to TQ training. They adopt policies to assure that school people receive necessary training to participate in TQ activities, and to ensure that they are not penalized for time off the job. Unlike more traditional school districts, TQ training is not routinely canceled to accommodate other requirements. Unlike school districts in really committed TQ organizations, "training is the last activity to be cut, not the first."

The pace and scope of TQ implementation will be constrained by the lack of funds for training if priorities are not clearly established. Therefore, it is essential that school districts that are beginning to implement TQ plan for the training costs up front. The school district should begin with its existing training budget, and to the extent feasible, re-deploy funds to support TQ. Also, previously budgeted leadership and management training, organizational development, and other training areas that are directly relevant to TQ can be tailored to support the TQ effort. Finally, the school district should estimate the total TQ training needs in relation to the implementation strategy, and reallocate accordingly.

Emphasizing Job Skill Training

School districts committed to delivering high quality services to their customers know that school people must be equipped with the skills and knowledge to perform their functions. As school districts establish their quality objectives, they routinely examine the skill requirements of the school people to meet new quality standards, and adjust their skills training accordingly.

For example, the Naval Supply Center in San Diego, California, gears the education and training program to each person's skill needs, which are tied to a competency-based certification. The center identifies skills, competencies, and tasks required for an occupation, and designs a structured-training program to ensure that the employee can satisfactorily perform the job. Since adoption of TQ, the center has modified the competency-based standards to reflect the quality standards established in the organization's strategic quality plan.

Assigning School People to Training

Once training resources have been identified, the school district should establish priorities and a plan for deployment of TQ training throughout. Most school districts have found that the ability of school people to absorb and retain TQ tools and techniques erodes quickly if substantial time lapses between the instruction and application of the new knowledge of the job. They often find it necessary to re-train school people when they begin to participate in a formal quality effort. In addition, long delay times between training in TQ practices and application in the school often generate cynicism and doubt about the quality effort. It then becomes difficult to resume the quality effort later. Therefore, successful TQ school districts usually provide TQ training beyond the initial awareness as the specific skills and knowledge will be used, e.g., on a "just-in-time" basis.

Scheduling Training

Most successful TQ school districts routinely schedule schools and communities to appropriate training when they are assigned to a formal TQ activity. Assignment to training is not a separate decision, but done as a matter of course. If the appropriate training is not available, assignment to the quality effort is frequently postponed until it becomes available.

It may not be possible to develop a detailed, phased schedule for training at the outset, because the schedule for TQ implementation has not yet been determined. Therefore, school districts frequently establish a formal policy and procedures for identifying specific training needs of schools and units, and arranging for the appropriate courses to meet the training needs as they arise.

Voluntary Vs. Mandatory Participation

As the TQ effort matures and spreads throughout the school organization, TQ becomes an integral component of the school organization's culture, and everyone participates routinely. However, in the start-up phase, participation in TQ is usually voluntary in order to maximize buy-in participants. It follows that participation in TQ training should also be voluntary in the early stages of a TQ effort, although appropriate training is required for those who do elect to participate in a formal TQ activity. The major expectations to this voluntary rule are orientation and awareness training, which frequently are provided to all school people, as well as selected training for central school administrators. Then if the school district has decided to implement TQ, all of the central school administrators' team may be required to participate in key training, such as TQ awareness, leadership, and organizational change, in order that they can effectively lead the overall effort.

PHASING TOTAL QUALITY TRAINING
THROUGHOUT THE SCHOOL DISTRICT

Timing of training is often critical to the success of TQ. The focus and concentration of training within the school district will vary as it progresses in its quality journey. The following are issues that school districts beginning a TQ effort should consider in phasing training throughout the school organization, including team orientation, school organization, and in-depth training.

Conducting Central School Administration Orientation

The first phase of TQ training is provided to the top leadership in order that they can direct the overall TQ effort, and usually consists of awareness training, which for the central school administration team is often the first formal action an organization takes to begin a TQ effort. An example of awareness training is a one-day session for the central school administration team. The session provides a general understanding of the basic concepts, principles, practices, and approaches of TQ, such as a guidance system, definition of quality, customer focus, interpersonal relations, and introduction to some of the basic statistical and problem-solving tools. Awareness training for the central school administration team is designed to provide participants with sufficient understanding of TQ to determine whether or not to proceed and to take some beginning steps.

Participation in a sampling of courses and conferences is also important. TQ practitioners differ in the specific approaches and emphasis that they advocate. For instance, some practitioners recommend a highly structured approach, starting with orientation and training for the central school administration team before implementing TQ activities at other school organizational levels. Others take a more flexible approach, tailoring the effort to the particular structure and culture of the school district.

In order to gain an appreciation for the variety of possible approaches to TQ implementation, the central school administration team often participates in several introductory courses and seminars provided by leading theorists such as Drs. Deming, Juran, and Crosby. Also, many private corporations, including several winners of the Malcolm Baldrige National Quality Award, offer TQ orientation courses to school districts.

One of the most effective ways to gain an understanding of TQ is to personally observe schools and other organizations that have already begun to implement TQ. Several factors should be considered in timing and selection of sites. One approach is to make a site visit shortly after an initial awareness session so that the general principles and ideas gained there can be translated into reality. An alternative approach is to wait until central school administrators have begun to wrestle with some of the initial implementation issues, such as establishing a quality steering committee, developing a vision statement, and establishing some early teams. After central school administrators have begun to deal with operational issues, a site visit can introduce ways to handle issues that emerge.

Independent reading and video viewing are also indispensable adjuncts to any education and training effort, particularly in TQ. A list of suggested readings on TQ training is included in the bibliography of this book.

Conducting School Organization Awareness

Many school districts provide either orientation (four to eight hours) or awareness (one to two days) for the entire school district long before any actual application of TQ. Some of these have found that the training created unfulfilled expectations, and set the overall quality effort back. Some say that if the organization is moving aggressively, letting everyone know something about TQ is a good idea, even if many of those trained do not participate directly in TQ initiatives for a while.

Conducting In-depth Total Quality Training

One of the earliest operating decisions a school district must make is where to target in-depth TQ training in the initial implementation phase.

After introducing the central school administration team to basic awareness, many school districts also concentrate their initial in-depth TQ training on central school administrators. School administrators may see the TQ effort as isolated tasks or as another program that can be delegated to schools, departments, and units, rather than a process that requires their active leadership and support. Also, many TQ practitioners believe that central school administrators should be familiar with specific TQ techniques, such as group problem solving and the basic statistical tools if they are to lead the TQ process. If central school administrators are not familiar with the practices and approaches toward team solutions before school, departments, and units use them, they are less likely to understand and accept the recommendations of QI and QA teams. Training at the top levels of the school organization is also necessary if the TQ deployment strategy is to focus on cross-functional issues rather than individual issues, since central school administrators normally control cross-functional decisions.

If the school district decides to focus its early quality efforts on specific operating issues at the school level, the training effort should be focused accordingly. The primary argument for focusing the early TQ efforts at the school level is to achieve quick successes that can be used to demonstrate the advantages of TQ throughout the school organization. In such a strategy, the focus of early in-depth training should be on team building, group problem-solving tools, and approaches for school people assigned to quality teams.

Many school districts have found that the greatest barrier to TQ implementation is the resistance of principals who feel bypassed and threatened by the effort. This resistance sometimes has been exacerbated by the initial implementation approach, which was to train other school administrators in TQ tools and techniques without involving principals. To overcome this resistance, many TQ practitioners recommend that all school people receive TQ training first, and that they be involved in the first teams. The principals so trained apply their team-based skills to cross-functional issues that span school organizational responsibilities. Such an approach frequently has the effect of making school administration champions of the quality effort, and they sometimes become the primary source of quality training in the school district.

Deciding where to focus TQ on a district-wide level will significantly influence the focus and direction of the early training. Major options include: 1) The TQ effort is phased in evenly throughout the school district, in which case all schools, departments, and units must become familiar with the TQ concepts, tools, and techniques more or less simultaneously; 2) Specific schools, departments, and units within the school district will be targeted first, in which case in-depth training for quality teams will be concentrated; and, 3) Focus the effort on specific operating issues or problems that span the school and units, but that require immediate attention, or give promise of quick payoff.

FOCUSING ON TOTAL QUALITY TRAINING

Many schools and other organizations who are implementing TQ have found a need for a common set of courses and instructional modules to support their TQ effort. Some of the more common subject areas and instructional courses adopted by school districts are indicated in this chapter.

The following summarizes major subject areas in which TQ school districts usually provide training as part of their quality effort.

Each school district needs to explain what TQ means to that school organization. The school district introduces school people to the fundamental principles of customer satisfaction; school people involvement and continuous improvement; and how the school intends to pursue those principles. The introduction includes the role of leadership, measurement/analysis, empowerment, rewards, recognition, teamwork, and customer focus. The training seeks to impart an understanding of work as a process; the impact of variation on quality; and many of the tools and techniques available for "managing by fact." As part of the introduction to TQ, the school organization will frequently begin developing and explaining the procedures and infrastructures that will be used to implement TQ, the implementation timetable, and the roles of the central school administrator's team, director, superintendent, principal, and other school people.

Many school districts find that their school administrators past training and experience is in relatively narrow technical areas. They have little awareness of principles of leadership and change that are fundamental to quality management. School districts therefore often provide training that introduces participants to quality management concepts like leading; managing, building, and sustaining trust and mutual respect; coaching and mentoring; encouraging risk-taking, openness, delegation, and empowerment; listening skills; systems thinking; and promoting organization change, while also understanding and handling resistance to change.

School organizations who are implementing TQ rely on a number of tools and techniques that have proven very helpful in assisting groups of school people to systematically improve their operations. They help ensure that problems are being attacked in an analytical way with reliance on data rather than feelings and opinions. The following are some of the key tools and techniques for which TQ school data often provide training.

Experience has shown that team problem solving can be a highly effective way to improve quality. The effectiveness of teams is enhanced considerably by using certain techniques to assist groups to identify and solve problems, such as brainstorming, nominal group technique, and multivoting. The techniques provide a structured way to ensure that everyone has equal voice in identifying problems and solutions, prioritizing suggestions, and reaching consensus on recommendations. Problem solving using a structured methodology following the Shewhart Plan-Do-Check-Act cycle is also an important element of training in this area. Other useful techniques include flow charts, stratification of data, force-field analysis, and matrices.

Statistical and Graphical Tools

A major practice of TQ—measurement and analysis— emphasizes use of data and statistical analysis to identify root causes of problems, identify solutions, and measure progress in meeting customer requirements. School districts should provide school people at all levels of training in several basic tools that allow them to analyze and display the data they have collected during their problem-solving sessions. Tools commonly used are the check sheet, Pareto analysis, cause-and-effect diagram, histogram, scatter diagram, control chart, and other graphs, such as line, bar, and pie charts.

Planning Tools and Techniques

School districts frequently rely on tools to aid in group planning, as well as problem solving. The tools are designed to systematically tap into the imagination and creativity of all participants in a group, and to provide a structured way to prioritize, organize, and plan for the deployment of the widest possible range of solutions. Among the tools commonly used for these purposes are seven management and planning tools, which are the control chart, histogram, scatter diagram, cause-and-effect analysis, run chart, flow chart, and Pareto chart.

Group Dynamics

Teamwork is one of the major ways to tap the skills and talents of everyone in pursuit of the quality objectives of the school district. School organizations provide school people at all levels with training in group dynamics, such as how a team takes on a personality of its own; how to work effectively in a group setting; personality differences; interpersonal relations and communication; respect for differences in perspective and point of view; and reaching decisions through consensus.

Customer Focus

School districts provide training to all school people in identifying both external and internal customers and suppliers, and what they need. Such training is designed to enhance school people's understanding of their products and services, who receives them (the customer), and what they think is important to the customer, as well as development of measure to know how well they are doing in meeting those customer needs.

Other specialized subject areas often included in formal TQ training are measurement of cost of quality, conducting effective team meetings, listening and communication skills, and advance statistical techniques.

TRAINING COURSES

School districts that are implementing TQ may use a variety of ways to educate and train school people in basic concepts and skills such as those summarized above. The typical training courses that many school districts provide for their school people are: orientation, awareness, quality team training, team leader training, and facilitator training.

Once the central school administration team has made a formal commitment to adopt TQ, the organization often introduces the entire school family to basic TQ concepts and approaches in four- to eight-hour lectures.

Many school organizations provide a one- to three-day course that introduces school people to the history, philanthropy, basic concepts, principles, and tools of TQ. School organizations beginning TQ usually provide such a course to their central school administrator's team as the first formal TQ activity, and often provide a course to all school people before they become actively involved in a formal TQ activity, such as setting up teams to improve processes.

A hallmark of TQ is use of quality teams. Teams of school and community people identify systematic operating problems and opportunities for streamlining operations, and ways to improve quality of processes or final outputs. They usually are comprised of a cross section of school people with particular skills and backgrounds relevant to the issues to be examined, and rely heavily on the expertise of the team members without regard to their position in the school district. Teams frequently are the most visible early expression of school people involvement in a TQ effort. They might be established temporarily to solve a specific problem, analyze cross-functional issues, or be a standing team of school and community people. Team members typically receive instruction over three to five days in the full range of TQ tools and techniques, such as leadership, group dynamics, interpersonal skills, group problem solving, and basic statistical and graphical tools.

In addition to training in the basic TQ tools provided to team members, team leaders often receive more advance training in leadership and management techniques, such as participative management, mentoring and coaching, group dynamics, effective meeting techniques, and techniques for guiding a team effort.

The effectiveness of quality teams is enhanced considerably by a facilitator (sometimes called a process observer) who helps to keep the team cohesive and focused on their objectives. Facilitator training, often a one- to two-week course, equips participants to be thoroughly familiar with TQ concepts and techniques, enables them to address the technical issues and languages of teams, and to handle the interpersonal dynamics, including values and personalities. The facilitator works closely with the team leader in helping to guide and focus the efforts of the quality team. Often either the facilitators or team leaders are also the primary trainers of team members.

TURNKEY TRAINING

Turnkey training courses may be provided for any of the specific areas of training that the school district provides to implement TQ.

Most school organizations adapt courses to fit their own needs. In some cases, school districts combine two or more of the subject areas into one course. For example, statistical training might be provided in a separate statistical course, integrated into the one-week team member instruction, or provided to teams as they tackle specific issues. Some school districts introduce concepts of leadership as a separate course, as well as a part of team training. Some school organizations provide all team leaders and team members with the same training, rather than a separate course for team leaders.

Also, the focus of each training area may vary depending on the particular training group. Central school administrators usually receive thorough training in leadership, organizational change, team dynamics, and the theory and concepts of TQ. Many also believe the entire school family should be thoroughly trained in statistical tools as well. Team leaders and team members usually receive thorough instruction in group problem solving and statistical tools so that they can apply the skills on the job. Figure 10.1 below summarizes the degree to which various groups of school people typically receive instruction in various training subject areas.

FIGURE 10.1
Education and Training Requirements

Superintendent	• TQ awareness	4-8 hrs
Central School Administrators	• TQ orientation	4-8 hrs
	• Deming's seminar	4 days
	• TQ parameters	1/2 day
	• TQ guidance system	1/2 day
	• Leadership and change	1/2 day
	• Basic statistics	1/2 day
	• TQ policies and procedures	1/2 day
	• TQ strategic planning	1-1/2 day
	• Interpersonal relations skills	varies
	• Problem-solving tools	2 days
	• Planning tools	1 day
	• TQ master plan	1/2 day
	• PCDA cycle	1/2 day
	• Graphic tools	1 day
	• Customer focus	1 day
	• Benchmarking	1 day
Quality Coordinator	• TQ awareness	4-8 hrs
	• TQ orientation	4-8 hrs
	• Deming's seminar	4 days
	• Facilitation skills	3 days
	• Coaching TQ participants	1/2 day
	• Evaluating TQ process	1 day
	• Benchmarking	1 day
	• TQ meeting coordination	1 day
	• Problem-solving tools	2 days
	• Interpersonal relations	varies
	• Basic statistics	1 day
	• Customer focus	1 day

FIGURE 10.1 (Continued)
Education and Training Requirements

	• TQ master plan	1/2 day
	• PCDA cycle	1/2 day
	• Graphic tools	1 day
	• Planning tools	1 day
	• TQ strategic planning	1/2 day
	• Leadership and change	1/2 day
	• Organizing quality steering committee	1 day
Quality Steering Committee	• TQ orientation	4-8 hrs
	• TQ awareness	4-8 hrs
	• Introduction to Deming's philosophy and System of Profound Knowledge	1 day
	• TQ guidance system	1/2 day
	• Interpersonal relations skills	varies
	• Developing TQ policies and procedures	1 day
	• Benchmarking	1 day
Quality Service Support Team	• TQ orientation	4-8 hrs
	• TQ awareness	4-8 hrs
	• Interpersonal relations skills	varies
	• Problem-solving tools	2 days
	• Planning tools	1 day
	• Graphic tools	1 day
	• Promotion and supporting services and products	1/2 day
	• PCDA cycle	1/2 day
	• Customer focus	1 day
	• TQ strategic planning	1-1/2 day
Facilitator/Process Observer	• TQ awareness	4-8 hrs
	• TQ orientation	4-8 hrs
	• Introduction to Deming's philosophy and System of Profound Knowledge	1 day
	• TQ guidance system	1/2 day

FIGURE 10.1 *(Continued)*
Education and Training Requirements

	• Problem-solving tools	2 days
	• Planning tools	1 day
	• Interpersonal relations skills	varies
	• Planning, conducting, and improving TQ meetings	1 day
	• Developing design team plans	1/2 day
	• Basic statistics	1 day
	• Developing quality School Improvement Plans	1-2 days
	• Customer focus	1 day
Quality Improvement Team	• TQ awareness	4-8 hrs
	• TQ orientation	4-8 hrs
	• Introduction to Deming's philosophy and System of Profound Knowledge	1 day
	• Graphic tools	1 day
	• TQ guidance system	1/2 day
	• Planning, conducting and evaluating TQ meetings	1 day
	• Developing School Quality Improvement Plans	1-2 days
	• Customer focus	1 day
	• Interpersonal relations skills	varies
	• Problem solving tools	varies
	• Planning tools	1 day
	• PCDA cycle	1/2 day
Quality Action Team	• TQ awareness	4-8 hrs
	• TQ orientation	4-8 hrs
	• Conducting team meetings	1 day
	• Planning, conducting, and evaluating presentations	1/2 day
	• Interpersonal relations	varies
	• Problem-solving tools	varies
	• Planning tools	1 day

FIGURE 10.1 *(Continued)*
Education and Training Requirements

	• Customer focus	1 day
	• Developing design team plans	1/2 day
Other School People	• TQ orientation	4-8 hrs
	• TQ awareness	varies
	• Problem solving tools	4-8 hrs
	• Interpersonal relations skills	varies

MANAGING TOTAL QUALITY TRAINING

This section discusses key principles and issues that school districts should consider in managing, organizing, and arranging for the delivery of TQ training.

First, virtually all TQ training should be structured and geared to how adults learn. Training should be experiential in nature where possible. Adults learn by absorbing concepts, ideas and facts through lectures, but they retain information best when they experience the application in real life situations. Some estimate that adults retain only 20 percent of what they hear, but 90 percent of what they do. Hence, training should stress practical application exercises for participants, including role playing and dealing with real-life case studies.

Training should be participative and interactive to the extent possible. In adult instruction, the participants themselves are often the teachers, while instructors facilitate the learning process, but are not necessarily the sources of all knowledge in the courses.

Above all, adult instruction should be non-threatening. The purpose is not to achieve a grade or otherwise coerce students to learn. The purpose is to facilitate learning that the student is assumed to actively desire and seek.

SELECTING TRAINERS

The knowledge and credibility of the trainers can significantly influence training effectiveness. Selecting and organizing the training staff is therefore crucial. In planning the TQ training effort, the school district should address several key issues. For instance, it should build internal training capability. some school districts beginning a TQ effort use outside training assistance, because they do not have the expertise internally. Most practitioners agree that ultimately school districts should develop their own internal training expertise, for the following reasons.

First, training in TQ takes on added meaning when the instruction is directly tied to operations of the school district. It is easier for the school district's own people to relate TQ to the school district and to operating issues.

The training is a critical driver of the TQ implementation effort. Only the school district's own staff fully appreciates the focus of the implementation effort.

Further, it is cost effective to develop internal training capability, because TQ training is an ongoing activity. The skills and techniques must be continually sharpened; new knowledge is developed; there are degrees of expertise (particularly in statistical application); and new school people enter the school district.

Finally, training is an excellent way for school people to learn about TQ. The trainer often learns more than the participants. For example, many successful private practitioners also have developed their own training expertise. The 3M company, Honeywell, and Federal Express have established their own quality colleges that are the primary sources of quality training for the corporation. Also, Westinghouse, Motorola, IBM, Xerox, General Motors, and Ford have established central TQ training facilities. Smaller organizations that do not already have core training staff also frequently develop their own TQ training resources by relying on their existing people as part-time trainers.

School districts are less likely to develop their own training capability in more advanced TQ practices, such as advanced statistical analysis, customer survey design, and benchmarking. Frequently, school districts seek outside assistance for such training if it is not already available in some other aspect of the organization's operation.

If the school district decides to develop its own training expertise, it must decide whether to use professional trainers or to reassign school people to TQ training.

Professional trainers have the advantage of experience in training. Some believe that professional trainers in related fields, such as organization development, statistics, and facilitation, can be brought up to speed relatively quickly in TQ, and thus should be the primary source of TQ trainers.

Some school districts find that school people, especially school administrators and supervisors, are the most effective trainers. Some of the advantages of using existing school people are:

- School people can relate the TQ instruction to operational issues confronted by the school district in day-to-day operations, and otherwise bring credibility to the TQ instruction.

- Frequently the most difficult people who enlist in the support of TQ are principals who feel their traditional roles and responsibilities are threatened. When school people are engaged in training TQ, they tend to become champions of the process, and can thus be influential in converting other school administrators as well.

- Training in TQ can be the most effective way to gain in-depth understanding and appreciation for the process, and thus a good way to enhance ownership by school people at all levels, and to influence their peers.

- If school people see their supervisors, who are trained in TQ become champions of the process, it can add credibility to the effort throughout the school district.

- Reliance upon school administrators and other school people for training place a premium on selecting prospective trainers—those who have good presentation skills and strong interest in TQ, and who can be made available for training either on a part-time or a full-time basis.

- Many organizations believe that use of school people as trainers is the best approach if the right people can be found. However, some organizations have found it difficult to find sufficient numbers of people with the right balance of training skills. They therefore use a combination of experienced trainers and school people.

Some TQ school districts indicate that they rely primarily on existing school people, rather than on professional trainers, for the reasons cited above. A few, however, take a balanced approach, selecting trainers from a variety of backgrounds, depending on the subject and training audience.

MANAGING THE OVERALL TRAINING EFFORT

A threshold issue that school districts must face early is how best to integrate and manage the various forms of training required. There are two alternative courses to follow: rely on an outside consultant or utilize school district management of training.

Many school districts beginning a TQ effort rely heavily at first on an outside consultant to help them develop a comprehensive implementation and training strategy. The consultant frequently assists in the design of the school district's implementation approach, trains central school administrators, and consults with them as they plan and manage the overall TQ effort. The external consultant is also frequently the primary source of training in the initial stages of TQ implementation.

Selecting an outside consultant at the outset of the TQ effort sometimes presents a dilemma to the school district. It is difficult for a school district to choose the appropriate strategy and consultant before it has become familiar with TQ and the alternative implementation approaches that are available. Some school districts use the process of selecting an outside consultant as part of their own education and orientation.

Because most school districts who are implementing TQ eventually find it desirable to develop their own training resources, they should be assured that the outside consultant has the expertise and willingness to train in-house trainers, and will work toward making the school district self-sufficient.

Under the school district management approach, the school district might arrange for training by outside consultants in specific courses, such as facilitation and team building. However, the consultant plans the overall TQ training and manages and integrates the various training courses.

In most TQ efforts, the quality coordinator plays a critical role in integrating the various sources of training, and in assuring that training is integrated with the overall implementation strategy. Typically, the quality coordinator reports to the chairperson of the QS committee. The coordinator usually is the person who maintains the overall implementation schedule, arranges the agenda, orchestrates all the activities of the QS committee, and identifies champions and resources to carry the quality effort throughout the organization.

If the school district decides to use a primary outside consulting and training firm to help guide its TQ effort, the quality coordinator usually is the primary point of contact. To be effective, the coordinator and the outside consultant must develop a close and mutually supportive relationship.

Because of the critical role of the quality coordinator, a consortium of school districts should organize to arrange for a comprehensive quality coordinator training course.

Tailor Training to Each School Organization

Some advanced TQ organizations have developed a TQ training curriculum that reflects its own culture and TQ implementation strategy. The content of the core training areas summarized previously is usually similar among other quality school organizations. Each school district, however, adapts the instruction to incorporate examples from its own operation, and modifies the length and mode of instruction to correspond to its particular implementation schedule and objectives.

If a decision is made to train existing staff development people to be trainers, a decision must be made as to how to take the trainers off their existing jobs. One approach is to establish a core group of experienced TQ trainers who become trainers of trainers. The bulk of training for school and community people is by staff development people who continue on their existing job assignments, but perform training on a rotating basis as a collateral assignment.

When a formal training program is not necessary, the quality coordinator may do the following to train individual members or the team as a whole:

- Provide mini-workshops to explain a function or activity.
- Initiate "think sessions" to assist the team in solving a problem.
- Call on specialists or experts to tutor a team member or team.
- Call on school administrators or others to present a seminar or workshop.
- Provide opportunities for either the principal or team leader to provide the education and training.
- Use a rich portfolio of team-building activities.

Evaluating Total Quality Training

Every training should have a built-in systematic evaluation and feedback system to ensure that the training objectives are being achieved, and that training continues to reflect emerging needs. Training for TQ is no exception. Because TQ training is such an integral part of the overall TQ effort, everyone in the school district has a high stake in assuring that it meets their needs. Many school districts rely on a variety of forms of training evaluation, surveys of school people who participated in the past, and monitoring of training courses by training specialists. The evaluation of training should be planned routinely in the design and deployment of the training strategy. It should attempt to address such issues as the cost-effectiveness of the training design; choice of contract and in-house courses; and use of media, manuals, and technology.

I use a wide range of indicators to evaluate my education and training activities when I conduct workshops. One of the most dependable sources is comments from the participants. Sometimes I hold brainstorming meetings with school and community people to improve training. School and community people feedback is used to modify course length, content, and timeliness, and has resulted in increased acceptance of the training.

For example, sometimes when I get carried away during the training process, participants will usually interrupt me to take a break. On other occasions, when participants feel that I need to dwell more on a given subject area, they will ask me to go over some of the essential points. I find that school administrators, teachers, and others who attend my training are not hesitant to give me constructive comments to improve my training. And I appreciate it very much.

There is one simple recipe to the effective management and deployment of TQ training. Each school district has a unique training need that reflects its existing management culture, existing mix of background and skills in school people, and quality deployment strategy. The school district should design its TQ effort to meet its own unique needs, particularly in relation to its overall TQ implementation strategy.

While each school district's particular TQ training needs are unique, most of them have found that some key operating principles and practices can significantly improve the effectiveness of their training. Many of those practices are summarized in this book. These practices will be useful as a general guide, particularly in the early stages of a TQ effort. School districts should also consult with other TQ practitioners, particularly those who have made good progress on the quality journey, to help them make their own decisions. The effort is not easy. However, if the quality journey is worthwhile, careful attention to the supporting training strategy and management is indispensable.

SUMMARY

Education and training is essential to the successful implementation of TQ. School people must receive training in skills to perform a variety of functions in TQ. They must also receive adequate knowledge about principles and practices associated with quality. In addition, they must receive attitude training that reflects the expectations and philosophies expected of all school people involved with the process.

If I had to identify one or two items that can doom a total quality process, I would say first that it would be a lack of commitment and support from the superintendent of schools, and second, an inadequate education and training program. As a national consultant and trainer, I maintain that all school districts should give more attention to maintaining and improving the knowledge, skills, and attitudes of their school people. In essence, I am echoing the sentiments of Tom Peters who said that creating a few good training programs is not enough. We need to develop a continuous learning environment. During a one-day seminar he gave in Philadelphia in September, 1988, he put it this way: "Training, training, retraining, then more training, and if I have to say it again, then you just don't get it."

Once an education and training program has been developed, attention must be focused on establishing a recognition and reward program to celebrate quality victories This is covered in the next chapter.

CHECKLIST FOR MAKING THE
TRANSITION TO TQ

In an effort to guide you to establish a comprehensive and healthy education and training program, I am recommending that you engage in the following activities:

1. Provide the necessary funds to support the TQ education and training program.
2. Emphasize job skills training, too.
3. Integrate training with on-the-job application.
4. Start with voluntary participation in TQ training, and as the process begins to blossom, make it mandatory.
5. Conduct training sessions for everyone in the school district, beginning with the board of education and ending with volunteers.
6. Gear the training to different groups of school people. Some groups need basic training only, while other groups need in-depth training.
7. Focus training on introduction to TQ, leadership, making organizational change, and planning and problem- solving tools and techniques. Focus coursework on orientation, awareness, quality team training, team leader training, facilitator training, and turnkey training.
8. Structure training according to how adults learn.
9. Build internal trainers.
10. Identify the role of quality coordinator.
11. Augment formal TQ training with various activities.
12. Establish a built-in system for TQ evaluation.

Chapter Eleven

Creating A Quality-oriented Recognition Program

Very few companies recognize their good performers. Many managers feel, somewhat cynically, that people are being paid to do their jobs and that's that. This attitude reflects an insensitivity to people that is trademark of many hockey-style managers. It is immature. The creation and development of a recognition program for executives and employees alike is a very important part of quality improvement. It is as important as supplier quality management or supervisor training or cost of quality discovery or the chief executive's comprehension of what quality really means and how to get it.

—Philip B. Crosby

The intent of this chapter is to describe the important steps for creating an effective recognition and reward program. The term recognition is used to refer to an integrated system of celebration, recognition, and rewards. It is a vital component to an effective TQ process. When accomplished appropriately, it makes school people feel good, and it provides an inducement and spirit for them to continuously improve. But, a recognition program does much more than that. It reinforces the quality culture, the quality beliefs, and shared values of the school district. A recognition process, that is, the events of the process, enable central school administrators to come together

with others in the school district on frequent occasions to celebrate progress made in TQ. As a result, central school administrators' visibility and communication create a bond among
all school organizational levels and promote esprit de corps.

IN THIS CHAPTER, I WILL
DISCUSS THE FOLLOWING:

- Citing the steps for developing a recognition program
- Using Maslow's Pyramid to prepare a recognition pro-
  gram
- Identifying principles of an effective recognition pro-
  gram
- Identifying what some of the best do

CITING THE STEPS FOR DEVELOPING
RECOGNITION PROGRAM

The primary purpose of a quality recognition program is to
reinforce those principles and practices in TQ to produce a
great school district. However, there are other reasons for establishing a recognition program, including the following:

1. To nourish the quality spirit so it will propel all school
   people to satisfy all customers
2. To surface quality champions
3. To improve the morale of QI teams
4. To encourage QI teams to go beyond the call of destiny to
   perform in an exemplary manner
5. To make QI teams feel at home, and provide an incentive
   to continuously make improvements
6. To recognize QI teams for achievement and results directly
   related to quality efforts
7. To provide a signal for the right road to follow
8. To create a greater bond between and among school organizational levels, and to promote esprit de corps

There are seven steps that should be taken to establish a quality recognition and reward program. These are described below.

Determine a List of Priorities and Values

Determining a list of priorities and values for establishing the quality recognition program is crucial, because it reinforces the principles and practices of TQ. Some of the priorities and values are:

- Acquiring the knowledge and skills to implement TQ
- Participating on a TQ team
- Achieving quality goals and objectives
- Completing quality projects
- Becoming trained and certified as a TQ facilitator
- Utilizing the problem-solving tools
- Upgrading quality standards continuously
- Improving the ability to meet customer needs
- Completing an unusual feat of quality

Cite the Conditions

When the practices and values that need reinforcement have been identified, the next step involves defining the conditions that qualify school people for recognition. The following are some examples:

- Successfully completing TQ training
- Successfully completing a TQ project
- Saving the school district or school money because of the TQ process
- Producing a factual demonstration of unusual student achievement as a result of the TQ process
- Having benchmarking success
- Meeting all quality goals and/or objectives

- Having 100 percent attendance at all team meetings
- Conducting an extraordinary number of customer (parental) visits

Allocate a Budget for the Quality Recognition Program

Some practitioners recommend allocating from five to ten dollars per school person on the payroll. This figure should be reviewed annually to determine if it is adequate.

Determine Accountability

Because in most cases the principal will be selecting either the individual or the team, he or she should be held accountable for the building of a quality recognition program. The QS committee has overall responsibility and accountability for the district-wide quality recognition program. The quality coordinator has the responsibility to make certain the program guidelines are followed.

Describe the Features, Benefits, and Procedures

Prepare a detailed document describing the recognition procedures, awards, and ceremonies to be held, the role of the superintendent of schools, and any other information QI teams need to implement and administer the quality recognition program.

Review the Quality Recognition Program With Each School

Once the essential components of the recognition program have been determined, consider the following two approaches:

1. Organize a focus group to receive feedback to complete the preparation of the written program.
2. Complete a draft of the total program and present it to the QI teams for their reaction and input.

Modify Based on Feedback

Assessing the recognition and reward program is an attempt to improve it to meet the needs of those participating in it. Ideally, several meetings should be held with all school people to resolve any problems and until a consensus can be reached. Remember, it is not the superintendent's recognition program but the school people who are deserving of recognition and rewards.

Once feedback regarding the approach selected has been collected, modify the program document accordingly. Get back to any groups that provided feedback, indicate the outcome of their input, and thank them for their assistance. Remember to present the completed document to the school as a whole for their acceptance.

USING MASLOW'S PYRAMID TO PREPARE A RECOGNITION PLAN

There are countless ways to recognize and reward QI teams and members for contributing to the success of the TQ process. One way that has been used by some organizations is the Abraham Maslow way; that is, recognition and rewards are classified according to the Maslow hierarchy of needs as illustrated in Figure 11.1. Organizations that used this method classify their rewards according to basic and motivational needs of people. Some people may be motivated by money, while others may be motivated through self-actualization. A sound recognition program accommodates the individual needs of people. It should be concerned with results and money saved, but also with the process, team effort, excellent performance, learning, and new skills. In addition, competition among QI teams should also be encouraged; after all, the beneficiaries of the competition are the students. Oh! Save me Dr. Deming!

FIGURE 11.1
Maslow Hierarchy of Needs

Using the Maslow way to recognize would link any financial rewards to the first level of the pyramid; the second level to promotion, sharing power, and being empowered; the third and fourth level to gifts, handshakes, trips, citations, photographs, lunch with the principal or superintendent, and ribbons; and, the fifth and highest level to free time, education, and training.

The Maslow way is an excellent process to design a quality recognition program, because some people value public acknowledgement or recognition. For others, material awards are their primary source of being rewarded for their efforts. While for others, the activity that serves both recognition and gratitude will be what drives them to continuous improvement. The idea that school people hear "thank you" in many different ways is due to their individuality, which should be considered and respected when designing a quality recognition program.

IDENTIFYING THE PRINCIPLES OF AN EFFECTIVE RECOGNITION PROGRAM

There are a number of important principles that should be observed when designing a quality recognition program. For one thing, make certain the recognition program is reality-oriented and relevant. School people will respond to a quality recognition program if they feel that rewards are provided for accomplishments that are related to long-range goals, priorities, and values. They will also favor a recognition program that rewards exceptional performance rather than routine performance, like a school person who goes beyond the "usual" to help a customer (student) to come to school each day for four-and-one-half months without an absence. However, on the other hand, do not design a recognition program so that only a few superhumans will be recognized through it.

The quality recognition program should be seen as a sincere expression of appreciation for quality efforts. When school people feel that they are being recognized for real and relevant accomplishments, the school administration is more likely to exhibit appreciation for what they have accomplished. In addition, others will also. Sincerity is a human trait that cannot be written into the recognition program; it must be felt to be perceived by school people.

A recognition program should not be limited to either a semi-annual or annual celebration. A just-in-time recognition program is more effective than an occasional one. Most school people enjoy being recognized soon after they have performed in an exemplary way. In fact, the ideal just-in-time recognition activities should occur within hours or days after the performance, rather than months later.

There are no doubt hundreds of ways to recognize school people. When developing the recognition program, a number of recognition methods should be incorporated. This variety demonstrates flexibility. The following are some recognition methods:

- Banner for office
- Catalog
- Cash
- Certificates
- Coasters
- Pick-your-own gift
- Picture in city newspaper
- Picture in district newsletter

- Decals
- Desk sets
- Dinner with spouse or friend
- Gift certificate
- Honor roll
- Lapel pin or jewelry
- Letter to personal file
- Letter from superintendent
- Logo items (hats, shirts, pens,)
- Mugs
- Paper weights
- Use of limousine

- Plaques
- Recognition by the board
- Savings bond
- Seminar attendance
- Shorts
- Special luncheon
- Special parking space
- Tickets to sporting events
- Trip (local or distant)
- Trophies

No recognition, presentation, or celebration should take place when the superintendent or his or her designee are not in attendance and involved in the ceremony. In addition, no recognition event should ever be postponed, because the superintendent or a representative is not present. To do so indicates that the highest official of the school district does not place much importance on recognizing school people for their quality performance efforts. As a result, the roles the recognition program reinforce will soon diminish.

Publicize the event, and involve school and community people. As stated previously, a quality recognition event reinforces the priorities and values of the school district. It also encourages similar quality efforts by other school people. However, if other school people do not hear about the accomplishments, they obviously cannot be influenced by it. If other customers (parents, students, senior citizens, etc.) are not aware of the accomplishments of the school district, how can they support it?

Below are five other tips for involving school and community people in the recognition program:

1. Involve peers of school people who will be recognized so they can be influenced by the spotlight treatment.

2. Unless the recognition is a district-wide celebration, hold the event in the school or on the site of those being recognized.

3. Request the superintendent or representative to go to the school or site of those being recognized. This demonstrates the superintendent's support for the TQ.

4. Publicize the recognition activities throughout both the school district and community.

5. Research school people's recognition needs.

The best way to do the latter is to go to the QA team or design team and ask them to outline their recognition needs and preferences, and to use that information as a base for designing the quality recognition program. Once a draft has been completed, return it to the QI team and review every detail of the recognition program, then revise accordingly and publicize it.

IDENTIFYING WHAT SOME OF THE BEST DO

Some organizations have established elaborate programs to recognize and celebrate outstanding feats of quality improvements. The following is a description of a few of these organizations:

Xerox Corporation, producer of office copier machines, recognizes team efforts through a Team Excellence Award and Excellence in Customer Satisfaction. In addition, individual team members are recognized for the President's Award and the Xerox Achievement Award. Nearly 50 percent of these awards are initiated by peer nomination.

Motorola, Inc., producer of electronic equipment, recognizes outstanding achievement through its CEO Quality Awards. Motorola also has a recognition program for its suppliers, known as the Pinnacle Awards.

Paul Revere, an insurance company, has established what is known as a Quality Value program to announce the Most Valuable Player and the Most Valuable Team winners and runners-up for the purpose of showing its appreciation for the enthusiastic support and involvement in the Quality Value process. This recognition program also gives people awards for certified ideas. Certification of an idea consists of a team leader explaining the idea to a quality analyst, and then demonstrating how it is implemented. The analyst has to answer two questions: Did the change take place? Did the change improve quality or is it a perception?

Once an idea is certified, it becomes eligible to be counted toward earning recognition. The recognition program provides orange, silver, and gold awards. For example, when a team initiates ten certified ideas, or saves $10,000 in annualized savings, its members receive a bronze cloisonne lapel pin, which recognizes each team members' contributions to "Paul Revere Quality." When a team initiates twenty-five certified ideas, or $25,000 in annualized savings, each team member receives a silver-plated lapel pin. In addition, each silver award recipient receives an opportunity to select a merchandise award from a Quality Awards catalog. When a team initiates fifty certified ideas, or $50,000 in annualized savings, each member receives a gold-plated lapel pin. Further, each member can select a merchandise award from the Quality Award Catalog F.

Philip Crosby, Dr. Philip Crosby's company, has established a Beacon of Quality Award by requesting its people to identify individuals that they feel serve as a beacon when it comes to quality. They ask, "What person do you see as the standard for quality performance?" The three winners who receive the recognition are presented with large brass candelabras properly engraved with their names and the title, "PCA Beacon of Quality."

Moore, the leading maker of business forms, has established a successful recognition program that is intended to foster a team approach to quality improvement. Groups of people can form a team to compete for the award. Participants are judged on their use of problem-solving techniques and how they apply to other solutions, creativity of the solution, cost savings, and how well the solution meets the needs of customers.

Conclusions of One of IBM's Recognition Programs

In February 1991, IBM hired the AdGap Group to study one of its recognition programs. The objective was to study their people's general perceptions of one of its recognition programs in addition to the following:

- Its strengths and weaknesses
- Their perceptions of the relationship between what they do and what recognition they receive
- Their opinions on how effective the recognition program is in improving performance
- How effective the recognition program was in motivating quality improvement efforts
- Based on the results and discussion, the following conclusions were reached:
- Providers and customers were not involved in the recognition program.
- There was only management—people recognition. There was no peer-to-peer recognition.
- People like money, but personalized awards were also appropriate.
- People did not understand the organization recognition program.
- Many people did not understand what they had to do to obtain recognition.
- Recognition was often not timely. Most recognition came at the end of the year.
- Winners in the program were not documented, and model behavior was not adequately publicized.
- Superiors were not trained in the theory and practice of recognition.

- The recognition program recognized only end-results, not the process necessary to attain them.
- The program failed to give the people an increased sense of dignity, self-worth, belonging, and value to the organization. Instead, it fostered a competitive environment in which there were winners and losers. The winners felt good; the losers did not.

As a result of the IBM study, the following was learned, and should be considered when a school district is developing its own recognition and reward program:

- It is easy to recognize top performers, but difficult to voice the performance of an entire school district.
- Teams must be continuously involved in every facet of a recognition program. Superior performance is indicated as superior learning.
- External consultants are required to evaluate an organization's current environment.
- Recognition must be deserved.
- Each level of the organization is unique, and requires a general set of guidelines, personal ingenuity, and creativity to implement a recognition program.
- Designing a new reward requires outside consultation.
- Often people are slow to learn, but quick to forget. As a result, organizations find it difficult to learn from mistakes.
- Different skills are needed from conception to implementation of a recognition program.

The results of the IBM recognition program led a company committee to establish the following:

1. The preparation and dissemination of a recognition workbook and video to educate IBM people.
2. A plan to make existing cash awards more effective.
3. The implementation of a peer-to-peer award.

4. The development of an award for quality improvement initiatives.

The IBM workbook and video describe how a unit can assess and modify its recognition program. The package was distributed throughout the organization and followed up with a survey to determine its effectiveness.

IBM continued its cash award, but extended it to include a gift (flowers, steaks, etc.), which is sent to the home to surprise the recipient. The recipient is also given show tickets, a complimentary dinner, or something else so he or she will always remember the event.

When someone exceeds the expectations of another person, he or she fills out a form and gives it to a process administrator. The person who fills out the form receives an envelope and card that contains twenty dollars to purchase a gift for someone exceeding the person's expectations. A personalized gift is purchased and presented to the recipient with the envelope and card that says, "Thank you for exceeding expectations."

The Professional Process Award is awarded to IBM teams in recognition of their using quality tools in their quality initiatives. Recipients are selected by a council of Market-driven Quality (MDQ) professionals based on nomination. All teams reaching a certification status are awarded a custom-designed medallion and letter from IBM's vice president and general manager. Award criteria include teamwork, use of management and planning tools, and use of problem-solving methods.

SUMMARY

Recognizing, celebrating, and rewarding school people for exemplary quality initiatives must first rest on a solid base of a competitive salary. It is not intended to be a substitute for inadequate salary. School people who feel underpaid in relation to other similar school districts will view the recognition program as a joke, and in some cases, with hostility. An effective way to determine if the present salary scale is adequate as a departure point for a quality recognition program is to survey school people to get their opinions. If the current salary is inadequate, then it should also be improved. If the current salary scale is adequate, organize a design team to plan, develop, launch, and evaluate your recognition program.

CHECKLIST FOR MAKING THE TRANSITION TO TOTAL QUALITY

Organizing a design team consisting of a cross section of school people (teachers, custodians, secretaries, etc.) to plan, develop, launch, and elevate the quality recognition program using the following as a guide:
1. Use the Shewhart/Deming Plan-Do-Check-Act cycle, and develop an outline for establishing a quality recognition program.
2. After completion of the outline, prepare a list of pertinent questions for conducting a focus group on the substance of the recognition program.
3. Complete preparation of the recognition program plan.
4. Forward the plan to each QI team, and request that they react to the plan.
5. Use the reactions to revise and modify the plan.
6. Prepare an article for the local newspaper on the quality recognition program. Circulate the final plan throughout the school district.
7. Send letters of appreciation to all who participate in the preparation of the recognition program.
8. When implementing the quality recognition program, it should dovetail with the celebration program, and the social setting where everybody gathers to celebrate quality feats.

Conclusion

A Final Word On
Total Quality

This book has been a blueprint for building a total quality (TQ) system in education. It is an attempt for all schools to reach a level of greatness that has escaped them in the past. To proceed, you must fully understand this blueprint, become possessed by the prospect of making the journey to greatness through TQ, and have the motivation to carry it through. If you think that TQ is similar to any other process, then, unfortunately, you do not have sufficient knowledge about the process to proceed and I highly recommend that you repeat Chapters One, Two, Three, Four, and Ten. TQ is like nothing we have learned in educational administration courses. If, on the other hand, you understand the full dimension of TQ, proceed with care considering everything discussed in these pages.

Reaching greatness through TQ will not be simple or easy. It will take guts, plenty of guts. Some school board members may not have either the desire or the stamina to even attempt the process. Some principals may object to the process out of ignorance, because they do not understand that when they share their power with teachers, they actually increase their power through the empowerment process. Teacher and teachers' associations/unions, too, may badmouth the process simply because they are not involved in the process from the onset.

Parents, too, may question the school district's attempt to implement TQ; that is, until they see the transformation of their children, and the joy they receive from the learning process. It is only natural for school people and parents to resist change. Outmoded ways have become too much of a habit for us to give them up without much pain. All of us have been comfortable for far too long with the manner in which our school districts are being managed. Yes, it will take guts for school administrators and teachers to reach for a seemingly unattainable level of performance such as greatness, but we must strive to do so, because children are our most valued assets.

Now, let us look back at some of the basic steps and key points presented since the beginning of this book:

1. Be mindful that TQ is a journey, not a destination. If you are looking for a quick fix or an easy process, then do not attempt TQ, because it is a long-range process that focuses on customers. It is aimed at continuous, research-based planning and a consistent understanding of the needs, requirements, and expectations of customers.

2. Explore the readiness of your school district for TQ. Introduce the central school administrators to TQ by having them explore the process through reading books and professional articles on quality; attending TQ workshops, seminars, and conferences; inviting consultants to appear in the school district to provide awareness sessions and more in-depth training; and, visiting TQ school districts and Malcolm Baldrige National Quality Award winners.

3. Make certain all school people are aware of all internal and external customers and providers. If your school district is ready for TQ, put in place the essential elements that demonstrate that central school administrators support TQ by installing it through a strategic planning process; focusing on the customers; developing a measurement and analysis system, committing schools to training; nurturing empowerment and teamwork among school people; and instituting quality assurance. Become aware of the three gurus of

TQ: Drs. W. Edwards Deming, Joseph M. Juran, and Philip B. Crosby. Practice their principles.

4. Use Dr. Deming's Fourteen Points, Seven Deadly Sins, Thirteen Obstacles, and the System of Profound Knowledge to guide your school district's transformation to TQ. Rework his principles to accommodate the needs and requirements of your school district. Perform a thorough search of your school district to eliminate any of his deadly sins and obstacles, and get rid of them once and for all. Train your school people and students to embrace Dr. Deming's System of Profound Knowledge so they are thoroughly knowledgeable, and embrace his theories of knowledge, systems, variation, and psychology.

5. Select an initial TQ implementation strategy that gets school people to do things better and differently. Use the strategy to develop an implementation plan, such as the one described below:

   a. Explore TQ.
   b. Understand Dr. Deming's philosophy and System of Profound Knowledge.
   c. Organize a quality steering (QS) committee.
   d. Organize for TQ on a district-wide level.
   e. Create a TQ guidance system.
   f. Establish a pilot study.
   g. Educate and train for TQ.
   h. Listen to customers and gather information.
   i. Develop a quality measurement system.
   j. Detect and close performance gaps.
   k. Implement TQ in the classroom.
   l. Develop a recognition and reward program.

6. Make certain that central school administrators are meaningfully involved in TQ by having them:

   a. Serve on the QS and QI teams.
   b. Participate in TQ training.
   c. Serve on QA teams.
   d. Review teams' project presentations.
   e. Participate in recognition and reward programs.

     f.   Speak directly with customers.
     g. Assist in planning and developing the quality service measurement system.
     h. Approve quality project ideas.
     i.   Support the efforts of all school people in their quest for TQ.
     j.   Conduct stump speeches on TQ throughout the school district and community.
     k. Attend team meetings.
     l.   Speak the TQ language.
     m. Demonstrate fanaticism for TQ.

7. Revisit your guidance system to determine if all the components are in place, such as the mission statements, strategic and school visions, shared values, service strategy, and quality policy. Communicate the guidance system through memos, stump speeches, video presentations, newsletters, and various other communiques. Evaluate school administrators partially on their ability to "walk the talk." Be mindful that teachers' behavior and attitudes inculcate a subculture in the classroom that should be monitored and corrected if necessary.

8. Implement TQ on a district-wide level by establishing a parallel structure consisting of a QS committee. Charge this committee with the responsibility of constructing a TQ model based on the needs of your school district and community. Include in your model a quality coordinator who will carry out the charge of the QS committee; a QSS team to provide professional assistance to the QS committee and teachers; QI teams that will plan, develop, and implement QI projects; QA teams that provide assistance to QI teams; and any other components based on the school district's needs. Realize that it will take a minimum of three years before you will have the basic TQ process in place.

9. Implement TQ on the school level by selecting pilot schools. Choose your best schools, and train school people and parents properly. Provide each pilot school with a budget to support their planning, education, and training

efforts. After a year, evaluate the progress of the pilot study, and modify it to correct any problems. Model the success of the pilot study by letting it in other schools. Do so deliberately, and eventually let TQ blossom throughout the entire school organization.

10. Listen to all your customers. Use a variety of methods to obtain feedback such as focus groups, surveys, "mystery customers," complaint or comment cards, customer panel, and visit customers. Researching your external customers is not enough; equally important is researching your teachers, who themselves are internal customers and know better than anyone else what is hampering a TQ school environment.

11. Develop a comprehensive quality service measurement system by identifying teaching and service areas; creating quality characteristics for each teaching and service area; describing measurements for each characteristic; and, matching standards for each measurement. Compare performance to quality standards, and correct and continually increase customer satisfaction.

12. Eliminate all performance gaps. Close the negative gaps between what customers expect from the service and what they perceive they require to close other potential gaps— the gaps between what customers expect and what school administrators think they expect; the gap between what the school administrators think customers expect and the service requirements established by the school districts; the gap between the service requirements and the service actually delivered; and the gap between the service actually delivered and what is said about the service in external communications.

13. Encourage teachers to implement TQ in the classroom by having them select appropriate TQ principles and practices from the three gurus. Educate both teachers and students about important concepts of TQ, such as the System of Profound Knowledge, the Shewhart/Deming cycle, and Dr. Deming's Triangle of Interaction. Join with other teachers

to create a host of TQ activities that can be integrated with course content to make learning fun and enjoyable. Generate a code of conduct for a TQ environment for students, teachers, and the principal.

14. Establish a recognition and reward program to drive the engine of TQ. The "psychology" of recognizing and rewarding school people for TQ efforts is powerful stuff. Have the QS committee and principals recognize and reward performance. How they celebrate quality victories can be even more important and more motivating than the size of the reward itself. Remember, recognition is the behavior of taking notice and saying, "Thank you." It comes in many forms, but always from the heart.

15. Train all school people in knowledge, skills, and attitudes for implementing and sustaining TQ. When implementing the training needs analysis, use the results to establish your own training program. Begin with quality education and training involving the central school administrators. Integrate quality with every skill and knowledge activity. Implement the training program from the top down, making certain all levels of the school organization are covered. Make certain training is placed on the agenda weekly. Use a variety of education and training opportunities and build education and training into staff meetings. The areas being covered by the training program should include introduction to TQ, leading and managing organizational change, planning and problem-solving tools and techniques, statistical and graphical tools, group dynamics, customer focus, and other TQ-related topics. Finally, make education and training the most crucial component of your TQ program.

As you continue down the road to total quality, your progress will become more and more effective. Eventually, your school organization will attain an outstanding record of achieving improvements in everything it does. As an outstanding school organization, you will become great at customer-focused quality planning, and your plans for both services and products, or for new procedures and systems will lead to quality performance when theories are conceived and put into place.

References

CHAPTER ONE:
NTRODUCINGTOTAL QUALITY IN EDUCATION

1. Some of the contents for this chapter are from a government document entitled, "Introduction to Total Quality Management in the Federal Government," as part of the *Federal Total Quality Management Handbook*.

2. Mary Walton, *The Deming Management Method*, Putnam Publishing Group: New York, NY, 1990.

3. Howard S. Gitlow, *Planning for Quality Productivity and Competitive Position*, Business One Irwin: Homewood, IL, 1990, pp. 1-47.

CHAPTER TWO:
UNDERSTANDING DR. DEMING'S PHILOSOPHY
AND THE SYSTEM OF PROFOUND KNOWLEDGE

1. Most of the contents of this chapter come from a document of the federal government, entitled "Management of Variation and TQM," by William E. Hughes, Jr., July 1991, pp. 6-29. U.S. ASDC Cost Analysis Office, P.O. Box 1500, Huntsville, AL.

2. W. Edward Deming, *Out of the Crisis*, Massachusetts Institute of Technology, Center for Advanced Engineering Study (1992), pp. 18-96; 319-370.

CHAPTER THREE:
IMPLEMENTING TOTAL
QUALITY IN EDUCATION

Most of the content for this chapter comes from:

1. Two booklets that are part of the *Federal Total Quality Management Handbook*:

   A. "How to Get Started," Booklet 1

   B. "How to Get Started," Appendix, Booklet 1A

   C. The Federal Quality Institute
       James L. Perine, Team Leader
       Colette Wickman
       Polly Mead

   D. The Office of Personnel Management
       Efstathia Siegel
       William Dooly
       Eugene Johnson
       Elaine Goddard
       Mary Moore

   E. The Department of Veteran Affairs
       John Scott McAlister

2. Thomas H. Berry, *Managing the Total Transformation*, McGraw-Hill, Inc.: New York, NY, 1991, pp. 28-38.

CHAPTER FOUR:
GAINING LEADERSHIP
COMMITMENT TO TOTAL QUALITY

1. Some of the contents of this chapter come from a booklet in the *Federal Total Quality Management Handbook*, entitled "How to Get Started," Booklet 1.

   2.Thomas H. Berry, *Managing the Total Quality Transformation*, McGraw-Hill, Inc.: New York, NY, 1991, pp. 1-38.

CHAPTER FIVE:
CREATING A GUIDANCE SYSTEM
FOR TOTAL QUALITY

1. Thomas A. Berry, *Managing the Total Quality Transformation*, McGraw-Hill, Inc.: New York, NY, 1991, PP. 25-26.

2. James Lewis, Jr., *Planning, Implementing, and Evaluating School-Based Management*, National Clearinghouse on School-Based Management, Jericho, NY: 1991.

3. J.P. Russell, *The Quality Master Plan*. ASQC Quality Press, Milwaukee, WI, 1990, pp. 27-29.

CHAPTER SIX:
ORGANIZING FOR TOTAL QUALITY

1. Some of the contents for this chapter come from one of the booklets of the *Federal Total Quality Management Handbook*, entitled, "How to Get Started," Booklet 1.

2. Thomas H. Berry, *Managing the Total Quality Transformation*, McGraw-Hill, Inc.: New York, NY, 1991, pp. 39-74.

CHAPTER SEVEN:
ESTABLISHING A QUALITY
SERVICE MEASUREMENT SYSTEM

1. Valerie A. Zeithamel, et al., *Delivering Quality Service*, The Free Press: New York, NY, 1990.

2. Leonard L. Berry, et al., *Service Quality*, Dow Jones-Irwin: 1989, pp. 38-80.

3. Richard C. Whiteley, *The Customer-Drive Company*, The Forum Cooperation: Reading, MA, 1991, pp. 149-176.

CHAPTER EIGHT:
DETECTING AND CLOSING
SERVICE PERFORMANCE GAPS

1. This chapter would not have been possible had there not been this book by Valerie Zeithamel, et al., *Delivering Quality Service*, The Free Press: New York, NY, 1990, pp. 51-134.

CHAPTER NINE:
APPLYING TOTAL QUALITY
IN THE CLASSROOM

1. George Dixon and Julie Swiler, *Total Quality Handbook*, Total Quality Newsletter, 1990, pp. 1-22.

2. This chapter is also based on an interview with Theresa Mary Hicks, a second grade teacher at Denver Mae Elementary School, Wilmington, Ohio.

CHAPTER TEN:
EDUCATING AND TRAINING
FOR TOTAL QUALITY

1. Some of the substance of the chapter comes from a booklet of the *Federal Total Quality Management Handbook*, "Education and Training for Total Quality Management in the Federal Government."

2. Howard S. Gitlow, *Planning for Quality Productivity and Competitive Position*, Business One Irwin: Homewood, IL, 1990, pp. 147-162.

CHAPTER ELEVEN:
CREATING A QUALITY-ORIENTED
RECOGNITION PROGRAM

1. Thomas H. Berry, *Managing the Total Quality Transformation*, McGraw-Hill, Inc.: New York, NY, 1991, pp. 159-170.

Bibliography

Aguayo, Rafael. *Dr. Deming: The American Who Taught the Japanese About Quality*. New York, NY: Simon & Schuster, 1991.

Albrecht, Karl. *The Only Thing That Matters*. New York, NY: HarperCollins Publishers, 1992.

Albrecht, Karl, and Ron Zemke, *SERVICE AMERICA!: Doing Business in the New Economy*. Homewood, IL: Dow Jones-Irwin, 1985.

AASA. *Total Quality for Schools: A Collection of Articles on the Concepts of Total Quality Management and W. Edwards Deming*. Arlington, VA: American Association of School Administrators, 1991.

Berry, Leonard L., et al. *Service Quality: A Profit Strategy for Financial Institutions*. Homewood, IL: Dow Jones-Irwin, 1989.

Berry, *Thomas H. Managing the Total Quality Transformation*. New York, NY:McGraw-Hill, Inc., 1991.

Block, Peter. *The Empowered Manager: Positive Political Skills at Work*. San Francisco, CA: Jossey-Bass, 1987.

Brassard, Michael. *The Memory Jogger*. Methuen, MA: GOAL/QPC, 1988.

Ciampa, Dan. *Total Quality—A User's Guide for Implementation*. Reading, MA: Addison-Wesley Publishing Co., 1992.

Covery, Stephen R. *Principle-Centered Leadership*. New York, NY: Summit Books, 1991.

Crosby, Philip B. *Let's Talk Quality: 96 Questions You Always Wanted to Ask*. New York, NY: Penguin Books, 1989.

Crosby, Philip B. *Quality Is Free: The Art of Making Quality Certain*. New York, NY: McGraw-Hill, 1979.

Crosby, Philip B. *Quality Without Tears: The Art of Hassle-Free Management*. New York, NY: McGraw-Hill, 1984.

Crosby, Philip B. *Running Things: The Art of Making Things Happen*. New York, NY: Penguin Books, 1986.

Deming, W. Edwards. *Out of the Crisis*. Cambridge, MA: Massachusetts Institute of Technology, Center for Advanced Engineering Study, 1986.

Dertouzos, Michael L., et al. *Made in America: Regaining the Productive Edge*. Cambridge, MA: MIT Press, 1989.

Dobyns, Lloyd, and Clare Crawford-Mason. *Quality or Else: The Revolution in World Business*. Boston, MA: Houghton Mifflin Co., 1991.

Ernst and Young Quality Improvement Consulting Group. *Total Quality: An Executive's Guide for the 1990s*. Homewood, IL: The Dow Jones-Irwin/APICS Series in Production Management, 1990.

Fiske, Edward B. *Smart Schools, Smart Kids: Why Do Some Schools Work?* New York, NY: Simon & Schuster, 1991.

Gabor, Andrea. *The Man Who Discovered Quality: How W. Edwards Deming Brought the Quality Revolution to America— The Stories of Ford, Xerox, and GM.* New York, NY: Penguin Books, 1990.

Garvin, David A. *Managing Quality: The Strategic and Competitive Edge.* New York, NY: Free Press, 1988.

Gitlow, Howard S. *Planning for Quality, Productivity, and Competitive Position.* Homewood, IL: Business One Irwin, 1990.

Gitlow, Howard S., and Shelly J. Gitlow. *The Deming Guide to Quality and Competitive Position.* Englewood Cliffs, NJ: Prentice Hall, 1987.

Glasser, William. *The Quality School: Managing Students Without Coercion.* New York, NY: Harper and Row, 1990.

Hammond, Joshua, and Jerry Bowles. *Beyond Quality: How 50 Winning Companies Use Continuous Improvement.* New York, NY: G.P. Putnam's Sons, 1991.

Harrington, H. James. *The Improvement Process—How America's Leading Companies Improve Quality.* New York, NY: McGraw-Hill, 1987.

Harris, John W., and J. Mark Baggett. *Quality Quest in the Academic Process.* Birmingham, AL: Samford University, 1992.

Hiam, Alexander. *Closing the Quality Gap: Lessons from America's Leading Companies.* Englewood Cliffs, NJ: Prentice-Hall, 1992.

Hunt, Daniel V. *Quality in America: How to Implement a Competitive Quality Program.* Homewood, IL: Business One Irwin, 1992.

Imai, Masaaie. *KAIZEN: The Key to Japan's Competitive Success.* New York, NY: Random House, 1986.

Ishikawa, Kaoru. *What Is Total Quality Control? The Japanese Way.* Englewood Cliffs, NJ: Prentice-Hall, 1985.

Ishikawa, Kaoru. *Guide to Quality Control.* Tokyo, Japan: Asian Productivity Organization, 1974.

Ishikawa, K. "Special Issue: Seven Management Tools for QC, Reports of Statistical Application Research, Union Japanese Scientists and Engineers." Rep. Stat. Appl. Res., JUSE 33, No. 2 (June 1986), ISSN 0034-4842.

Jablonski, Joseph R. *Implementing TQM: Competing in the Nineties Through Total Quality Management.* Albuquerque, NM: Technical Management Consortium, 1992.

Juran, Joseph M. *Juran on Leadership for Quality: An Executive Handbook.* New York, NY: Free Press, 1989.

Juran, Joseph M. *Juran on Planning for Quality.* New York, NY: Free Press, 1988.

Juran, Joseph M. *Juran on Quality Planning.* Wilton, CT: Juran Institute, Inc.: First Draft, April 1985.

Juran, J., and Gyrna, F. *Juran's Quality Control Handbook.* 4th ed. New York, NY: McGraw-Hill, 1988.

King, Bob. *Hoshin Planning: The Developmental Approach.* Methuen, MA: GOAL/QPC, 1989.

Kinlaw, Dennis C. *Continuous Improvement and Measurement for Total Quality: A Team-Based Approach.* Homewood, IL: Pfeiffer & Co., 1992.

Mann, Nancy R. *The Keys to Excellence: The Story of the Deming Philosophy*. Los Angeles, CA: Prestwick Books, 1989.

Maslow, Abraham H. *Motivation and Personality*. New York, NY: Harper and Row, 1970.

Neave, Henry R. *The Deming Dimension*. Knoxville, TN: SPC Press, Inc., 1990.

Peters, Tom. *Thriving on Chaos: Handbook for a Management Revolution*. New York, NY: Alfred A. Knopf, 1987.

Rinehart, Gary. *Quality Education*. Milwaukee, WI: Quality Press/ASQC, 1992.

Russell, James P. *The Quality Master Plan: Quality Strategy for Business Leadership*. Milwaukee, WI: ASQC Quality Press, 1990.

Scherkenbach, William W. *Deming's Road to Continual Improvement*. Knoxville, TN: SPC Press, 1991.

Scherkenbach, William W. *The Deming Route to Quality and Productivity: Road Maps and Road Blocks*. Rockville, MD: Mercury Press, 1988.

Senge, Peter M. *The Fifth Discipline: The Art and Practice of the Learning Organization*. New York, NY: Doubleday/Currency, 1990.

Townsend, Patrick L. *Commit to Quality*. New York, NY: John Wiley & Sons, 1990.

Townsend, Patrick L., and Joan E. Gebhardt. *Quality in Action: 93 Lessons in Leadership, Participation, and Measurement*. New York, NY: John Wiley & Sons, 1992.

Tunks, Roger. *Fast Track to Quality: A 12-Month Program for Small to Mid-Sized Businesses*. New York, NY: McGraw-Hill, 1992.

Walton, Mary. *The Deming Management Method*. New York, NY: The Putnam Publishing Group, 1986.

Walton, Mary. *Deming Management at Work*. New York, NY: Putnam, 1990.

Whiteley, Richard C. *The Customer-Driven Company: Moving From Talk to Action*. Reading, MA: The Forum Corporation, 1991.

Zemke, Ron, and Dick Schaaf. *The Service Edge*. New York, NY: Penguin Books, 1989.

Zeithaml, Valarie A., et al. *Delivering Quality Service: Balancing Customer Perceptions and Expectations*. New York, NY: The Free Press, 1990.

Index